KU-068-446

The Treasury of NATURAL HISTORY

The *Treasury* of NATURAL HISTORY

by Bertha Morris Parker

Galley Press

© Copyright 1968 by Western
Publishing Company Inc.
This 1985 edition designed and produced
by Autumn Publishing Limited,
10 Eastgate Square, Chichester, England.
Published in this edition by Galley Press, an
imprint of W H Smith & Son Limited
Registered No 237811 England.
Trading as WHS Distributors, St. John's House,
East Street, Leicester, LE1 6NE
All rights reserved. No part of this publication may
be reproduced, stored in a retrieval system,
or transmitted in any form or by
any means, electronic, mechanical,
photocopying, recording or otherwise,
without prior written permission
from the publishers.
ISBN 0 86136 717 0
Printed in Czechoslovakia

Illustrations from the Basic Science Education Series
(Unitext), written by Bertha Morris Parker and
published by Harper and Row, used by permission.

Contents

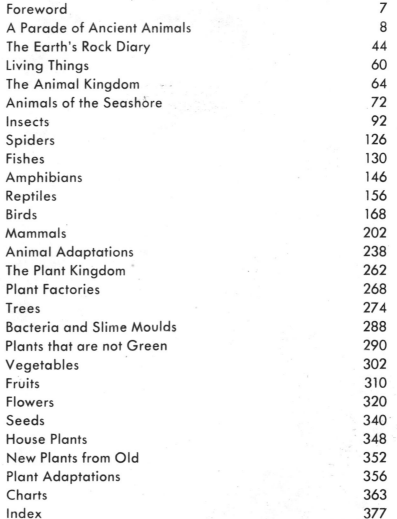

Illustrators

PAULINE BATCHELDER ADAMS
GEORGE BAKACS
NORMAN BARBER
DOROTHEA AND SY BARLOWE
JUANITA BENNETT
ROBERT D. BEZUCHA
VIRGINIA BRADENDICK
MATILDA BREUER
WALTER BUEHR
LOUISE FULTON BUSH
ARTHUR D. CUSHMAN
MRS. LOIS DARLING
RACHEL TAFT DIXON
WALTER DOWER
ANDRE DURENCEAU
E. JOSEPH DREANY
OLIVE EARLE
WALTER FERGUSON
RUDOLF FREUND
BYRON GERE
MARJORIE HARTWELL
HANS HELWEG
LOWELL HESS
ROBERT HODGELL
WALLACE HUGHES
ARCH AND MIRIAM HURFORD

WILLIAM HUTCHINSON
JAMES GORDON IRVING
NORMAN JONSSON
MATTHEW KALMENOFF
ROBERT KISSNER
ENID KOTSCHNIG
OLGA KUCERA
BOB KUHN
JACK J. KUNZ
JOSEPH LOMBARERO
HARRY McNAUGHT
G. I. McWILLIAMS
RENE MARTIN
REBECCA MERRILEES
ERIC MOSE
ARTHUR MUELLER
ELIZABETH NEWHALL
RICHARD ORR
RAYMOND PERLMAN
CRAIG PINEO
RAY PIOCH
FRED POFFENBERGER
HAROLD PRICE
LORELLE MARIA RABONI
DON RAY
ALLIANORA ROSSE
MARY ROYT
WILLIAM De J. RUTHERFOORD
ROD RUTH
ARNOLD W. RYAN
LLOYD SANFORD
KATHERINE SAMPSON
MARITA AND GEORGE SANDSTROM
SAM SAVITT
WILLIAM SAYLES
ALEX SEIDEL
NED SEIDLER
ARTHUR SINGER
FREDERICK E. SEYFARTH
RUSS SMILEY
ELMER SMITH
DARRELL SWEET
VALERIE SWENSON
JAMES TEASON
ALTON S. TOBEY
ANN OPHELIA TODD
DAN TODD
PAUL WENCK
ELOISE WILKIN
BARBARA WOLFF
JEAN ZALLINGER
RUDOLPH F. ZALLINGER

Foreword

What the earth is made of, the seemingly countless kinds of plants and animals about us, and the life of past ages—these are subjects in which young people have a natural interest. To take advantage of that interest and build up an understanding of the world of nature is the aim of *The Treasury of Natural History*.

Young people ask many questions about their environment: How do we know that once there were dinosaurs? How can we tell a butterfly from a moth, or a toad from a frog? Is a tomato a fruit or a vegetable? Could you cross a cabbage with a rose? And so on. The author has used such questions as a help in selecting, from the vast amount of nature

knowledge, the topics to be included in this book.

The wonderful colour illustrations will help the reader to recognize many of the rocks, plants, animals, and fossils he sees. The book is not designed as a nature guide: no section is sufficiently complete to serve that purpose. But the pictures will nevertheless help in identification and, more importantly, will illustrate many basic facts and ideas about the world of nature.

The book makes the reader's experiences with nature much more meaningful. A shiny pebble is no longer just something pretty to add to one's collection; it is a bit of one of the rock pages on which the earth has written its diary. A garden is not just a source of vegetables to eat and flowers to cut; it is also a collection of plant immigrants from many foreign lands, and of the results of experiments in plant breeding.

In science, 'truth changes', because better scientific instruments and methods are constantly revealing more of nature's secrets. But one can foresee little change during the coming years in the basic idea presented in this book—that the story of the earth is indeed one of great changes, that animals and plants are adapted in wondrous ways for living as they do, and that there are undreamed of things still to be discovered about our earth and its long yesterday.

BERTHA MORRIS PARKER

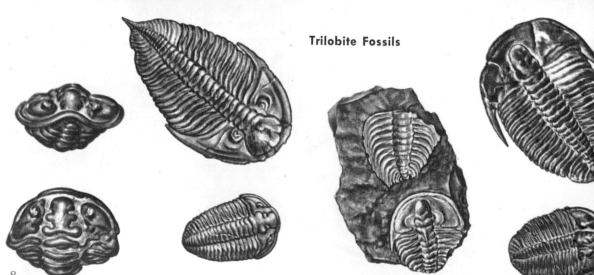

Trilobite Fossils

A Parade of Ancient Animals

Six hundred million years ago there were already a great many kinds of living things on the earth. The big picture shows a number of them. Of course, it was not painted from life, for the plants and animals pictured lived long, long before there were any people. Scientists have found out about the living things of long ago from traces of them in rocks. Such traces are called fossils.

A parade of the animals of six hundred million years ago, if there could be one, would not be exciting. For one thing, it would have to be underwater, for all the animals of that time—at least all that we know about—lived in the sea. All of them, moreover, were fairly small.

The animals that held the centre of the stage in those long-ago days were the trilobites. Although few trilobites were more than three or four inches long, they were large in comparison with their neighbours, and there were huge numbers of them.

The name trilobite was given to these animals many millions of years after the last ones died. They had no name at all while they were alive because there were no humans to name them. 'Trilobite' means 'three-lobed'—their hard covering was divided into three long lobes.

The trilobites belong to the enormous group of jointed-legged animals, called the arthropods, but they were not closely related to any of the jointed-legged animals of today. They lived in the shallow water of the seashores. Feathery gills helped them to swim as well as breathe. Long feelers and, as a rule, big compound eyes helped them to find food. They ate other animals, probably both living and dead ones. They also ate plants. When in danger, many curled themselves up. Others simply folded in the middle and closed up like a book.

Compared with the higher animals of

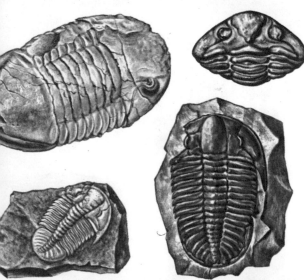

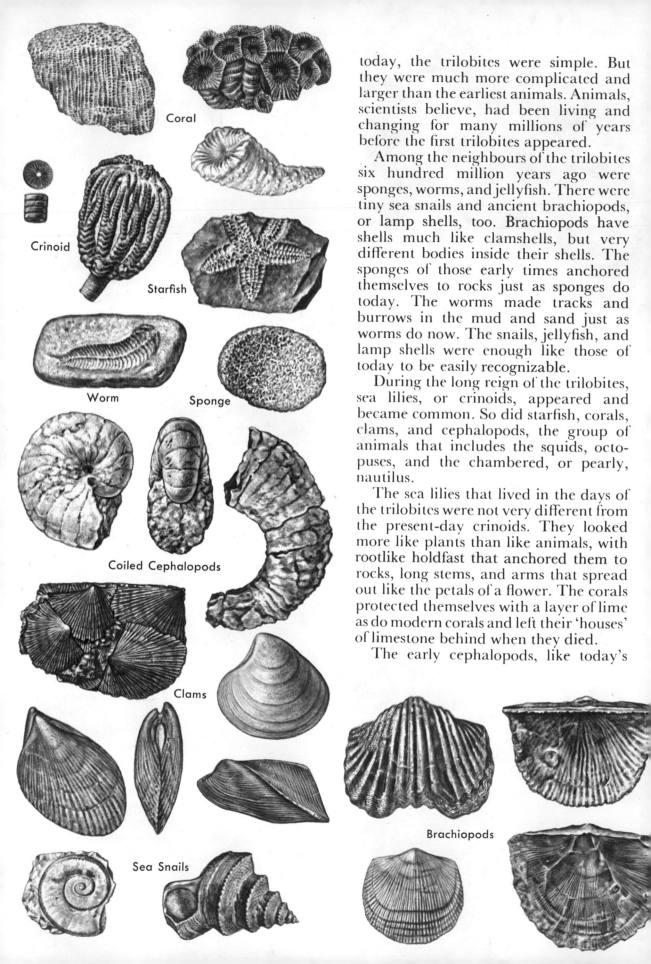

Coral

Crinoid

Starfish

Worm

Sponge

Coiled Cephalopods

Clams

Sea Snails

Brachiopods

today, the trilobites were simple. But they were much more complicated and larger than the earliest animals. Animals, scientists believe, had been living and changing for many millions of years before the first trilobites appeared.

Among the neighbours of the trilobites six hundred million years ago were sponges, worms, and jellyfish. There were tiny sea snails and ancient brachiopods, or lamp shells, too. Brachiopods have shells much like clamshells, but very different bodies inside their shells. The sponges of those early times anchored themselves to rocks just as sponges do today. The worms made tracks and burrows in the mud and sand just as worms do now. The snails, jellyfish, and lamp shells were enough like those of today to be easily recognizable.

During the long reign of the trilobites, sea lilies, or crinoids, appeared and became common. So did starfish, corals, clams, and cephalopods, the group of animals that includes the squids, octopuses, and the chambered, or pearly, nautilus.

The sea lilies that lived in the days of the trilobites were not very different from the present-day crinoids. They looked more like plants than like animals, with rootlike holdfast that anchored them to rocks, long stems, and arms that spread out like the petals of a flower. The corals protected themselves with a layer of lime as do modern corals and left their 'houses' of limestone behind when they died.

The early cephalopods, like today's

nautilus, had shells. Some of the shells were coiled, like that of the nautilus. Others were long and straight. The animal's head and arms protruded from its shell.

In time the scorpionlike eurypterids, close relatives of the trilobites, appeared. The most conspicuous animal in the picture below is a eurypterid. You will recognize the trilobites, starfish, and corals in the foreground. A cephalopod is just appearing at the right near the two snails.

For a tremendously long time—a hundred million years perhaps—the trilobites had no real rivals. Then, although trilobites continued to be very common, the cephalopods gradually overshadowed them. Many grew to be larger than any of the trilobites. Some of those with straight shells were 20 feet long. Since they were meat-eaters, the cephalopods probably devoured vast numbers of the trilobites.

Trilobites lived on for many, many millions of years after they were no longer masters of the sea. Some of the later ones developed long, and seemingly useless, projections. Approximately 230 million years ago the trilobites died out completely. We say that they became extinct.

It would be a mistake to think of the animals of the ancient seashores as living just where the seashores are today. Land and sea were not always as they are now. For many millions of years the British Isles were joined onto the continent of Europe. The English Channel and the

Straight Cephalopod

North Sea did not exist then. And many places that are now far from the sea were part of the sea-bed.

The time when the trilobites and the cephalopods were the leading animals is sometimes called 'the heyday of animals without backbones', for these animals had no backbones. They had no bones of any kind. Neither did any of the other animals pictured here. Another name for the time is the Age of Invertebrates. 'Invertebrate' means 'without a backbone'.

Scientists divide the story of the earth into long stretches of time called eras. The Age of Invertebrates was the first part of the Palaeozoic era. The word 'palaeozoic' means 'ancient life'.

The early Palaeozoic era was a quiet time. Not an animal in the world had a voice. There were, as you know, no land animals to make a noise by running about. Almost the only sounds were thunder and the noises of wind and waves.

Europe 450 million years ago (Ordovician Period)

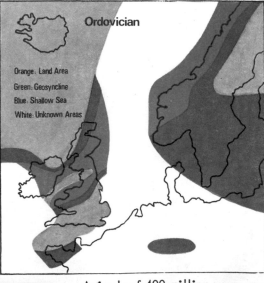

Ordovician

Orange: Land Area
Green: Geosyncline
Blue: Shallow Sea
White: Unknown Areas

Animals of 400 million years ago (Silurian Period)

Lobe-finned fish climbing up on land

The first animals with backbones to appear on the earth were fishes. They appeared in the days when the cephalopods were the masters of the seas. The early fishes were successful. Within 50 million years or so there were so many of them that they quite overshadowed the simpler animals. The time when they were the leading animals of the earth is called, in everyday language, the Age of Fish.

Many of the early fishes were jawless, just as the lampreys of today are. Like the lampreys, moreover, these jawless fishes had no paired fins. But they were very different from lampreys in one way —they had armour made of thick plates of bone.

There were many different kinds of armoured fish. Some were little; others were very large. Pterichthys ('wing fish') was only about six inches long. Dinichthys, on the other hand, was between 20 and 30 feet long. Its name means 'terrible fish', and it was terrible. Its jagged jaws could snap shut with great force. Both Dinichthys and Pterichthys had paired fins. So did the other fishes in the picture with Dinichthys. One kind is much like the little 'wing fish'. The other is an early shark. Sharks were common in the Age of Fish.

Notice the limbs of the fish climbing up on shore in the picture at the top of the page. Fishes like these are called lobefins because of their limbs, which certainly do not look much like fins. A lobefin differed in another way from most other fishes—in addition to gills it had simple lungs, which allowed it to spend some time out of water. There were other fishes with lungs—the lungfishes—living at the same time.

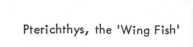

Pterichthys, the 'Wing Fish'

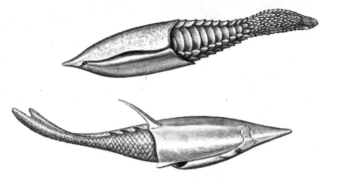

For all its size and fierceness and stout armour the 'terrible fish' could not hold its own. Neither could the little 'wing fish'. They and all their close relatives were replaced in time by fishes more like the common fishes of today. The lobefins, the lungfishes, and the jawless fishes were not completely replaced, but they became far less common than they had been. For millions of years the sharks flourished. There came to be hundreds of species. Sharks are still fairly common, but their heyday ended about 300 million years ago.

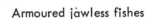

Armoured jawless fishes

Dinichthys pursuing a primitive shark

The Coal Age followed the Age of Fish. It, too, was a part of the Palaeozoic era.

At the beginning of the Coal Age much of Europe was low and swampy. So were

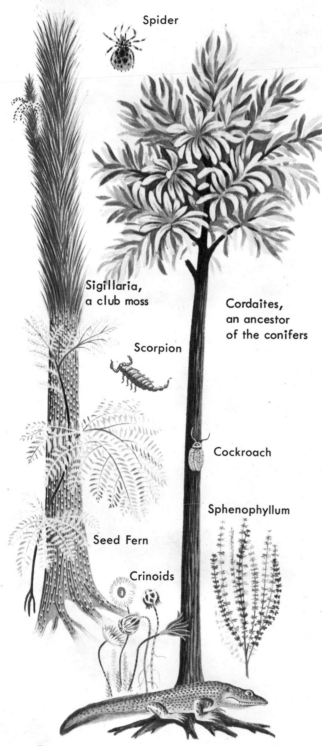

Spider

Sigillaria, a club moss

Cordaites, an ancestor of the conifers

Scorpion

Cockroach

Sphenophyllum

Seed Fern

Crinoids

Diplovertebron, an early amphibian

some other parts of the earth. Forests grew in the swamps. The forests were luxuriant, for the climate was mild and the air as well as the ground was very moist. The trees that died and fell into the swamp water did not rot away entirely. Instead, they formed a thick layer of rotting plant material, like peat.

In many of the swamps, the water gradually grew deeper. Perhaps the land was slowly sinking. Perhaps the sea was rising and overflowing into the swamps. The change was very slow, but at last the forests were drowned. The drowned trees were added to what was left of the trees that had fallen before. Wet mud flowed in over the thick layer of dead trees.

Later, much of the water that covered the old swamps drained away. Again there were swamps with forests growing in them. In time these forests, too, were drowned and buried under mud and water. Time after time the same changes took place. At last in many regions there were several layers of buried forest. As millions of years went by, these layers changed to coal.

The trees that made up the Coal Age forests were not oaks and elms and pines. They were not any of the forest trees common now. Instead, they were chiefly giant club mosses, horsetails, ferns, seed ferns, and cordaites. The pictures here will give you an idea of what some of them looked like.

The pictures show, too, seven kinds of Coal Age animals. Clearly an important change in the animal world had taken place, for six of the animals pictured lived all, or at least most, of their lives on land. The moment when an animal first succesfully crossed the dividing line between water and land was one of the most important times in the earth's long history.

Perhaps the first animal to live on land was a scorpion. As you know, earlier there had been scorpionlike animals in the sea. Now, in the Coal Age, there were scorpions on land. There were spiders and insects, too. Scorpions, spiders, and insects of several kinds were well established on land at the beginning of the

Coal Age. They were common during all that long time.

Some of the insects that lived during the Coal Age were larger than any insects of today. There were 'dragonflies' measuring two and a half feet from wingtip to wingtip. There were giant cockroaches four inches long. Cockroaches were so common that the Coal Age is sometimes called the Age of Cockroaches.

Scorpions, spiders, and insects have no backbones. The first backboned animals to live on land were amphibians. Toads and frogs are among our common amphibians of today. Toads and frogs begin their lives in water. The tadpoles that hatch from the eggs are very much like little fish. Later they become air-breathing animals and can live on land. The first amphibians also began their lives in water but were able to live successfully on land when fully grown.

Scientists now believe that the amphibians originally descended from fishes like the strange lobefin pictured on page 12.

Diplovertebron was one of the earliest amphibians we know about. At a glance it does not look very different from its lobefin ancestors. It probably did spend much time in the water. But its salamander-like legs show that it was able to walk about on land. Diplovertebron grew to be from one to three feet long.

Late in the Coal Age there were reptiles, too. The strange-looking pelycosaur pictured below was one of them. It is easy to see why these reptiles are called sailbacks. There are many guesses as to what the 'sail' was used for. One guess is that it helped to keep the animal's body at the right temperature.

The pelycosaurs with their big 'sails' and mouthful of teeth, looked rather terrifying. But they were strictly plant-eaters.

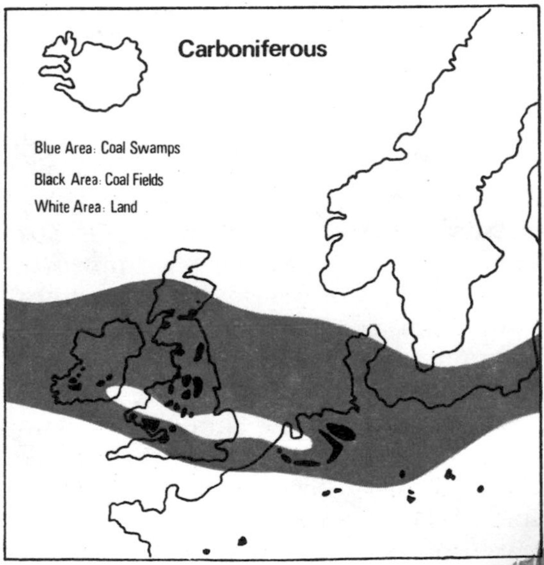

Europe in the Coal Age
(Carboniferous Period)

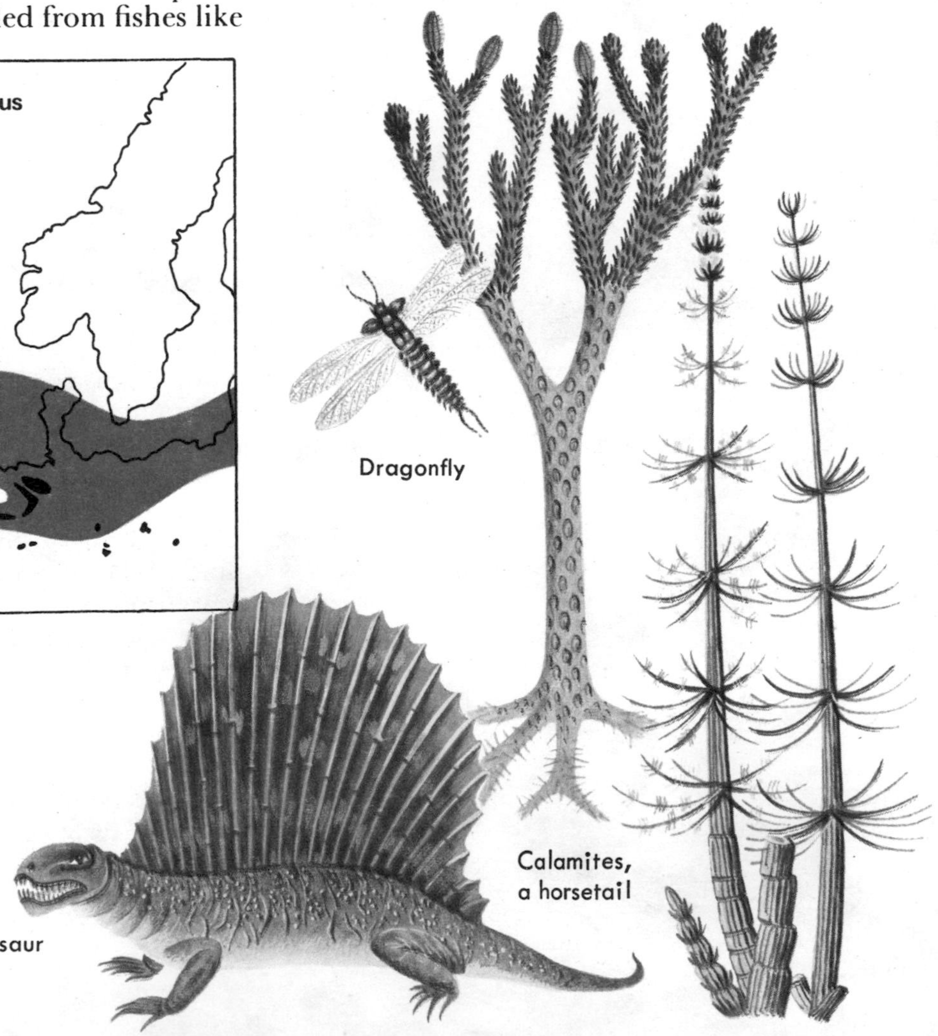

Lepidodendron, a club moss

Dragonfly

Calamites, a horsetail

Sailback Pelycosaur

Eryops

Seymouria

It was about 50 million years from the end of the Coal Age to the end of the Palaeozoic era. There is a common name for this long period. Scientists call it the Permian. During the Permian period great changes took place in the surface of the earth and in its climate. Vast areas of land were pushed upwards. Long mountain chains were formed. Many arms of the sea became dry land, and many swamps disappeared. Some regions grew to be much cooler, and some to be very arid. The number of plants and animals on land was greatly reduced.

Conifers had become the leading land plants. The leading land animals were amphibians and reptiles. None of them were big compared with the gigantic reptiles and mammals of later times.

Eryops was a big amphibian of the

Limnoscelis

period. It grew from six to eight feet long. As you see, it looked much like a huge frog with a tail. Like the other amphibians of its time, however, it had something which no amphibian has today — a third sensitive eye on its forehead.

Eryops megalocephalus is the full scientific name of this creature. The second part of the scientific name means 'big-headed'. Its head was truly big, and its mouth was enormous.

Eryops could walk, but not at all fast. Its legs, although stout, were so short that its body was close to the ground. It probably spent most of its time sunning itself at the edge of a swamp. It did not have to hurry to get food. 'Minnows' and water plants could be scooped up easily at the water's edge. Besides, Eryops, with its many sharp teeth, could capture some of its smaller amphibian relatives.

Although Eryops had a big skull, its brain was not very large. Instead, the bones of the skull were very thick. We can be sure that this big animal, as it sunned itself, did not do any thinking about the changes that were taking place on the earth. Perhaps it just let out a hoarse croak now and then, for it may, like today's toads and frogs, have had a voice.

Even though some amphibians lived on, Eryops disappeared long ago. In the end, size did not mean success. The largest amphibian now, the giant salamander of Japan, is only about half as big.

The reptiles descended from the amphibians. Seymouria was an amphibian, but it was much more reptilelike than Eryops. In fact, from fossils it was not easy for scientists to say whether Seymouria was an amphibian or a reptile — it had certainly almost changed enough from its amphibian ancestors to be classed as a reptile. Limnoscelis was a reptile. Probably, however, it spent much of its time in the water and lived on fish just as Seymouria probably did.

At a glance it is hard to tell the difference between the sailback you met in reading about the Coal Age, and Dimetrodon, the sailback pictured here. The

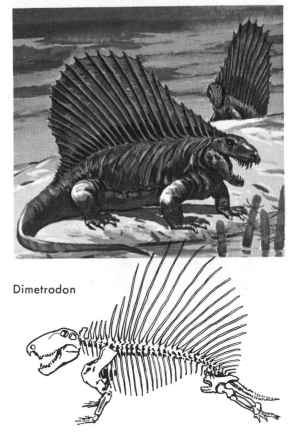

Dimetrodon

two were much the same shape. Dimetrodon lacked the crossbars in its sail which the other sailback had. The biggest difference between the two, however, is that Dimetrodon had very long, sharp teeth — it was a meat-eater. This pelycosaur was, in fact, one of the leading meat-eating land animals of its time. It was also by far the most common of all the reptiles in North America. Many fossils have been found there.

In the regions that were becoming desert, reptiles had a big advantage over amphibians. The amphibians all began their lives in water. The reptiles began theirs on land. The eggs of the amphibians were covered with a layer of jelly and were kept damp by being in water. The eggs of the reptiles had a shell around them. This shell protected them from drying out. The little reptiles that hatched from the eggs were not like little fish. They were very much like their parents. They could live on land because from the time they were hatched they had lungs to breathe with, not gills.

Compsognathus

As the long Palaeozoic era ended, the Mesozoic, or 'middle life', era began. This era, which lasted for some 165 million years, was the Age of Reptiles. During the long Mesozoic era, reptiles flourished amazingly. They practically took over the earth.

The Age of Reptiles is sometimes called 'the days of the dinosaurs', for this great group of reptiles appeared early in the era and the last ones died as the era ended.

The word 'dinosaur' means 'terrible reptile'. It is not a particularly good name, for not all the dinosaurs were terrible. Many were rather small animals, and some, though big, were gentle plant-eaters. But there were some dinosaurs that were truly terrible.

Stegosaurus

In all, there were thousands of different species; probably at least 5,000. One species would disappear and another species would take its place. For most of the thousands of species of dinosaurs there are no common names. They have only scientific names.

Plateosaurus was an early dinosaur. It was big—from the end of its nose to the tip of its tail it measured about 20 feet—but it was not terrible. It ate nothing but plants. Plateosaurus was rather clumsy. It must have been stupid, too. In its small head there was not much room for a brain.

The other three dinosaurs pictured came later. They all lived at about the same time, but they were not at all close relatives. As you might guess, Compsognathus and Allosaurus were much more closely related to each other than either of them was to Stegosaurus. All three were land animals—all dinosaurs were.

Compsognathus was small—no bigger than a cockerel. This little dinosaur could run fast on its two long hind legs, catching smaller reptiles and the mouse-like early mammals to eat. Its front legs were so small that they look as if they had not grown properly.

Allosaurus was a dinosaur that really deserves to be called terrible. It was a fierce meat-eater about 35 feet long—far larger than any meat-eating animal on land today. It, too, walked on its hind legs. Allosaurus means 'leaping reptile'. This meat-eating dinosaur, it is thought, used its powerful hind legs to go leaping about after its prey.

With such a creature as Allosaurus on the lookout for prey, life for other land animals must have been dangerous. It is not surprising that some of the plant-eating dinosaurs developed armour.

Stegosaurus, the 'plated reptile', was one of the armoured dinosaurs. It had a double row of bony plates all down its back and sharp spikes on its tail. Swinging its tail from side to side was like swinging a gigantic battle-club.

Stegosaurus, like many other dinosaurs, was built on the pattern of big bodies—it was 20 feet long—and small

Plateosaurus

brains. Its brain was not very much larger than a man's fist—too tiny to control the muscles of the hind legs and tail. These muscles were controlled by an enlargement of the spinal cord at the base of the tail.

The enlargement of the spinal cord at the base of the creature's tail gave rise to

what we call thinking. This armoured dinosaur, moreover, was not the only dinosaur that had two 'brains'. Some of the others that needed an extra 'brain' were the monstrous plant-eating dinosaurs you will find out about on the next two pages—the giants of the reptile world.

Allosaurus

the idea that Stegosaurus had two brains. A well-known jingle tells that Stegosaurus could think 'upon both sides of every question': it could think on one side of the question with the brain in its head and on the other side with the brain in its tail. It could, the jingle says, make 'both head and tail' of every problem. Actually, Stegosaurus did not do any of

19

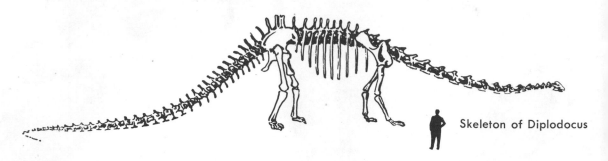

Skeleton of Diplodocus

The titanic Diplodocus was the longest animal ever to walk on land. It measured nearly 90 feet from the end of its nose to the tip of its tail.

Diplodocus only ate tender plants. It did not eat grass—there was not yet any grass in the world for it to eat. Many of the plants it ate grew in the numerous lakes and swamps. It must have taken this creature all day long to gulp in enough food for its enormous body. Probably it spent most of its life in lakes and swamps. Getting food was easy there, and the water helped to hold up its huge body.

The head of Diplodocus was small. There was not much room for brains. Indeed, its brain weighed only about a pound—not much of a brain for a body of 25 tons or so.

Diplodocus, like all the dinosaurs, hatched from eggs. We know that the eggs of one nine foot dinosaur were nine inches long. If Diplodocus followed the plan of an inch of egg for every foot of body, how enormous its eggs must have been!

Brachiosaurus was not quite so long as Diplodocus, but it was much heavier. So far as anyone knows, it was the heaviest animal that ever walked on land—it weighed 50 tons! Notice that in the picture Brachiosaurus is standing with only the top of its head above the water. Its nostrils were in the crest on top of its head. Many of the dinosaurs had nostrils at the top of their heads. Brachiosaurus, you can see, had front legs longer than its hind ones. With its long front legs and its long neck, this giant of the dinosaurs, if it could walk down a city street today, could easily look into third-storey windows.

Probably the best known of all dinosaurs is Brontosaurus. Its name means 'thunder reptile'. This dinosaur was not given its name because it had a voice like

Diplodocus

Brachiosaurus

thunder. No one knows what kind of sounds it may have made, if any at all. The scientist who named it chose its name, it is said, because he thought that when so huge an animal walked about, the ground would shake and make a noise like thunder. The picture of its skeleton on page 45 shows that Brontosaurus was a giant. It was about 70 feet long and weighed over 30 tons.

There were many other dinosaurs much like these three giants. They were not armoured as Stegosaurus was. They were all good prey for Allosaurus and the other big meat-eating dinosaurs of the time. They could not run easily, for their legs were like tree trunks and their long, heavy tails were certainly not easy to pull along. Probably their habit of spending much of the time in lakes was their best protection. They had thick skins too.

These giant dinosaurs were the biggest four-footed animals of all time. However, they were not the largest animals that ever lived. No dinosaur was as big as the blue whale of today.

Corythosaurus (in the foreground)
and Parasaurolophus, duck-billed dinosaurs
with strange crests that probably helped make underwater
feeding possible

Trachodon,
a very common duck-billed dinosaur

Styracosaurus

Ankylosaurus

The dinosaurs pictured here all appeared rather late in the Age of Reptiles. Most of them were plant-eaters. Only Tyrannosaurus and the little turkeylike dinosaur at the far left in the picture with Tyrannosaurus ate meat.

Tyrannosaurus—the name means 'tyrant reptile'—looked rather like its ancient relative Allosaurus, but it was larger. Tyrannosaurus grew to be almost 50 feet long and was from 18 to 20 feet tall as it walked about. It was the largest flesh-eater ever to live on land. Its jaws were so big that it could open its mouth to form a hole more than a yard long. Some of its sharp teeth were six inches long. The toes on its huge hind legs had sharp claws like an eagle's. But its 'arms' were ridiculously small and weak. The heavy tail of Tyrannosaurus helped this giant meat-eater to walk upright.

Triceratops means 'three-horned'. This armoured dinosaur had three sharp horns on its head. As a matter of fact, it had all its armour on its head and neck.

As long as it could face up to an enemy it was well protected, but behind the great bony frill around its neck, Triceratops' only protection was its thick skin. No doubt Triceratops won some battles, but often fell prey to the giant meat-eaters.

Styracosaurus was another horned dinosaur. It, too, had to face up to an attacker if its horns were to help.

Ankylosaurus was a sort of armoured tank. Its back and head were covered with plates of bone. Rings of bone covered its tail. Both its legs and its tail were protected with bony spikes. At the end of its tail there was a bony club. Except for some of the turtles, no other reptiles have ever been so well armoured. This dinosaur was about 15 feet long and five feet high.

The other three dinosaurs are so-called duckbilled dinosaurs, a very common group. Because of their big and often strangely shaped skulls, the duckbilled dinosaurs have been called 'Nature's biggest boneheads'. They must have provided many a meal for Tyrannosaurus and the other big meat-eating dinosaurs of their time.

Trachodon was about 30 feet long. On its toes and most of its 'fingers' it had little hoofs. Its 'hands', and probably its feet as well, were webbed. Trachodon spent much of its time in the water eating the plants growing there. Its name means 'rough tooth'. In its mouth this big plant-eater had almost a thousand teeth!

Tyrannosaurus attacking Triceratops

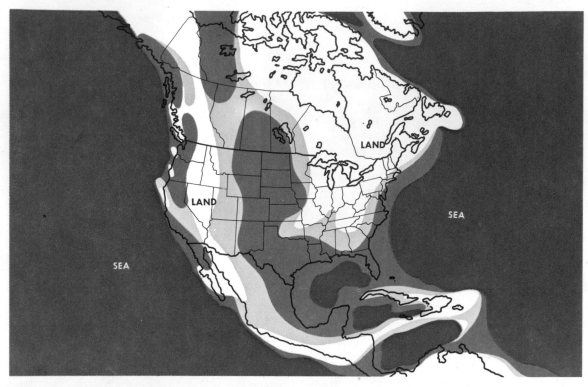

North America late in the Age of Reptiles (Cretaceous Period)

About 65 million years ago the dinosaurs all became extinct. Why they did, after being the lords of the land for 125 million years, is a mystery. With their disappearance the Age of Reptiles came to an end.

Perhaps the reason why many of the giant dinosaurs died is that their bodies were too big for their brains. With smaller bodies and bigger brains they might have

Oviraptor, an ostrich dinosaur

lived on. They were successful for a very long time because conditions on the earth remained almost the same for millions of years. When conditions changed, the huge creatures were not suited to their changed surroundings, and they were not intelligent enough to adapt to the new ones.

One of the changes that played a part in bringing about the end of the dinosaurs was the drying up of many of the lakes and swamps. There were fewer places in which water could help the giant plant-eating dinosaurs to hold up their huge bodies. There were also fewer plants to serve as food for them and for the other plant-eating dinosaurs. And as the plant-eaters became fewer and fewer, there was less food for the flesh-eaters.

Changes in temperature were also against the dinosaurs. Like today's reptiles, they were cold-blooded. Their temperature was the same as the temperature of their surroundings. The climate became colder in many regions. The dinosaurs living there had no way of keeping their bodies warm. Getting cold made

Protoceratops

them sluggish and less able to fend for themselves. The eggs of the dinosaurs, moreover, probably did not hatch as well after the climate began to change.

The drying up of lakes and swamps in North America and the change in climate were partly caused by the rise of the Rocky Mountains. The Rockies are, then, partly to blame for the death of the dinosaurs which were very common in the region corresponding to North America.

The habit of some dinosaurs of eating the eggs of others probably played a part in bringing an end to the dinosaurs. The small ostrichlike dinosaurs that ran about on two legs could cover ground fast. Many of them are thought to have got a part of their food by stealing eggs from the nests of other dinosaurs. If so, having two free feet to serve as hands must have been a great help in digging up the eggs. Their speed was needed to escape from the bigger dinosaurs whose nests they robbed. The name of Oviraptor means 'egg robber'.

When a nest of eggs and a skeleton of the small dinosaur Protoceratops were found in desert land in Mongolia many years ago, the crushed skull of an ostrichlike dinosaur was found with them. Perhaps the ostrichlike dinosaur was trying to eat the eggs when it was killed.

The rise of more advanced animals, the mammals, doubtless also played a part in the killing off of the dinosaurs. Early mammals probably ate dinosaur eggs. But many of the reptile relatives of the dinosaurs lived on.

Early mammals eating dinosaur eggs

Plesiosaurus

Ichthyosaurus

Geosaurus

During the Age of Reptiles by no means all the reptiles lived on land. There were also many in the sea. Among the reptiles in the sea were plesiosaurs, crocodiles, ichthyosaurs, turtles, and lizards.

The plesiosaurs were descendants of early land reptiles, but they certainly did not look like land animals. They were very different even from the big plant-eating dinosaurs that lived in lakes. They had stiff, rather flat bodies, and their four legs had become powerful paddles.

Some of the plesiosaurs had long necks and small heads, others short necks and long heads. Plesiosaurus, as you can see, was a long-necked plesiosaur. The mouth of this ancient reptile was full of sharp teeth—clearly Plesiosaurus was a meat-eater.

Geosaurus was like a crocodile. But with its fish-fin tail and paddle-shaped limbs it was very different from its four-footed land relatives. Some of the ancient

sea crocodiles were 50 feet long—twice as long as the biggest crocodile we know today.

'Ichthyosaur' means 'fish reptile'. This name was well chosen, for the ichthyosaurs certainly looked like big fishes. Their bodies were streamlined so that they could push their way through water easily, and their tails, like that of Geosaurus, were fishlike. In place of legs they had paddles much the shape of fishes' fins. They swam with their tails and bodies and steered with their 'fins', just as fishes do.

Ichthyosaurus and all the other ichthyosaurs had enormous eyes—bigger than those of any other animal of any time. A 25-foot ichthyosaur's eyes were as big as a man's head. If your eyes were as big in proportion to your size as an ichthyosaur's were to its size, they would be as big as cricketballs. Their huge eyes helped the ichthyosaurs to find prey in the dim light of the deep seas.

Flopping their way up on shore to lay their eggs must have been hard for many sea-reptiles. It was impossible for the ichthyosaurs. But reptile eggs will not hatch in water. The ichthyosaurs solved the problem in the only possible way: they kept their eggs in the mother's body until the eggs hatched. Little ichthyosaurs were born alive. No one knows whether baby ichthyosaurs followed their mother after they were born.

The ichthyosaurs died out before the end of the Age of Reptiles. They had copied fish so well that it is difficult to understand why they did not live on. Fish had been in the seas long before the ichthyosaurs, and the seas are still swarming with them now.

Ichthyosaurs were already scarce by the time the reptiles in these pictures appeared. These reptiles lived in the sea when Tyrannosaurus was 'tyrant' of the land reptiles.

Like the earlier long-necked Plesiosaurus, Trinacromerum and Kronosaurus were plesiosaurs. But they belonged to the group of plesiosaurs with short necks and long heads and beaks.

Apparently, long jaws were as good as long necks for catching fish. Kronosaurus was very large—nearly 50 feet long. Its head alone measures more than three yards. It was the giant of the plesiosaurs. One of the long-necked plesiosaurs of the time was almost as big. Its long, snakelike neck was twice the length of its body.

The tails of the plesiosaurs were not much use for pushing these big reptiles along. Their limbs, however, were wonderfully built paddles. Some of their toes had over a dozen joints! The plesiosaurs rowed through the water with their paddles.

Archelon was an early sea turtle. It looked much like some of the sea turtles of today, but it was larger than any that are living now. It measured up to 12 feet long and 12 feet across from flipper tip to flipper tip.

Tylosaurus belonged to the group of marine reptiles called mosasaurs. They were sea lizards, distant relatives of the big monitor land lizards now found in the Far East. Tylosaurus measured nearly 30 feet. All the mosasaurs followed the marine reptile pattern of having

Archelon   Trinacromerum

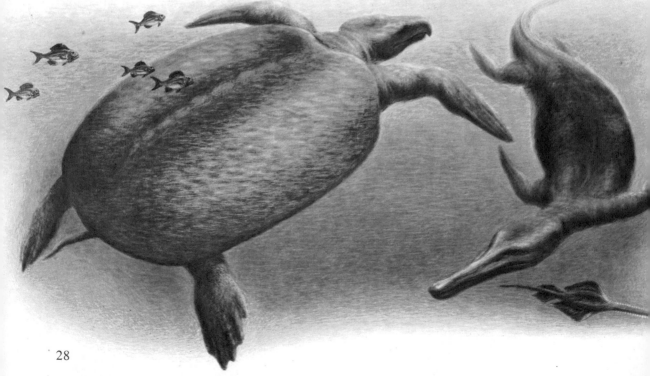

28

Kronosaurus

Tylosaurus

paddles instead of legs. Like snakes, they had scaly skins, and jaws with extra joints that let them swallow big prey. The mosasaurs were probably the greatest fish-eaters of the Mesozoic seas.

At the close of the Age of Reptiles the plesiosaurs and mosasaurs, disappeared too. No one knows why, since the turtles survived. But, whatever the reasons, all the great sea reptiles except the turtles completely disappeared like the dinosaurs.

29

Rhamphorhynchus

Some of the descendants of the early reptiles, instead of taking to the sea, took to the air. These were the pterosaurs. 'Pterosaur' means 'wing reptile'. The wings of the pterosaurs were formed from sheets of skin, like those of bats. Each 'hand' had one long 'finger' to which the front edge of the wing was fastened. The wing finger of the later pterosaurs was very long. Another name for these pterosaurs is pterodactyl. 'Pterodactyl' means 'wing finger'.

The body of a large pterodactyl was about the size of a goose or turkey, but the wings were huge. The largest had a wingspread of 27 feet, more than twice that of the wandering albatross, the largest of the present-day birds and four times that of any bat we know. The earliest flying reptiles known, had wings that spread out a little more than twice the length of their body.

One of the earliest of the pterosaurs had a fairy-tale-sounding name—Rhamphorhynchus. Rhamphorhynchus was about a foot and a half long. Its wingspread was about four feet. The long, thin tail of this pterosaur ended in a leaf-shaped piece of skin that served as a kind of rudder as the creature soared through the air.

Rhamphorhynchus seldom rested on the ground. Instead, it usually clung to a cliff or to the trunk or a branch of a tree. Perhaps it hung head down, just as bats often do now. It could clamber around in trees easily because it had claws at the front of each wing. The skin of the wing was fastened to the fourth finger, leaving three fingers free for holding on. The 'little finger' was missing.

Rhamphorhynchus had sharp teeth. Oddly enough, they pointed forwards. Teeth pointing backwards ought, it would seem, to have been much better for catching the fish that this flying reptile ate, but apparently its teeth made good spears.

Pterodactylus was one of the first of the pterodactyls. It was smaller than Rhamphorhynchus—in many cases no bigger than a sparrow—and it did not have a long tail. Nor did it have so many sharp teeth. But its wings were much, much longer in proportion to its body.

Pteranodon lived much later, at the same time as Tyrannosaurus and the duckbilled dinosaurs. With its 13-foot wings it was the giant of the flying reptiles. The long finger of each wing was nine feet long.

Pteranodon's head was big in proportion to its body. At a glance it would seem that this reptile was an exception among the reptiles, most of them having small brains. As a matter of fact, the brains of all the pterosaurs were rather large for reptiles. But Pteranodon's brain was not so large as one would imagine from the size of its skull. Most of its strange anvil-shaped head was full of air.

Scientists are not sure how well this giant pterodactyl could fly. Its hollow bones—many of the bones of the pterosaurs were hollow—and its great wings were perfect for soaring through the air. But since the only way it could move its wings was by flapping them, most scientists do not believe that it could fly nearly as well as most birds.

It is certain that a bad tear in the wing would make the wing useless. It would not be at all like the loss of a feather or two from the wing of a bird. Probably many a Pteranodon on a fish-catching expedition tore a wing and fell into the sea, where it was soon gobbled up. It is quite certain, too, that if Pteranodon, in

Pterodactylus

swooping down, had to make an emergency landing on level ground, it would have been almost impossible for it to get into the air again.

Pteranodon had no teeth at all, even though it was a meat-eater. But it had, as you see, a very long, stout beak.

This giant flying reptile may be thought of as a last fling of the pterosaurs. Its disappearance towards the close of the Age of Reptiles was the end of these creatures of the air.

The birds of today do not look much like crocodiles. But scientists say that the birds and the crocodiles, together with the dinosaurs and the flying reptiles, descended along separate lines from the same group of early reptiles. The birds, then, although distantly related to the flying reptiles, are not their descendants. Instead, the ancestors of the birds, scientists believe, were small reptiles that ran about swiftly on their hind legs. Perhaps they mostly lived in the trees,

leaping lightly from branch to branch. Gradually, it is thought, the scales of these reptiles became feathers and the front legs developed into wings. The reptiles that became birds changed in another important way, too: they became warm-blooded.

The first bird we know about is Archaeopteryx. Archaeopteryx was still so much like its reptilian ancestors that scientists could not be sure it was a bird if it were not for its feathers.

Archaeopteryx was very different from any bird of today. It had no bill, and it had jaws with teeth. No bird today has teeth.

The bony part of the tail of a bird of today is very short. In those days, though, the tail feathers spread out from this bony part like the ribs of a fan. There were many bones in the long tail of Archaeopteryx. Along this bony tail, feathers were arranged in pairs, one pair for every joint in the tail.

Pteranodon

Archaeopteryx

Archaeopteryx means 'ancient wing'. The wings of this ancient bird were not, however, true wings. Although they were feathered, they still ended in hands much like those of the meat-eating dinosaurs. Probably Archaeopteryx used its clawed fingers for climbing about in the trees it lived in and its outspread 'wings' to glide

Hesperornis

down to the ground or from tree to tree.

Archaeopteryx was about the size of a crow. For all we know, it may have been as black as a crow. Artists have to guess at the colour of all prehistoric animals.

This first bird appeared in the early days of the dinosaurs—about 150 million years ago. Many other birds, too, appeared in the Age of Reptiles. One was Hesperornis, the first known water bird. It appeared much later than Archaeopteryx.

Hesperornis was probably better fitted for diving than any bird of today. Its body, which was more than four feet long. was very slender, and its beak was long and sharp. It had powerful legs that made excellent oars, and big webbed feet. Like Archaeopteryx, Hesperornis had many teeth; it could hold on to the fish it caught.

This big diving bird could not fly. The reason is simple—it had the merest traces of wings. It could not walk well, either—its feet turned out at right angles to its body, and its legs were set too far back.

Hesperornis was large, but the true feathered giants of the past were ground birds. None of these really giant birds could fly.

Diatryma appeared soon after the end of the Age of Reptiles. It was seven feet tall and had powerful legs and a huge beak. There were other big birds much like it. If anyone could have looked down on the earth in those days, he might very well have thought that the birds were about to take over the earth, just as the reptiles had done many millions of years earlier. But they did not do so.

Phororhacos was much like diatryma. It lived in Patagonia, at the southern tip of South America, some 20 million years ago, long after the days of the dinosaurs. Phororhacos had a head as large as the head of a modern horse. Even though the bird was from seven to eight feet tall, its head was out of proportion. A sharp hook at the end of its beak served to tear flesh to bits.

The largest bird living today is the ostrich. Some of the flightless giants of the past were rather like it and its relatives, the cassowaries and kiwis. Aepyornis and the moas of New Zealand were among them.

Aepyornis is sometimes spoken of as the 'elephant bird', in Madagascar. It was much the size of an ostrich, but it laid eggs as big as footballs. One would have been equal to several dozen hen's eggs.

The tallest birds that ever lived were moas. Some of these birds were 12 feet high. The moas are not very ancient. When the first missionaries went to New Zealand they heard stories of birds big enough to trample men to death. Apparently man had appeared on the earth before the moas disappeared. The early Maori inhabitants of New Zealand may have helped to bring about the extinction of the moas by killing them for food.

It has been suggested that the ancient flightless birds, as well as those we have

Diatryma

Moa

Aepyornis

Phororhacos

now, descended from primitive birds that were never able to fly. But scientists do not agree. They say that in the beginning all birds could fly but that some lost the power to do so. Perhaps these no longer needed to fly, either to get food or to escape meat-eating enemies.

Borhyaena

Borophagus

Merycoidodon, an oreodont

The first mammals were not very important-looking creatures. In the Age of Reptiles, no one, if he could have seen these little furry animals—most of them the size of rats and mice—would have had any idea that their descendants would one day dominate the birds and take the place of the reptiles as the lords of the earth. But they did. Scientists call that era that followed the Age of Reptiles the Caenozoic era. 'Caenozoic' means 'recent life'. The common name for the era is Age of Mammals.

At the end of the Age of Reptiles the climate in many parts of the world had become much colder. This change caused great hardship to the cold-blooded reptiles. But it was not nearly so much of a hardship for the warm-blooded birds and

for the mammals, also warm-blooded. Their bodies stayed warm even in cold surroundings.

Their hair was a big help to the early mammals. Hair, or fur, is a very poor conductor of heat. It served to keep the heat of their bodies from escaping. With hair to keep them warm, the mammals could be active all the year round.

The early mammals, moreover, were built so that they could move very fast. They had to be quick to keep out of the way of the much bigger meat-eating dinosaurs. Besides, they, too, were meat-eaters, and being fast gave them a great advantage.

Another great advantage the early mammals had over reptiles was the better care they took of their young. Most of

A grassland of 20 million years ago (Miocene Period)

the reptiles laid their eggs and then went off and left them. The eggs, and the young reptiles that hatched from them, were at the mercy of meat-eating animals and the weather, but the mammals' young were born alive. They carried their eggs in the mother's body until the eggs developed into young animals. After they were born the babies were fed with milk from the mother. They were guided and fed until they were able to look after themselves.

Most important of all, the mammals had bigger brains in proportion to their size than the reptiles. They were better able to adapt in a changing world.

The scene above shows some of the mammals that grazed on the prairies of North America 20 million years ago.

The two animals at the left are giant 'pigs'. In the centre foreground there is a 'deer', with a strange pair of horns on its nose. A small rhinoceros is behind the deer. The horses in the background are easy to recognize. The giraffelike animal on the far right is an early camel. Notice that it has no hump. The clumsy-looking animal near the centre of the picture is a chalicothere. The group it belonged to became extinct thousands of years ago.

Only one of the strange mammals pictured separately has any close relatives still living. It is Borophagus, an early dog. Borhyaena was a meat-eating pouched mammal. Merycoidodon an oreodont ate plants. Like many other grass-eaters, it chewed cud.

During the Age of Mammals—the age

we are still in—mammals of thousands of species have developed. As one would expect, since the Age of Mammals has lasted for some 65 million years, many kinds have appeared, flourished, and then disappeared. Some of the extinct mammals were very large. It was not long, as time goes in the story of the earth, after the giant dinosaurs disappeared before there were giants among the mammals. Baluchitherium, Uintatherium, and Brontops are three that deserve a place in any parade of ancient animals.

Baluchitherium, the 'Baluchistan beast', was a rhinoceros. But it was horn-less and much larger than any of today's rhinoceroses. It was, in fact, the largest land mammal of all time—a tall giraffe would just come up to its shoulders—and it was very heavy. Imagine trying to fit this big beast into a room in your house. It would need a room 30 feet long with a ceiling of over 20 feet high!

Uintherium, the 'Uinta beast' gets its name from the Uinta Mountains of the western United States of America, where fossils of it are found. It lived much earlier than Baluchitherium and was not nearly so enormous as that largest of all land mammals, but it was the giant of its time. Uintatherium specialized in horns. It had three pairs at various places on its homely face.

Brontops belonged to the group of mammals called titanotheres, or 'giant beasts'. It, too, specialised in horns, but it had only one pair, just behind its nose. They were, however, very large. Its name means 'thunder face'. This big mammal's skull curved downwards behind its nose so that its face was the shape of a soup dish. As one would guess, the 'giant beast' was not the brainiest of animals. It lived at the same time as Baluchitherium.

Not all the giant mammals of the past lived on land. When Uintatherium was the giant on land, Zeuglodon, an early whale, lived in the open sea. It grew to be 70 feet long, but was very slender. If

Baluchitherium

Uintatherium

Brontops

Zeuglodon had not disappeared long before there were any people, we would know where early sailors got their stories of enormous sea serpents.

We can trace the ancestry of many of our mammals back through millions of years. We can see what changes, in some cases very great ones, that have taken place in them since they first appeared on the earth.

We have a very complete record of the ancestry of the horse. The story begins with Hyracotherium, better known as eophippus, the 'dawn horse'.

Eohippus, a little animal no bigger than a fox, lived early in the Age of Mammals. Its home was in the woodlands of Europe and western North America.

The 'dawn horse' had a short neck, a short face, and teeth that could only chew tender leaves. On each forefoot it had four toes—the 'thumb' was missing

and on each hind foot it had three. Each toe ended in a little hoof. Tiny bones in the feet of this little dawn horse, relics of its missing thumb and big and little toes show that its ancestors had once been five-toed animals.

Eohippus was well equipped for living in wooded country. It could run in and out among the trees easily and hide in the shadows from its meat-eating enemies. It could reach and eat the leaves on bushes and on low branches of trees. The feet of this little horse were suitable for walking on soft, spongy ground.

As time went by, conditions changed in the regions where eohippus lived. The ground was not so soft as it had been. As its surroundings changed, eohippus, generation by generation, changed, too.

After many centuries it had changed so much that scientists give it a new name— Mesohippus, the 'middle horse'.

Mesohippus was about the size of a red setter. Its neck and its face were longer than those of eohippus and so were its legs. Its feet had also changed.

Eohippus

Hyracotherium Mesohippus Merychippus Pliohippus

Mesohippus had three toes on each foot. The middle toe was larger than the other two, but all three reached the ground.

Conditions on the earth kept on changing. The climate became much drier in the places where Mesohippus lived.

Much of the woodland disappeared. In its place there was grassland. If mesohippus had not been able to change, too, we would never have had our horses of today.

But, generation by generation, Mesohippus did change. With low-branching trees scarce, its teeth changed so that instead of eating leaves it could graze on grass. It grew taller and swifter, and its neck and face grew longer. It changed so much that it is called Merychippus, the 'cud-chewing horse'. Size and speed were a help now that woods to hide in were scarce. Merychippus could run much faster than its ancestors because it ran on only one hoof on each foot. The two side toes dangled.

By some 10 million years ago Merychippus in turn had changed in so many ways that it has a new name, Pliohippus. The name means 'more (like a) horse'.

Pliohippus had only one hoof on each of its feet. Its face was long and horselike, and its teeth were even better than those of Merychippus for chewing grass.

From Pliohippus came the horses, zebras, and wild asses of today. All of them carry about with them evidence of their early ancestors' several toes. Hidden under the skin there are small splinters of bone left from the vanishing toes.

The story of the elephant is very different from the story of the horse. It has to be pieced together from a much less complete record. The story begins in

African Elephant

Mastodon

Trilophodon

Equus,
the modern
horse

Africa about 40 million years ago with a small animal that looked somewhat like a pig or a tapir. No man ever saw this animal alive. If anyone had, he would never have guessed that it would have descendants with long trunks, enormous ears, and great ivory tusks weighing more than 100 pounds apiece.

The name of this ancestor of the elephants is Moeritherium. Its name is taken from Lake Moeris, an ancient lake in Egypt where fossils of this animal have been found.

Moeritherium was stocky. Its legs were thick and short and its body was long. It had two small tusks in its upper jaw—they were simply extra-large, sharp-pointed teeth—and two in its lower jaw. These tusks were useful in raking up plant food.

Generation by generation, some of the descendants of Moeritherium grew taller. As they did, other changes took place that made it easier for them to eat from the ground. Both jaws grew longer, and so did the tusks. The nose and upper lips became longer, too. The elephant's trunk had begun to develop.

Later descendants grew still taller. Their heads got bigger and their necks became shorter. Their jaws and tusks kept on growing longer and the snout stretched enough to make up not only for the longer legs but also for the shorter necks. They came to look like Trilophodon.

Then a strange thing happened. The lower jaws, after having become longer, grew shorter again until there was nothing left but a 'chin'. The lower tusks disappeared and the long upper ones curved upwards instead of downwards. With no lower jaw to rest on, the stretched-out snout was left to hang down over the chin. It was a real trunk.

The descendants of Moeritherium that became elephants were not the only ones with trunks. Down the long road from Moeritherium to the elephants there were many sidelines. Dinotherium was one. The mastodons were others. The Mastodon, as you can see, was very much like an elephant.

Indian Elephant

Dinotherium

Moeritherium

PACIFIC OCEAN

ATLANTIC OCEAN

Woolly Mammoth

Sabretooth

Mastodon

About two million years ago, the time that we call the Ice Age began. It is named for the parts of it when vast sheets of ice spread from the regions around the North Pole down over much of the northern hemisphere. By this time the elephant tribe had spread far and wide. Two of them—the mammoth and the mastodon—were common in northern lands.

The biggest mammoths grew to be 14 feet tall at the shoulder. The huge curved tusks measured 13 feet. Some mammoths were covered with coarse hair. Great herds of these woolly mammoths roamed about, often very close to the edge of the ice. Their hair protected them from the cold.

No one knows exactly when man first appeared on the earth. We do know that there were people in parts of Europe during the last part of the Ice Age. These people lived in caves. There were woolly mammoths in Europe at that time. The cavemen drew pictures of these vanished elephants on the walls of some of their caves.

The mammoths were a great help to the cavemen. They provided them with food. Perhaps some of the pictures of mammoths on the walls of caves were ment to be prayers for a successful mammoth hunt.

The cavemen also drew pictures of the woolly rhinoceros. This big hairy creature, too, was found in Europe in the Ice Age.

The mastodon, like the woolly mammoth and the woolly rhinoceros, was well protected from the cold. How strange these big furry animals would look beside their almost hairless relatives of today.

The mammoth, mastodon, and woolly rhinoceros were plant-eaters. The sabretooth was an Ice Age meat-eater. Its name comes from the big cat's two enormous fangs, which were like swords, or sabres. With them it could make deep stabs into the bodies of animals with thick hides. Mastodons were probably the chief food of this meat-eater. About the time the mastodon disappeared—first in Europe and then in North America—the sabretooth, too, became extinct.

Woolly Rhinoceros

41

Boreostracon

During much of the Ice Age, the climate of the part of North America that is now the United States was mild. There were long, warm periods between the times of spreading ice sheets. Many animals that had moved up from South America flourished.

One that became very common was Megatherium. Its name means 'giant beast'. Megatherium was a ground sloth. The sloths of today are all tree dwellers. They are strange, clumsy beasts that hang from the limbs of trees without moving very much. Although they have four feet, these feet are not at all well adapted to walking. Megatherium spent its whole life on the ground. It was far too heavy to live in trees.

This 'giant beast' was a harmless plant-eater. It had a thick tail and heavy hind legs. When it sat up on its haunches, as it often did, it could use its front legs with their strong claws as arms to dig out roots or to slash off branches of trees. It was so strong that it could break down whole trees to get the leaves from them. When it sat up, it was about twice as tall as a man. It had a long, powerful tongue that it used to strip leaves off the trees.

Megatherium's sharp, curved claws were helpful in digging up roots, but they were rather a nuisance when the animal walked. They had to be doubled under in an awkward way, since they could not be pulled in as a cat's can. Perhaps they were one of the reasons why this great ground sloth became extinct.

Boreostracon was another immigrant from the south. It was one of the glyptodons, ancient mammals related to the armadillos of today. They had some hair, but they were not at all furry.

Boreostracon sometimes grew to be as big as an ox. Like all the glyptodons, it was almost completely covered in armour. On its back it had a shield much like that of an armadillo. In addition to the shield on its back, Boreostracon had a bony plate on its head, bony rings around its tail, and many spikes at the end of its tail. It could not roll up like an armadillo.

The picture above shows how some of the animals of the Ice Age met their death in a part of the United States not covered

Megatherium

A tar pool trap

by the ice. Here oil welled up out of the ground and formed pools of sticky tar. After rain, water would collect on top of the tar in these pools. Animals such as mammoths, horses, and camels would wade out into the pools to get a drink. Then they would be trapped in the sticky tar.

The cries of the trapped animals would attract the sabretooth, the giant condor, and other meat-eaters. The weapons of these big meat-eaters were of no use when they found themselves sinking into the tar, too. Many sabretooths and birds of prey were trapped. So many animals were caught in these tar pools that they are often called the 'death-trap' tar pools.

A number of mammals beside the mammoth provided food for the cavemen. Among them were reindeer, musk oxen, wild horses, and wild sheep.

The animals that provided the cavemen with food might be thought of as friends. The cavemen had many animal enemies, too. One was the cave bear. The cavemen lived in caves during the winter to protect themselves from the cold. The cave-bears sought shelter in the same caves. Many a fight must have been fought between the cavemen and the big cave-bears. Of course, if a caveman won a fight with a cave-bear, he had a warm bearskin for a blanket or for clothing. The cavemen had to depend on wild animals for winter clothing as well as for food.

We are still in the Caenozoic era—the Age of Mammals. The Ice Age and the time since then, often called the Age of Man, form parts of it. Man, you probably know, is a mammal. Will mammals, you may very well wonder, continue to be the earth's leading animals? Or, a hundred million years or so from now, will most of the kinds of mammals of today belong to a parade of ancient animals? Will the elephants, the antelopes, and the whales, to name but a few, come to an end as the dinosaurs did? No one can tell. At the moment there is little to make us think that man himself is in danger of being crowded off the earth by other animals. Man is more likely to kill off many of the other species of animals.

The Earth's Rock Diary

If it were not for fossils, no one would know about the trilobites, the dinosaurs, the chalicotheres, or any of the other prehistoric animals that are extinct. We know about ancient plants from fossils, too.

The name 'fossil' comes from the Latin word for 'dig'. Many of the fossils we find are in solid rock so that they have to be dug out. But not all fossils are, because they are not all made in the same way.

A fossil may be a whole animal that was buried in such a way that the body could not decay. Many mammoths have been found in the far north, frozen in great blocks of ice left from the Ice Age. So have bodies of the woolly rhinoceros. Of course, the meat begins decaying once these animals are broken out of the ice. Bodies of the woolly rhinoceros have turned up in tar pools too.

Many insects of long ago were trapped in the resin of ancient pine trees. Later the resin was buried underground and became amber. Although for the most part the buried insects have almost dis-

Ancient Fish

Trilobites

Insect in Amber

Petrified Wood

Fossils

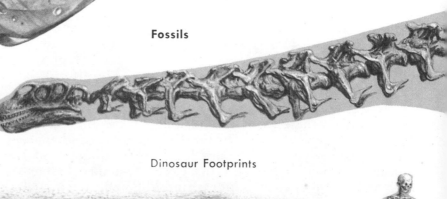

Dinosaur Footprints

appeared, their shapes show as sharp hollows in the amber. In many museums there are pieces of amber containing fossil insects. From them we see what the insects looked like when they were trapped millions of years ago.

Many fossils are casts. One of the pictures shows a piece of rock on which there are several trilobite casts. The story of every trilobite cast is something like this: a trilobite died, and its body fell to the muddy bottom of the sea. Soon the soft parts of its body decayed. Then the hard covering served as a mould. It filled with limy mud. In time the hard covering itself decayed and the space it had taken up was filled with limy mud. Later, no one knows how much later, the mud hardened, just as the mud around it did, into solid rock.

The fossil fern leaf pictured is a cast, too. The leaf was pressed down in some way into mud. It decayed but left its imprint in the mud. More mud washed into the imprint. All the mud hardened into solid rock. When the rock was later split in two, there was a raised cast of the leaf on one surface and the imprint in which it was made on the other.

Fossil footprints are imprints. Those in the picture were made when a dinosaur walked across a layer of soft mud.

Ordinarily such prints would have been washed away or trampled out. But conditions were such that they were not. When the mud became solid rock the footprints remained.

The bones in the skeleton of the great dinosaur Brontosaurus are petrified. 'Petrified' means 'turned to stone'. They were petrified in this way: the dinosaur died and fell into a lake or swamp. It was promptly covered up with sand or mud. The soft tissues of the body decayed rather rapidly, but the bone tissue of the skeleton was left. Then, little by little, water brought minerals that filled up all the tiny hollows in the bones and made them solid as stone. The minerals then preserved the bone itself by shutting away the air and water that would have destroyed it. The fish skeleton pictured is also petrified, but it has not been separated from the rock in which it was found.

In the petrified wood there is no wood left at all. As the trunk of an ancient tree lay covered with mud, water took away the wood, particle by particle, and gradually replaced it with mineral deposits. At last the trunk was rebuilt in stone.

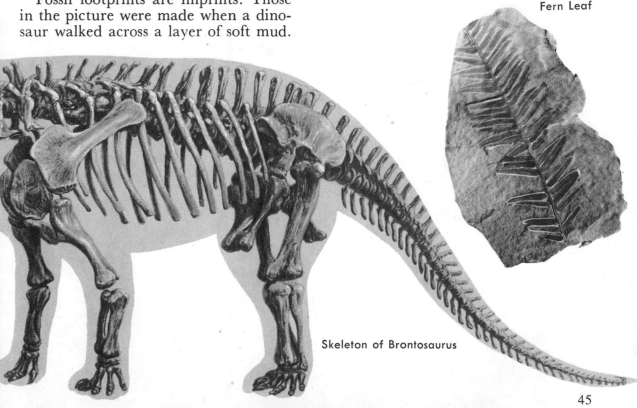

Fern Leaf

Skeleton of Brontosaurus

In our museums there are many skeletons built of the petrified bones of ancient animals. It takes an enormous amount of work to free the bones of a big animal from the rock in which they are found. The rock must be chipped away piece by piece. If the fossils are rather small, blocks of rock containing them may be cut out and taken to a museum. The fossils are not freed until they reach the museum workshops.

Large fossils may be so heavy that they are difficult to transport. Just the skull of one dinosaur, when it was in a box and ready to be delivered, weighed 3,650 pounds. Imagine what a whole petrified skeleton of a diplodocus would weigh! And think how hard it would be to fasten the bones of a dinosaur back in place.

A skeleton like the one pictured on this page is sometimes found with the bones in almost the right position. In many cases, however, the bones are scattered about and mixed in with the bones of other animals. It is not always easy to tell which ones belonged together or when all the bones of a creature have been found.

Often a fossil bone is broken. The collector may put such a bone in a plaster cast for transportation.

Some fossils are simply the hard parts of plants or animals that have been kept as they were. A fossil may, for example, be a bone that has remained unchanged without being petrified. Great quantities of fossil bones have come from peat bogs, tar pits, and quicksand.

The outside 'skin' or crust of the earth is made up of rocks of many different kinds. Some of them are made from sediments, such as sand and mud, that settle on the floor of lakes and seas or from shells that fall to the bottom of the sea. These rocks are often spoken of as water-made rocks. *Sedimentary rocks* is the scientific name for them.

Other rocks are made from hot, liquid rock that comes from deep in the earth. Such rocks are called *igneous rocks*. This name is from the Latin word for fire. Sometimes igneous rocks are called volcanic rocks. It is easy to see why they are, since many of them are made from the hot, liquid rock that pours from the craters of volcanoes.

There are also rocks that have been much changed since they were first formed. These are the *metamorphic rocks*. 'Metamorphic' means 'changed'.

The different layers of rock that make up the earth's crust may be thought of as pages in the earth's diary. They tell the story of the earth during the long ages before there were any people who could write of living things or take note of changes in the appearance of the earth. A deep cut in the earth's crust, like the Grand Canyon in America, opens up rock pages covering millions and millions of years for scientists to 'read'.

The layers of water-made rocks are the pages that tell most of the story of ancient life. It is not surprising that they are, because mud and water play such an important part in the making of fossils.

Skeleton of the dinosaur Hadrosaurus

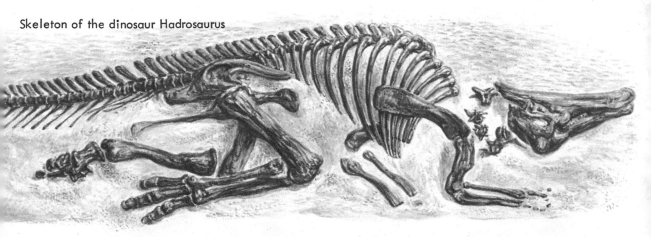

Shale

Sandstone

Limestone

Conglomerate

The rocks pictured on these pages are all water-made, or sedimentary, rocks. There are outcrops of such rocks in many places.

Shale is made from mud. A piece of shale smells like mud when it is wet. It feels rather like soap.

Sandstone, as its name suggests, is made of grains of sand cemented together. You can feel the grains if you rub your fingers over a piece of sandstone. A layer of sandstone sometimes provides a clue about its formation by having ripple marks on it.

Limestone may be made of lime that has settled on the bottom of a lake from the water itself. Anyone who has seen the lime that collects on the inside of a kettle knows that water can have a great deal of lime in it. Limestone may, instead, be made of the shells of water animals. Vast numbers of animals take lime from the water of lakes and seas to make shells for themselves. When they die they sink to the bottom of the water. The soft parts decay or are eaten up. Animals with shells have lived and died in such numbers that in many places thick layers of limestone have been built by their shells. A piece of limestone may be a great mass of fossil shells. Some limestones make excellent building stone.

Conglomerate is usually part sandstone, but it also contains pebbles. One nickname for it is 'puddingstone'.

A pebble is a small piece of rock that has been knocked about so that it has lost its rough edges. A handful of pebbles picked up on a beach usually includes some bits of sedimentary rock, some igneous rock, and some metamorphic rock. Many of them have been carried a long way from the mass of rock they came from, perhaps by waves, perhaps by long-gone glaciers of the Ice Age.

Sometimes pebbles are so worn by their journeys that it is hard, unless they are cracked open, to tell what rock they are made of. Those pictured below are all pieces of water-made rocks. One is sandstone, four are limestone, and four are shale.

Beach pebbles

A Salt Mine

Rock Salt

Lignite

Rock salt and coal are other water-made rocks. They are both so useful that we mine them in great quantities.

Since sea water contains salt, it is not surprising that in places, layers of salt have been formed at the bottom of the sea. Rock salt seldom contains fossils, for although many plants and animals live in the salt water of the oceans, life becomes scarce when the sea water is salty enough for a layer of salt to settle from it.

As you know, coal was formed, not from sediments washed down into a lake or sea, but from buried forests. The diagrams below tell the story of how coal was made. Many plant fossils are found in coal. It is from them that we can tell what trees grew during the Coal Age.

Layers of water-made rocks tell us much more about the earth's history than what plants and animals once lived there. They tell where lakes and seas used to be. Land and sea have not remained the same through the ages. The map on page 15 shows that in the days when the coal was being made the sea spread over hundreds of square miles of what is now dry land. The map is based on layers of water-made rocks which scientists have found—rocks made during the Coal Age.

Those who know how to read the earth's rock diary can also read from water-made rocks about changes in climate during past ages. Rock salt, for example, is much more likely to be formed when the climate is dry and water evaporates fast from lakes and seas. Fossils found in water-made rocks help, too, to tell the story of changes in climate. Fossils of coral and such tropical or semitropical plants as figs and palms found in Greenland, for example, show us that Greenland was once, millions of years ago, much warmer than it is today.

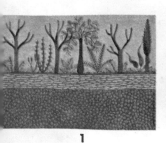

1

2

3

4

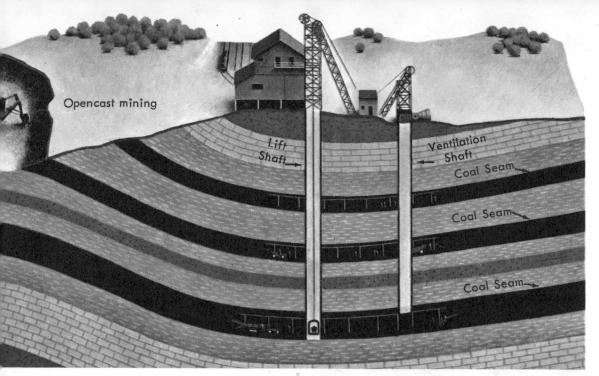

Opencast mining

Lift Shaft

Ventilation Shaft

Coal Seam

Coal Seam

Coal Seam

A Shaft Mine

1. Back in the Coal Age dense forests grew in vast swamps.

2. The land sank and trees were drowned.

3. The trees were covered with mud.

4. The land rose and forests grew again.

5. Again the land sank and once more the trees were drowned.

6. Again the drowned trees were covered with mud.

7. In time, after perhaps several ups and downs, the regions of the buried forests became dry land. Deep underground the forest layers changed to coal.

8. Now men dig into the ground to get the coal formed from the buried forests of millions of years ago.

Soft Coal

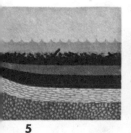

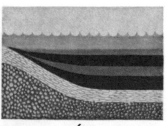
5

6

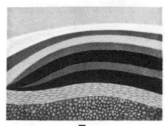
7

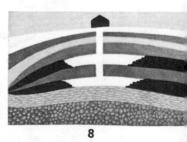
8

Basalt

All the rocks pictured on these two pages are igneous, or volcanic, rocks. Several of the specimens are basalt or granite, which are very common igneous rocks.

The diagrams on the next page show how a volcano can build itself into a mountain. Hot liquid rock is squeezed up to the surface from deep beneath the earth. While it is underground it is called magma. When it pours out on the surface it is called lava. At times a volcano erupts so violently that lava is shot high into the air and shattered into pieces. The pieces cool and harden into cinders and bits of ash, most of which fall near the opening the lava came from. Gradually they build a cone-shaped hill around the opening. And more and more lava, cinders, and ash make the hill into a great mountain.

Lava that pours out of a volcano may cool very quickly. It may have many spaces in it just as slag does that comes from steel mills. These spaces were filled with hot gases as the lava poured out. Two of the rocks formed in this way are pumice and scoria. Pumice is so light that it will float in water. If a volcano in or near the sea erupts, pumice may cover the water for miles around. Scoria is much coarser.

Obsidian and rhyolite are other rocks formed from lava that cools quickly. They have no spaces in them. Obsidian looks like smooth glass. In fact, it is often called volcanic glass. As a rule it is black. Rhyolite is light-coloured and rather glassy.

Basalt is formed from lava that is slower to cool. It is a dull-black rock, as the pictures show. In some places there are layers of basalt hundreds of feet thick. A layer may break up into six-sided columns. Anyone who has visited the Giant's Causeway in Ireland has seen columns of basalt like this.

Pumice

Rhyolite

Porphyry

Obsidian

Scoria

Diorite

Granite

Magma may cool when it comes near the surface and harden into solid rock underground. Granite is formed from magma that hardens beneath the surface. This common igneous rock may be pink, red or grey in colour. It has dark crystals in it that give it a speckled look. Although formed underground, granite is often found at the surface, because the rocks which originally were above it have been worn away. Granite is so hard that it has been called 'the rock everlasting'. It takes a high polish and is an excellent building stone.

There are a great many other igneous rocks. Some, like granite, have cooled so slowly underground that crystals large enough to be seen have formed in them. Among these are diorite and porphyry. Some of the crystals in porphyry are especially large. Other rocks, like pumice, obsidian, rhyolite, and basalt, are made from lava that pours out over the surface of the ground. The crystals, if there are any, in these rocks are very tiny.

From the igneous-rock pages in the earth's diary, scientists can tell that in parts of the world there were once active volcanoes where there are none today. They can tell, too, that at times in the past great cracks opened up in the earth and allowed lava to pour in floods from them.

How a volcano builds itself

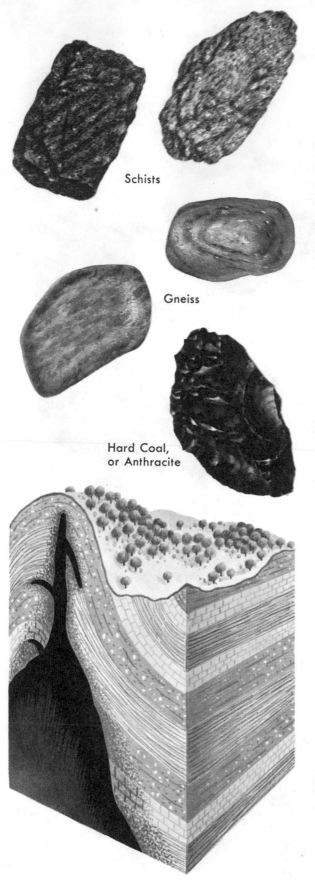

Schists

Gneiss

Hard Coal,
or Anthracite

The metamorphic rocks in the earth's crust are like pages of the diary which have been re-written. After layers of rock have been formed, they are sometimes squeezed into great folds. They are sometimes bulged up by magma pushing from underneath. The squeezing, pushing and heating bring about changes in the rocks.

The diagram on this page shows magma being forced up through layers of rock of different kinds. Around the magma there is a zone where the rocks are being changed.

Marble, slate, quartzite, and hard coal are simple metamorphic rocks. They are not greatly changed from the rocks they came from. All marble was once limestone, all quartzite was once sandstone, all slate was once shale, and all hard coal came from soft coal.

Gneiss of the kind pictured is a simple metamorphic rock, too. It is so much like the granite it came from that it is often called banded granite. Some gneisses are more complicated.

The schists—there are many kinds—are rocks greatly changed. Just looking at them does not give us much of a clue as to how they began. A schist may be formed from shale or from conglomerate or from any one of several other rocks.

Many of the metamorphic rocks are very useful. Hard coal, for example, is a much cleaner fuel than soft coal. It is not dusty, and it produces little smoke.

Slate can be split into very thin sheets with smooth surfaces. It has long been used for blackboards and for roofing slates. This common metamorphic rock may be red, green, blue-grey, brown, or purple.

Marble is the most beautiful of the metamorphic rocks. It can be given a high polish. The purest marble is white, but marble may be grey, green, pink, red, or black. Much marble is streaked. Many statues and fountains are made of marble.

Quartzite is an extremely durable rock. In the days of brick pavements some of the 'bricks' used were blocks or quartzite instead of true bricks of baked clay.

Slate

Marble

Quartzite

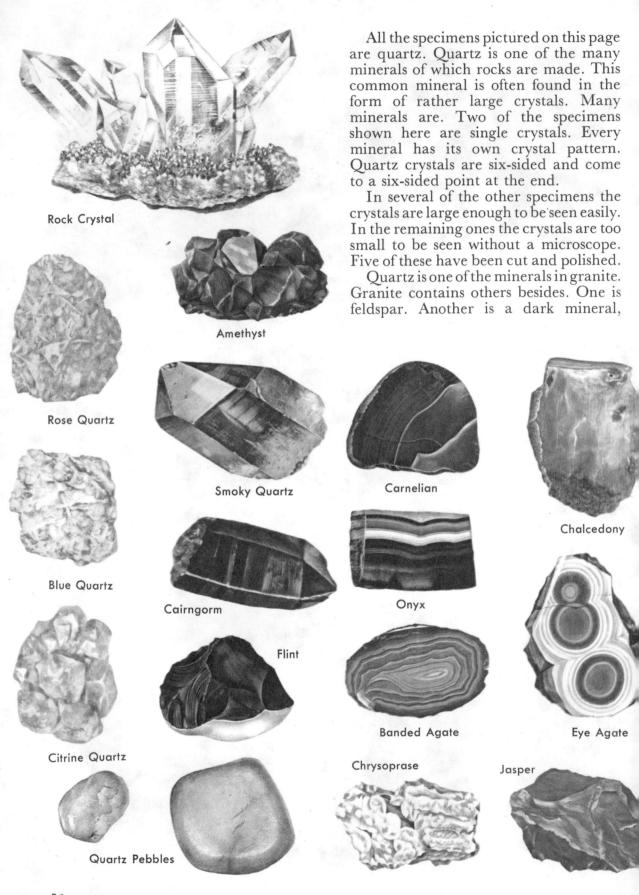

Rock Crystal

All the specimens pictured on this page are quartz. Quartz is one of the many minerals of which rocks are made. This common mineral is often found in the form of rather large crystals. Many minerals are. Two of the specimens shown here are single crystals. Every mineral has its own crystal pattern. Quartz crystals are six-sided and come to a six-sided point at the end.

In several of the other specimens the crystals are large enough to be seen easily. In the remaining ones the crystals are too small to be seen without a microscope. Five of these have been cut and polished.

Quartz is one of the minerals in granite. Granite contains others besides. One is feldspar. Another is a dark mineral,

Amethyst

Rose Quartz

Smoky Quartz

Carnelian

Chalcedony

Blue Quartz

Cairngorm

Onyx

Citrine Quartz

Flint

Banded Agate

Eye Agate

Chrysoprase

Jasper

Quartz Pebbles

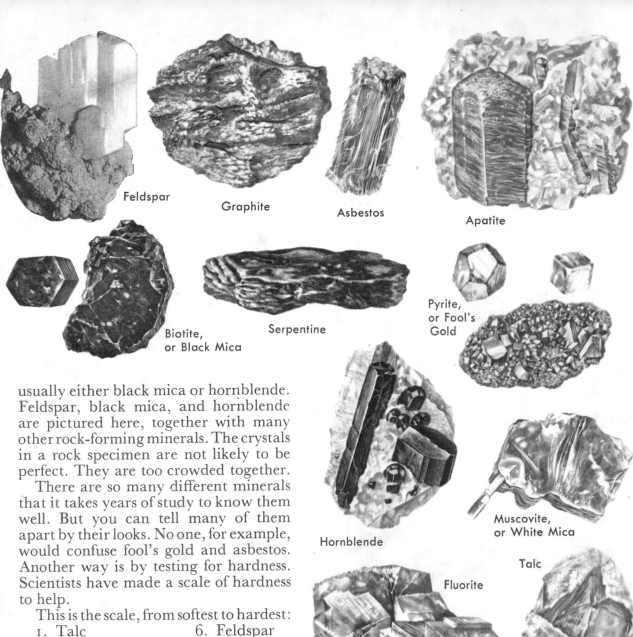

Feldspar

Graphite

Asbestos

Apatite

Biotite,
or Black Mica

Serpentine

Pyrite,
or Fool's
Gold

Hornblende

Muscovite,
or White Mica

usually either black mica or hornblende. Feldspar, black mica, and hornblende are pictured here, together with many other rock-forming minerals. The crystals in a rock specimen are not likely to be perfect. They are too crowded together.

There are so many different minerals that it takes years of study to know them well. But you can tell many of them apart by their looks. No one, for example, would confuse fool's gold and asbestos. Another way is by testing for hardness. Scientists have made a scale of hardness to help.

This is the scale, from softest to hardest:

1. Talc
2. Gypsum
3. Calcite
4. Fluorite
5. Apatite
6. Feldspar
7. Quartz
8. Topaz
9. Corundum
10. Diamond

Talc, as you see, is the softest mineral and diamond is the hardest. You can scratch talc with your thumbnail. Books about minerals usually give their hardness ratings. If you have a mineral specimen you are trying to identify and you find that quartz will scratch it but that it will scratch apatite, you know that it must be one with a rating between five and seven. Some other ways of identifying mineral specimens can be used only in specially equipped laboratories.

Talc

Fluorite

Sulphur

Tourmaline

The crystals of some minerals are so beautiful that we use them as jewels, or gems. Some of the varieties of quartz you have already seen are gemstones. The most popular of them is amethyst. Opal, a variety of quartz which does not form crystals, is also a popular gemstone.

Most of the other gemstones shown here are in crystal form. Some of the pictures show the crystals as they are found. Others show them after they have been cut into jewels. Emeralds, rubies, and diamonds are the most valued gems —emeralds and rubies for their colour and diamonds for their brilliance. These gems are very durable. Diamond, you remember, is the hardest mineral.

Jade seldom occurs as crystals. Its value as an ornament depends upon its

Opal

Topaz

Aquamarine

Zircon

Spinel

Chrysoberyl

Garnet

Emerald

Ruby

Sapphire

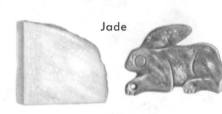

Jade

Diamond

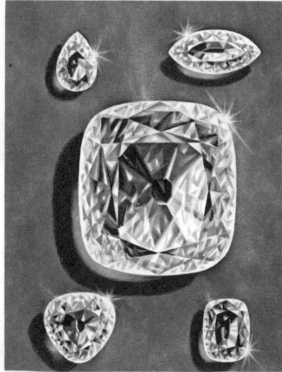

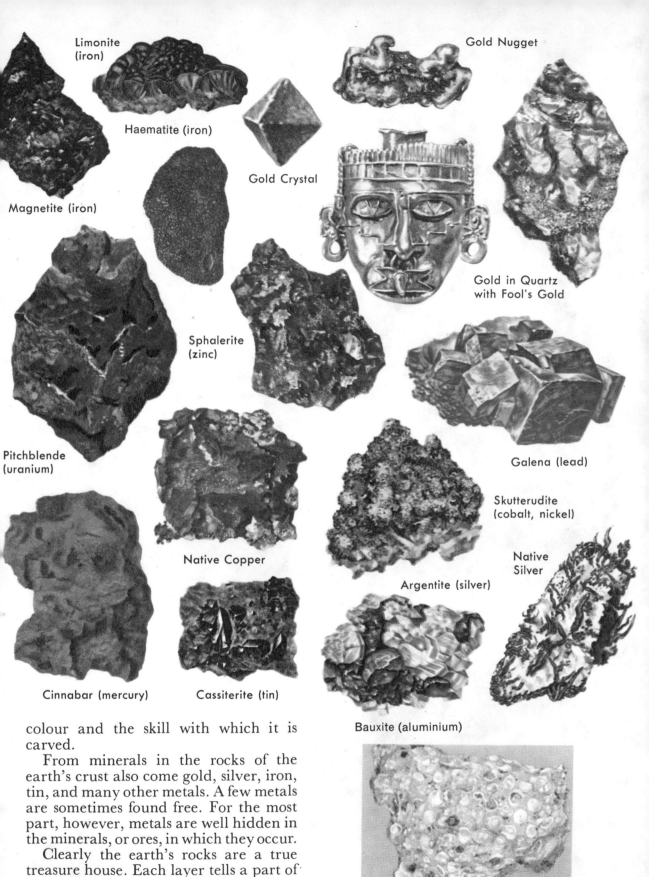

Limonite (iron)

Haematite (iron)

Magnetite (iron)

Gold Crystal

Gold Nugget

Gold in Quartz with Fool's Gold

Sphalerite (zinc)

Pitchblende (uranium)

Galena (lead)

Native Copper

Skutterudite (cobalt, nickel)

Argentite (silver)

Native Silver

Cinnabar (mercury)

Cassiterite (tin)

Bauxite (aluminium)

colour and the skill with which it is carved.

From minerals in the rocks of the earth's crust also come gold, silver, iron, tin, and many other metals. A few metals are sometimes found free. For the most part, however, metals are well hidden in the minerals, or ores, in which they occur.

Clearly the earth's rocks are a true treasure house. Each layer tells a part of the earth's history.

59

Living Things

In the world today there are hundreds of thousands of kinds of living things. Many scientists classify all of them as either plants or animals. Others divide living things into three kingdoms: plants, animals, and protists. In the protist kingdom they put many small organisms not easy to classify as either animals or plants.

Living things differ greatly in size. Some, like the germs that cause typhoid, are so tiny that they cannot be seen without a powerful microscope. Others, like elephants and whales, weigh tons. Some living things have very short lives. The mayfly lives less than a day after it reaches its grown-up stage. The giant sequoia, on the other hand, can easily live for a thousand years. Living things come in almost every shape you can imagine. But in certain ways all living things are alike.

They are all built of tiny blocks, or cells, of that mysterious living material called *protoplasm*. Some organisms are single cells. The biggest plants and animals, on the other hand, are made up of millions and millions of cells.

All living things show some organisation into different parts for different purposes. An oak tree has roots, a trunk, branches, leaves, flowers and seeds. A

Giant Sequoia

tiger has a body, head, tail, legs, eyes, ears, and a mouth, to say nothing of many organs inside its body. Even the simplest one-celled organism has different parts of its one cell that carry on different kinds of work.

All living things must have food and water. They all need oxygen, too.

Chemical changes go on in all living things. Food is used up to provide energy. New living material is made. Old living material is worn out. Waste is produced that must be got rid of.

All living things have the power of growth. They can all produce other living things like themselves. They all move to some extent. Even living things that stay in one place may be seen to move parts of their bodies. Barnacles, for example, after swimming freely when young, settle down for life, but their feathery legs are still very active. And though a living thing may appear to be motionless, you may be sure that some movement is going on inside it.

All living things, moreover, show change in response to changes that go on around them. The leaves of a sensitive plant fold up if touched. A kitten scratches when annoyed. A sunflower turns towards the sun. Your own hair stands on end and you get gooseflesh when you are either cold or frightened.

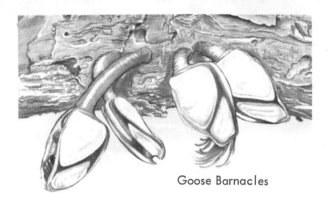

Goose Barnacles

Mayfly

Sensitive plant

The things that stand out most clearly in the picture above are a toad and a toadstool. Although a toad and a toadstool are alike in many ways, you can easily tell one is an animal and the other is a plant. But it is very hard to give a definition of an animal that will fit all animals. It is even harder to give a definition of a plant that will fit all plants.

There are dozens of ways in which toads and toadstools are different, but these ways would not hold for all the different plants and animals that there are.

One of the big differences between a toad and a toadstool is that a toad can move about over the ground, while a toadstool must live its whole life in one place. But there are plants—some small

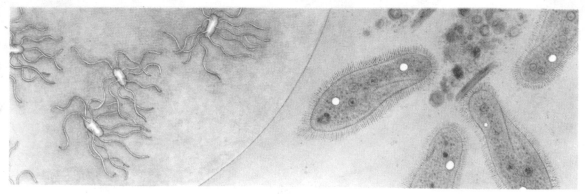

Typhoid Germs

Paramecia

seaweeds, for example—that move about freely. And many animals, like the barnacle, spend most of their lives in a single spot.

A toad has eyes, ears, bones, muscles, and a brain. A toadstool has none of these things. But neither does a sponge or a coral, and they are classed as animals.

The plants we are most used to seeing have leaves. But a toadstool has no leaves. Neither does a cactus or a duckweed.

Probably you think of plants as green, and most of them are. But toadstools are not green.

Most animals change faster than plants with any change in their surroundings. But the leaf of a sensitive plant folds up quickly.

Most plants have cell walls made of cellulose. But not all of them do. Clearly this is not a sure way to tell a plant from an animal.

Even though it is very hard to put in words exactly what makes some living things plants and what makes others animals, fortunately not very many of

those we are used to seeing are puzzling. Most are as easy to classify as a sunflower and a bear. But the classification of some is in dispute. The pictures on this page show a few of the puzzling organisms. They are among those often classed as protists.

Typhoid germs are bacteria, long thought of as plants. These bacteria have, as you see, hairlike projections. With these projections they can move fast in water. A typhoid germ, projections and all, is a single cell.

The paramecium is often called the slipper animalcule because of its shape and size. It belongs to the protozoa, long called animals. The paramecium is only a single cell, though it is very much larger than a typhoid germ. It is big enough to be seen in a good light without a microscope.

For a part of their lives slime moulds move about and act more like animals than plants. Then they stop moving and act more like plants than animals. No wonder some scientists call them protists.

Slime Mould

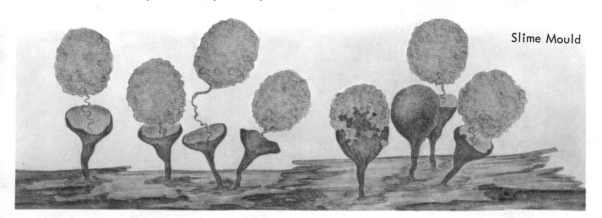

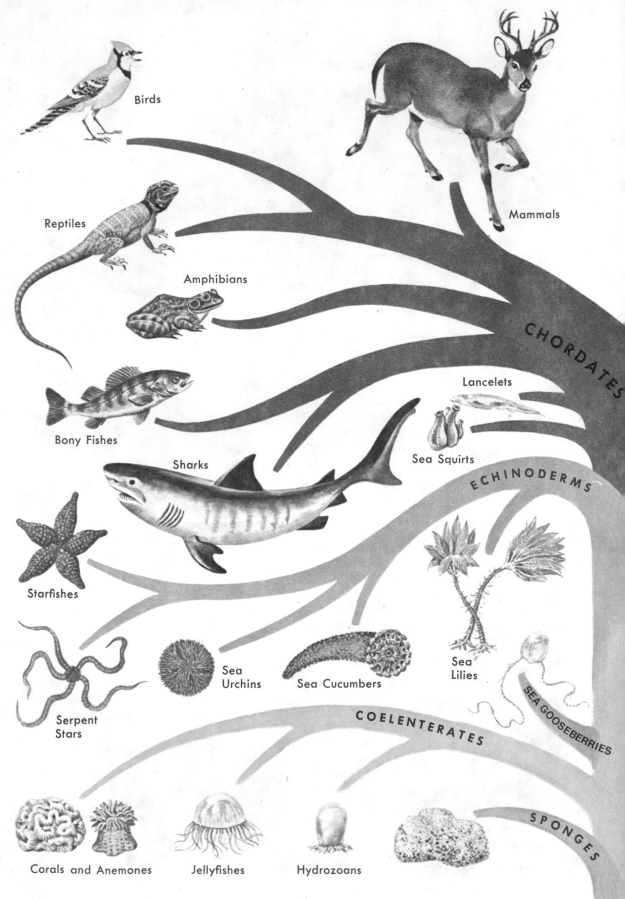

Birds

Mammals

Reptiles

Amphibians

CHORDATES

Lancelets

Bony Fishes

Sharks

Sea Squirts

ECHINODERMS

Starfishes

Sea Lilies

Serpent Stars

Sea Urchins

Sea Cucumbers

SEA GOOSEBERRIES

COELENTERATES

SPONGES

Corals and Anemones

Jellyfishes

Hydrozoans

64

The Animal Kingdom

Today about a million kinds of animals are known. There may be many more not yet discovered. Some animals are so small that they cannot ordinarily be seen. Therefore it is not surprising that new kinds are constantly being discovered.

The tree diagram gives us an overall picture of the organisation of the animal kingdom. Only the most important branches of it are shown. The simplest animals are near the bottom of the tree, while the most advanced are at the top. All the animals of today are believed to have come from one-celled organisms of long ago.

Notice that the lowest branch is marked 'protozoa'. Protozoa are among the organisms classified as protists.

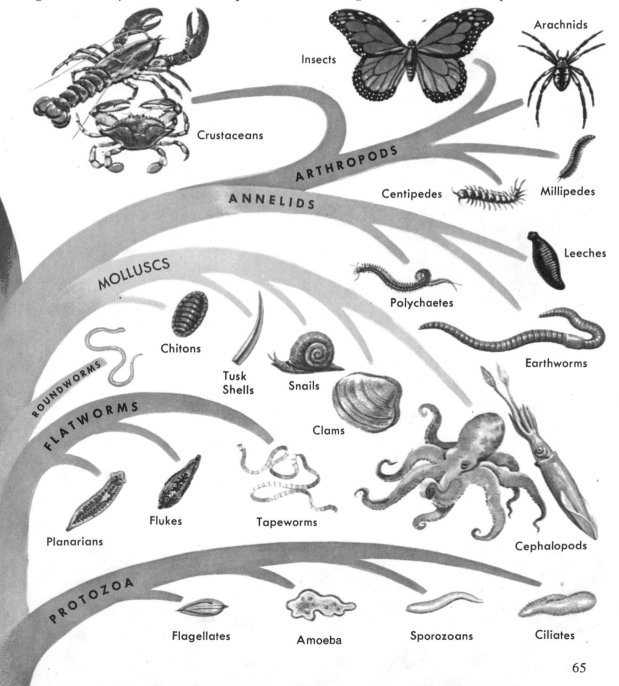

Insects

Arachnids

Crustaceans

ARTHROPODS

ANNELIDS

Centipedes

Millipedes

Leeches

MOLLUSCS

Polychaetes

Chitons

Tusk Shells

Snails

Earthworms

ROUNDWORMS

FLATWORMS

Clams

Planarians

Flukes

Tapeworms

Cephalopods

PROTOZOA

Flagellates

Amoeba

Sporozoans

Ciliates

Banded Garden Spider

Red Admiral
Butterfly

Painted Lady
Butterfly

The chief divisions of the animal kingdom are called *phyla*. There are about 25 altogether, many made up of little-known animals. The tree shows less than half of them.

Phyla are divided into *classes*. Classes in turn are divided into *orders*, orders into *families*, families into *genera*, and genera into species. Each separate kind of animal is a species.

Every animal has a scientific name. The scientific name of the red admiral butterfly is *Vanessa atalanta*. The first part of the name tells us its genus, the second part its species. The name of the painted lady butterfly is *Vanessa cardui*. The two butterflies are in the same genus.

The *Vanessa* butterfly belongs to the family of brush-footed butterflies. This family is in the order of *Lepidoptera*, the 'scaly wings', a division of the class of insects. The insects are a part of the phylum of jointed-legged animals, or arthropods, by far the largest of all the phyla.

The animals pictured on these two pages are in seven different phyla. The spider, lobster, and shrimp, together with the butterflies, are arthropods. The earthworm is an annelid. The sea urchin and sand potato are echinoderms, the 'spiny-skinned' animals. The coral is a coelenterate, and the paper nautilus a mollusc. Sea-gooseberries, often called comb jellies, have a phylum to themselves.

Although scattered among several phyla, the animals in these pictures are all invertebrates. They have no backbone.

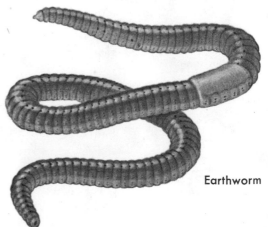

Earthworm

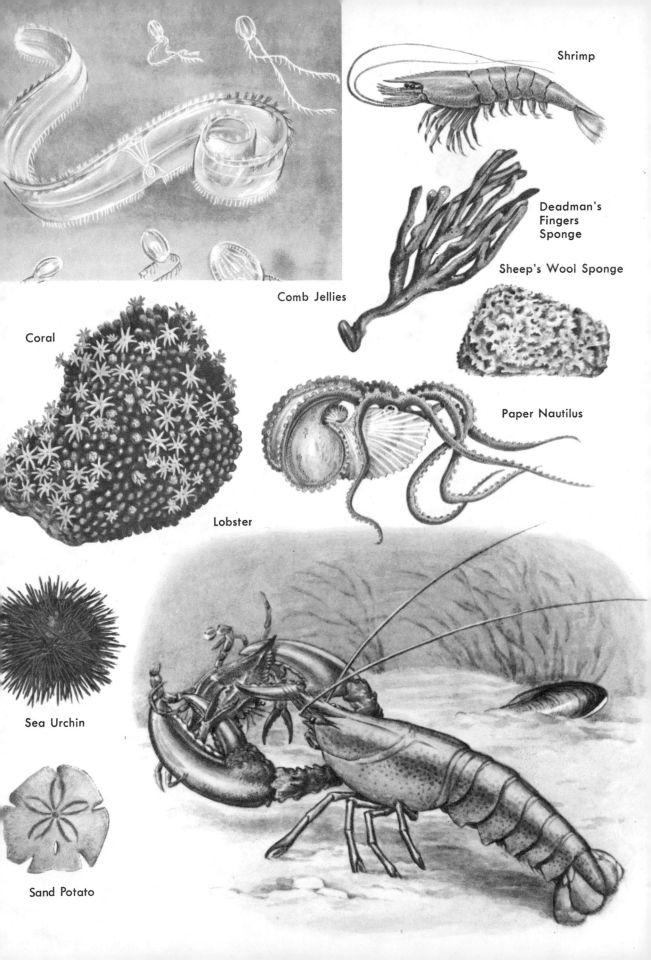

Shrimp

Deadman's
Fingers
Sponge

Comb Jellies

Sheep's Wool Sponge

Coral

Paper Nautilus

Lobster

Sea Urchin

Sand Potato

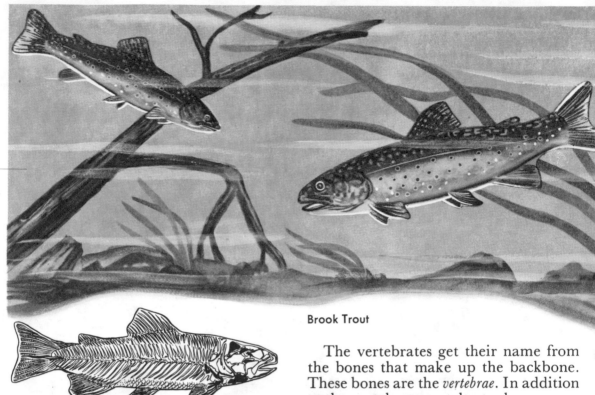

Brook Trout

There were invertebrates on the earth for millions and millions of years before any animals with backbones appeared. Even though they have lost the high place in the animal world they held for ages, animals without backbones are still far more common than vertebrates, the animals with backbones. In number of species the invertebrates outnumber the vertebrates by about 25 to 1. The vertebrates, however, are far more conspicuous, chiefly because of their size.

The vertebrates get their name from the bones that make up the backbone. These bones are the *vertebrae*. In addition to the vertebrae, vertebrates have many other bones. All their bones together make up their skeleton, which forms a framework for their body and gives them their shape.

There are five big groups of vertebrates. The animals pictured here represent three of them—fishes, amphibians, and reptiles.

The brook trout, needless to say, is a fish. Fishes are all water animals. They have fins, not legs. Fishes breathe with gills. A few kinds have additional ways of getting oxygen. Most fishes, but not all,

Green Frog

Crocodile

are covered with minute, silvery scales.

The green frog is an amphibian. Amphibians get their name from their life history. 'Amphibian' means 'living a double life'. A green frog starts its life in water. It gets oxygen from the water with gills, just as a fish does. It has no legs. Later it becomes an air-breathing creature. It develops legs as well as lungs. This is the general amphibian pattern. Amphibians have no scales. Their skins are bare, and, as a rule, moist.

The crocodile and the snake are reptiles. The word 'reptile' comes from a Latin word which means 'to creep'. Reptiles have short legs, or no legs at all.

No big new groups of sea reptiles have appeared to take the place of those that disappeared with the dinosaurs. Most reptiles of today are land animals. Even those that spend most of their time in the water—except for a few whose young are born alive—come up on land to lay their eggs.

Reptiles are built something like adult amphibians, but they differ from amphibians in two important ways: they breathe with lungs all their lives, and, with very few exceptions, their skins are covered with scales. Contrary to the common idea, the scales are dry, not slimy.

Fishes, amphibians, and reptiles are cold-blooded. Being cold-blooded does not mean always being cold. Instead it means having to get warmth from the surroundings. A cold-blooded animal may be very warm indeed if it is in the hot sun. But in freezing temperatures the animal is sure to be cold and inactive. In being cold-blooded, the fishes, amphibians, and reptiles are like insects, molluscs, worms, and all the other animals without backbones.

Gaboon Viper

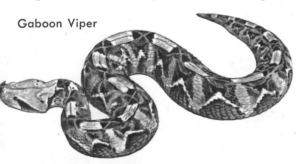

The mourning dove and the pig represent the other two groups of vertebrates. These two groups differ from the fishes, amphibians, and reptiles in being warm-blooded. Their bodies are warm inside even in cold surroundings.

The mourning dove, of course, is a bird. Birds can be told from all other animals by their feathers. A bird's body is truly warm. The normal temperature of some species is 112 degrees Fahrenheit, compared with 98.4 degrees for the human body. Birds have hearts with four rooms, or chambers.

All birds are air-breathing. They have lungs all their lives. Although the earliest birds had teeth, the birds of today do not. Instead, they have a gizzard in which their food is ground into small pieces.

The pig is a mammal. Mammals get their name from their mammary, or milk, glands. All mammals feed their young with milk.

Like the birds, the mammals have hearts with four chambers. They breathe with lungs all their lives. In this way they are like both the birds and the reptiles. They all have some fur, or hair, even though some of the biggest mammals— the elephant, hippopotamus, rhinoceros, and whale—have very little. Their hair, as well as their milk glands, serves to set the mammals apart from the other vertebrates.

One might expect that each of the five big groups of animals with backbones would be put in a separate phylum. But in spite of their differences the five are sufficiently alike in important ways for them all to be included in the same phylum. They do not even make up one phylum on their own. The sea squirts and a few other little-known animals are grouped with the vertebrates in the phylum of chordates.

Two pictures on page 71 show sea squirts. These small animals are not much more than living sacs anchored fast in one place. They have no bones. The body of each one has two openings. Water, bringing with it tiny plants and animals which serve as food, comes in through one opening and, having picked up waste, leaves through the other. The animal gets its name from these openings. If it is disturbed, its squirts a jet of water from each of them.

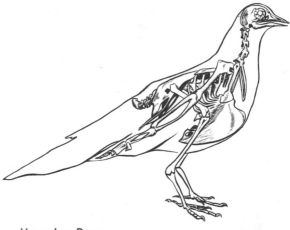

Mourning Dove

Sow and piglets

Man, of course, since he is a mammal, is a chordate. It is hard to believe that scientists put the sluggish sea squirts in the same phylum of animals with us. To understand why, we have to know something about a sea squirt's life history.

When a sea squirt is young, it looks much like a tadpole. It swims freely about in the water. Its body is almost transparent. The tadpolelike creature has an eye that can tell light from darkness and a nerve cord that extends backwards from a small, hollow brain. Below the nerve cord there is a rod that stiffens the little animal's body. This rod is called a notochord. It is its notochord which puts the lowly sea squirt into the phylum of chordates.

In its very early stages every animal with a backbone has a notochord. No animal in any other phylum ever has one. Therefore, even though a sea squirt loses its notochord as it grows up and never develops a skeleton, the brief period in its life when it has a notochord earns it a place in the phylum at the top of the animal tree.

After a short period of swimming about, a sea squirt stands on its 'face' and attaches itself to a solid surface. It then loses, together with its notochord, its tail, its eye, its brain, and all but a small portion of its nerve cord.

The sea vase pictured is also sometimes called the tube sea squirt. It is only about two inches high.

The sea peach gets its name from its shape and its orange-red colour. The colour makes it stand out from its neighbours in the cold coastal waters where it lives.

Some kinds of sea squirts never grow up and settle down. They spend their whole lives in the 'tadpole' stage, moving about in the sea. One kind forms cylinder-shaped colonies several feet long. These colonies shine vividly at night.

The lancelet, a small ribbon-shaped animal that comes to a point at each end, is another of the chordates that do not have a backbone. But it has a notochord even when it grows up. Lancelets often plunge tail first into the sand of a seashore with only their mouths above the surface. They never, however, follow the sea squirt's fashion of anchoring themselves in one spot for the rest of their lives.

Sea Vase   Sea Peach

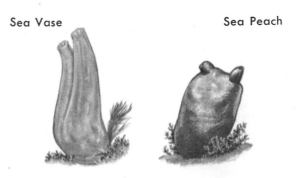

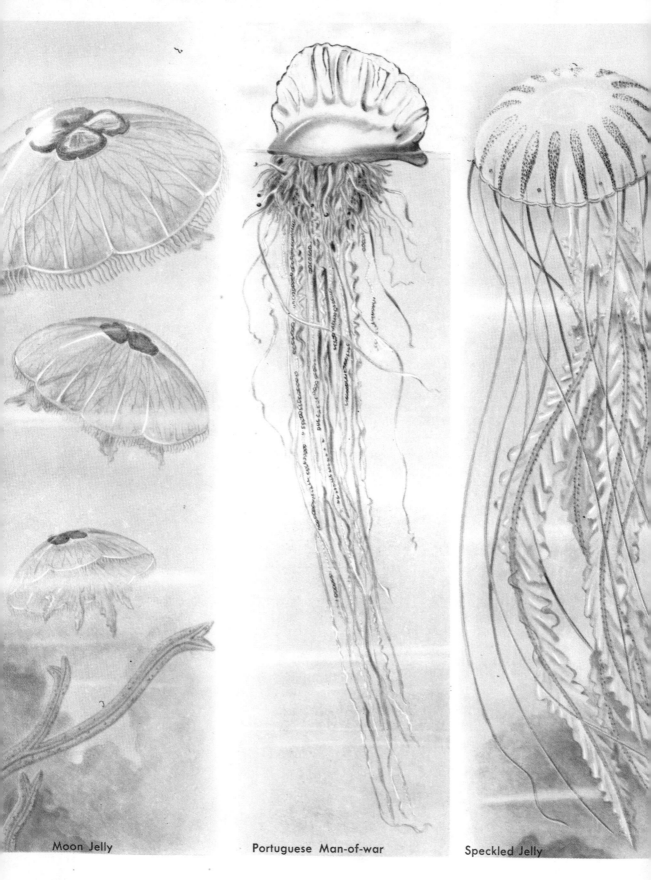

Moon Jelly   Portuguese Man-of-war   Speckled Jelly

Animals of the Seashore

The seashores of the world are the homes of thousands of species of animals without backbones—*invertebrates*. These animals live where the tides flow in and out and where great waves buffet the shores. Some of them move with the waves and the tides. Some bury themselves in the sand or mud when the tide goes out and wait for it to come in again. Some anchor themselves for life to rocks along the shore. A great many are protected by hard coverings. The jellyfish is among those with no hard parts at all.

The common jellyfish and speckled jellyfish are much alike except that the speckled jellyfish has longer streamers hanging down from around its mouth, and longer feelers, or tentacles. These streamers and tentacles help a jellyfish to catch its food. On its tentacles there are many threads, or darts, filled with poison. When an animal comes near enough to touch a tentacle it is shot at once with poison darts. Jellyfish swim lazily about by opening and closing like an umbrella, or else they simply float.

The Portuguese man-of-war is a jelly-fish, too, but it is not a single animal. It is a whole colony of animals. The separate animals are not all alike, and they do not all do the same kind of work. Some of them do the eating and digesting of food. Some serve as fishing lines and as protectors of the colony. Others are for feeling only. Still others have the task of producing a new generation of jellyfish.

The 'sail' of the Portuguese man-of-war is a bag filled with gas. It keeps the colony afloat. This 'many-in-one' jelly-fish got the 'man-of-war' part of its name because it reminded people of a tiny battleship as it sailed along. Its 'guns' are its darts.

Often a Portuguese man-of-war has some little fish travelling with it. These fish, called man-of-war fish, are immune to the poison of their companion.

The graceful sea fan pictured below is a horny coral. It is actually a colony of tiny, eight-tentacled animals. In the picture you do not see the animals themselves. They are hidden in the horny

Sea Fan

Stalked Sea Anemone

branches of this intricate 'fan'.

But at night and on dark days the tiny animals of a sea fan come out of hiding and gather in food with their tentacles. Digestive canals inside the horny skeleton connect the animals of the colony.

The jellyfish and the sea fan belong to the group of animals called coelenterates. So do the hydroids, sea anemones, and stony corals. All the animals of the group have poison darts, or threads, like those of jellyfish, that help them get food.

The hedgehog hydroid, too, is a colony of tiny animals. The picture shows the different kinds that make up a colony. The tall ones with long tentacles do the eating and the snakelike ones the stinging. Those with 'balloons' produce new animals.

Sea anemones look much like flowers. Some of them have beautiful colours. Like the Portuguese man-of-war, some sea anemones have fish companions that are not hurt by the anemone's poison threads. An adult sea anemone holds fast to something solid, but it is not anchored there. It can glide slowly from place to place.

Although a single stony coral is shown

Hedgehog Hydroid
(greatly enlarged)

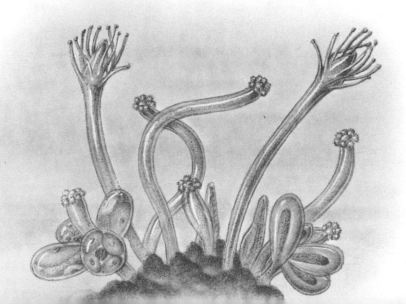

here, nearly all of these stony corals exist in colonies like the ones which comprise the sea fan. Each animal builds a rock cup for itself out of the lime in the seawater. It keeps adding lime and building its cup higher. Together all the animals of a colony build a big house of stone. Different species of coral build houses of different patterns. Often its common name comes from the shape of house a coral colony builds. Thus we have such names as star, brain, tree, and staghorn coral. Corals have been building rock houses in the seas for millions of years. No wonder there are great coral reefs and even islands.

Sea gooseberries (often called comb jellies) can be mistaken for small jellyfish, and were once classed with the coelenterates. However, as we can see from the diagram on pages 64 and 65, sea gooseberries form an independent branch of the animal kingdom. They are frequently stranded on beaches when the tide goes out, and in the dark they create a luminous glow.

There are worms of many kinds along the seashores. The pictures show one, the bristle worm, that swims about freely, and three that stay in one place in tubes they build for themselves. Some sea worms have beautiful, bright-coloured plumes. The plumes are gills with which

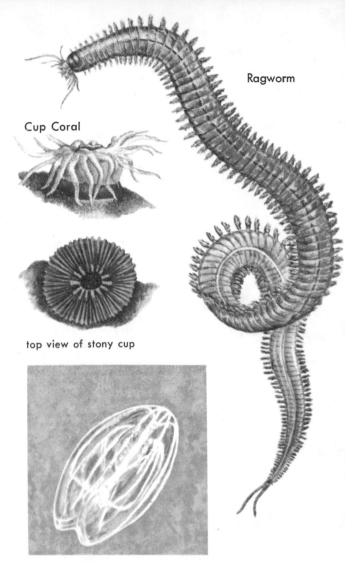

Ragworm

Cup Coral

top view of stony cup

Rainbow Comb Jelly

Fan Worm

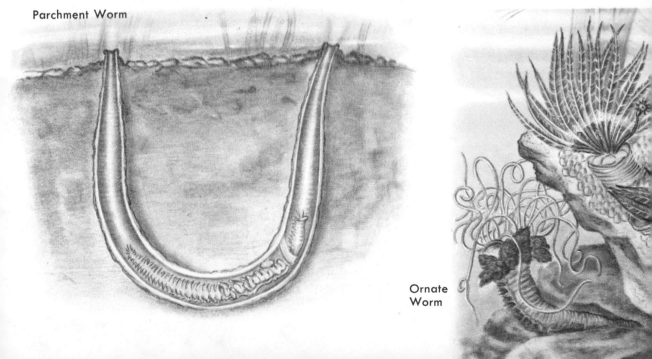

Parchment Worm

Ornate Worm

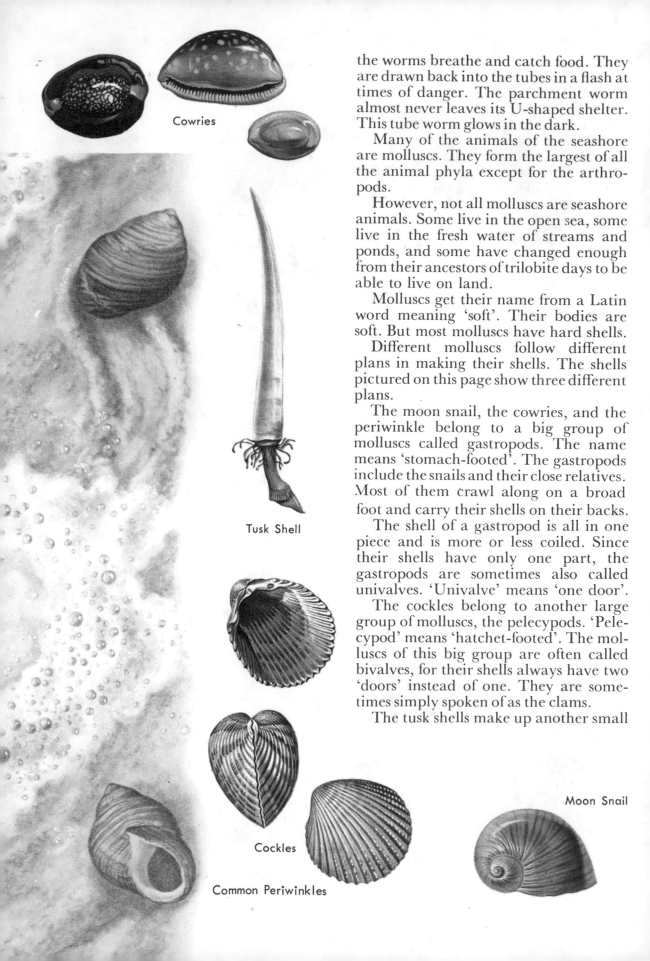

Cowries

Tusk Shell

Cockles

Common Periwinkles

Moon Snail

the worms breathe and catch food. They are drawn back into the tubes in a flash at times of danger. The parchment worm almost never leaves its U-shaped shelter. This tube worm glows in the dark.

Many of the animals of the seashore are molluscs. They form the largest of all the animal phyla except for the arthropods.

However, not all molluscs are seashore animals. Some live in the open sea, some live in the fresh water of streams and ponds, and some have changed enough from their ancestors of trilobite days to be able to live on land.

Molluscs get their name from a Latin word meaning 'soft'. Their bodies are soft. But most molluscs have hard shells.

Different molluscs follow different plans in making their shells. The shells pictured on this page show three different plans.

The moon snail, the cowries, and the periwinkle belong to a big group of molluscs called gastropods. The name means 'stomach-footed'. The gastropods include the snails and their close relatives. Most of them crawl along on a broad foot and carry their shells on their backs.

The shell of a gastropod is all in one piece and is more or less coiled. Since their shells have only one part, the gastropods are sometimes also called univalves. 'Univalve' means 'one door'.

The cockles belong to another large group of molluscs, the pelecypods. 'Pelecypod' means 'hatchet-footed'. The molluscs of this big group are often called bivalves, for their shells always have two 'doors' instead of one. They are sometimes simply spoken of as the clams.

The tusk shells make up another small

group of molluscs. A tusk shell buries itself in sand with only the smaller end of the shell showing. Its foot, which looks a little like a tiny horse's hoof, digs into the sand. Around the mouth there are tentacles that gather food.

Many people make collections of sea shells. Most of them know much more about the shells than about the animals inside them. The shells pictured on this page are gastropod shells. Three of the pictures show living animals.

The spindle shell is a typical snail. The one in the lower picture is moving along. Its head, eyes, and feelers show clearly. Notice the disc at the back of the foot. If there is danger, a spindle shell pulls its head and foot into its shell and closes the opening tight with this disc.

The spindle shell also has a peculiar 'tongue'. A gastropod's tongue, called a radula, is very long and narrow, and on it there are rows of tiny teeth. With its radula a gastropod can scrape little plants off stones, tear larger plants to pieces, and even drill through the hard shell of another animal in order to eat it.

The abalone is a sea snail found in large numbers round the Pacific coasts of North America, Australia, China and Japan. With its powerful foot it can attach itself so firmly to rocks that even the heaviest seas cannot dislodge it. When detached from a rock its foot curls up at the edges, as shown below.

The abalone is considered a great delicacy as a food, like the oyster. And also like the oyster, the inside of the abalone's shell is beautifully coloured.

Black Abalone

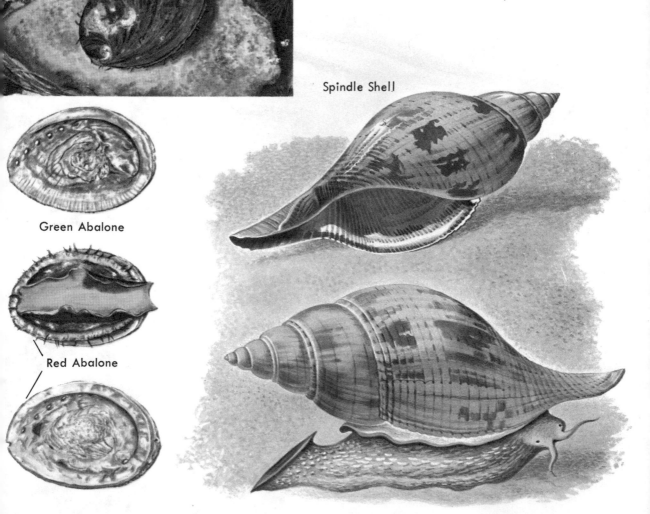

Green Abalone

Red Abalone

Spindle Shell

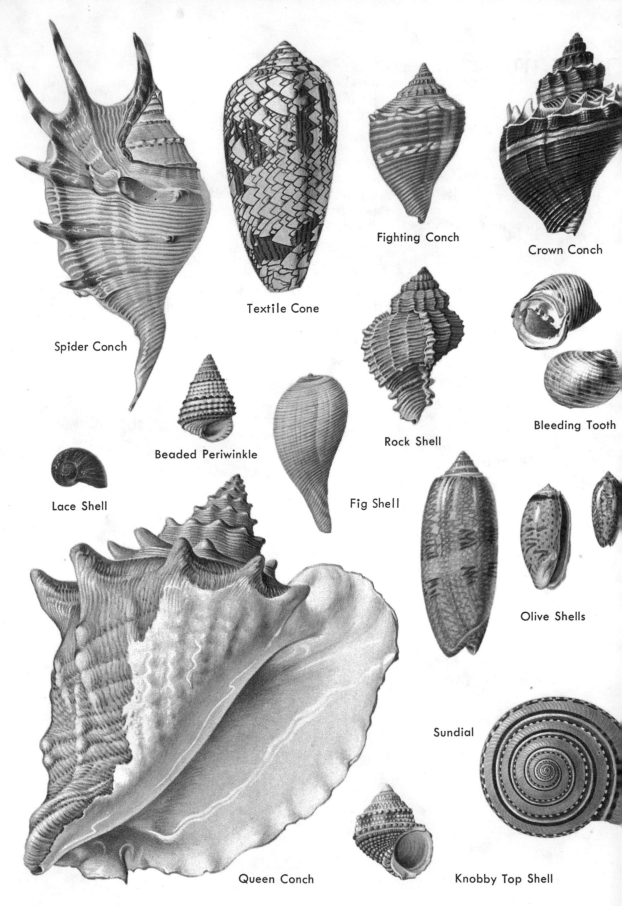

Fighting Conch

Crown Conch

Textile Cone

Spider Conch

Bleeding Tooth

Beaded Periwinkle

Rock Shell

Lace Shell

Fig Shell

Olive Shells

Sundial

Queen Conch

Knobby Top Shell

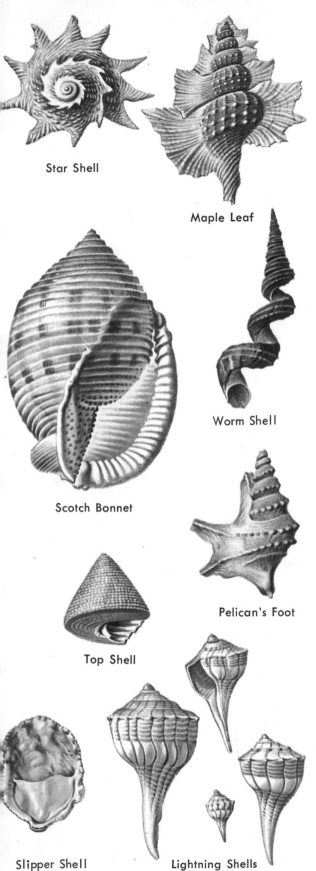

Star Shell

Maple Leaf

Baby Tooth

Bubble Shell

Giant Button
or Top Shell

Keyhole Limpet

Worm Shell

Flat Periwinkle

Screw Shell

Scotch Bonnet

Pelican's Foot

Top Shell

Slipper Shell

Lightning Shells

All these shells are gastropod shells. There are gastropods in fresh water and gastropods on land—there are hundreds of kinds of tree snails, for example—but all these shells are from gastropods of the sea.

Notice the names of these shells. In many cases it is easy to see how they came about. Even if the names were not given, you would probably be able to pick out the star shell, and the maple leaf.

The queen conch is one of the largest gastropods. In real life the queen conch shell is much larger than the illustration on the opposite page. Perhaps you have held a conch shell up to your ear to hear the 'roar of the sea'. The soft roaring sound you do hear has nothing directly to do with the sea, of course. It is caused by the special acoustical properties of the shell itself. Nevertheless, it is a pleasant piece of make-believe to associate with this wonderful specimen of the seashore.

Gastropods never grow too large for their shells. Although the shells seem hard and inflexible like stones, they do, in fact, grow in proportion to the animal inside them.

Hard–shell Clam

Most of these pictures show live pele-cypods, the 'hatchet-footed' animals. The common cockle is typical of the group. It has no head—no pelecypods do. And it has a hatchet-shaped foot it uses to burrow in the sand. You can see in the picture the cockle's water tubes, or siphons, extending a little way beyond the shell. Water moves in and out of the cockle's body through them.

The cockle also uses its foot to move across sand. The pictures below show how it achieves this. Firstly it extends its foot forward. Then it swells up the foot, which acts as an anchor. And finally it pulls itself forward after its extended foot.

Many bivalves, after a short babyhood swimming about, settle down in one place and never move again. Oysters

Giant Clam

behave like this. So does the giant clam. This settles, hinge down, in a coral reef and the coral growing up around it builds a made-to-measure nest.

This big clam is the largest of all bivalves. It may measure more than a yard across and weigh 500 pounds. It can clamp the two parts of its shell shut with great force. More than one underwater explorer has had an unpleasant adventure with this creature. In contrast with the giant clam, the tiny clams called basket shells are only half an inch across.

Bivalves provide us with a great deal of food. Oysters, clams, scallops and mussels are harvested in huge numbers. Some bivalves, especially the pearl oyster, are

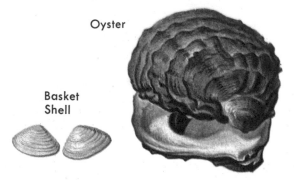

Oyster

Basket
Shell

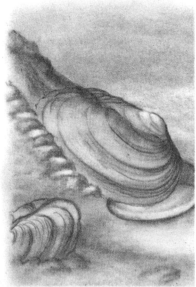

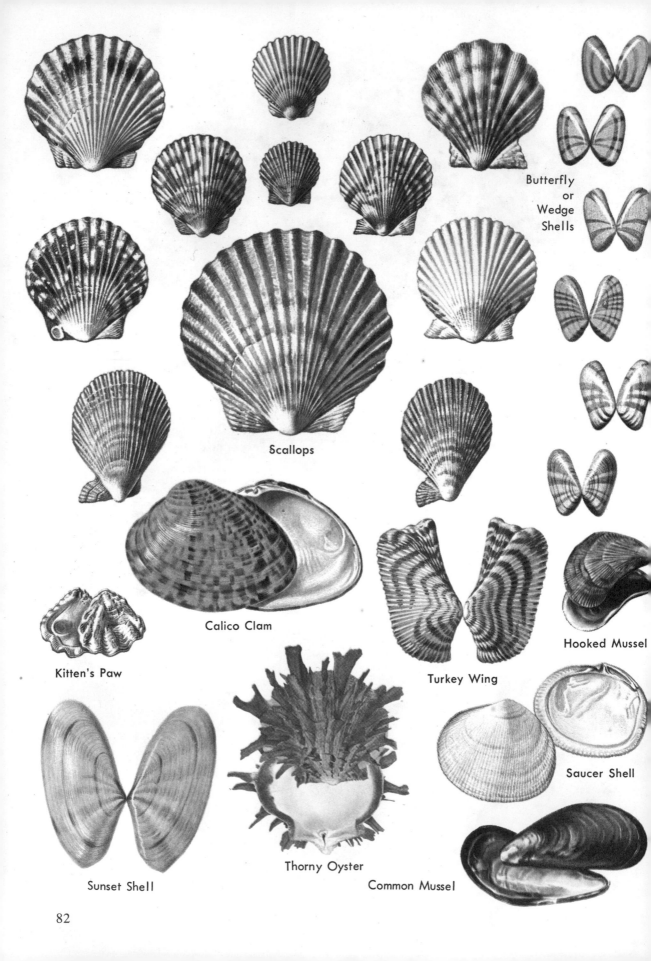

Butterfly
or
Wedge
Shells

Scallops

Calico Clam

Kitten's Paw

Turkey Wing

Hooked Mussel

Saucer Shell

Sunset Shell

Thorny Oyster

Common Mussel

82

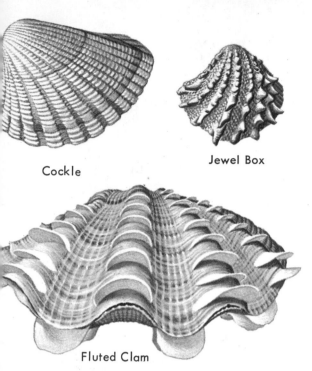

Cockle

Jewel Box

Fluted Clam

valuable for quite another reason. They are the source of all true pearls.

Here is another selection of shells to further illustrate the amazing variety and beauty of these types of mollusc. As you can see, some of them also have very pictorial names, such as sunset shell and kitten's paw.

Scallops are an interesting kind of clam. They swim by opening their shells and snapping them shut, thus creating for themselves a simple kind of water propulsion.

The beautiful little butterfly shells are also called wedge shells, bean shells and coquinas. The coquina limestone found along some coasts is made of these shells.

Shells have been used as money by many peoples. For example, the Red Indians used strings of shell beads as money. Much of the shell money, called

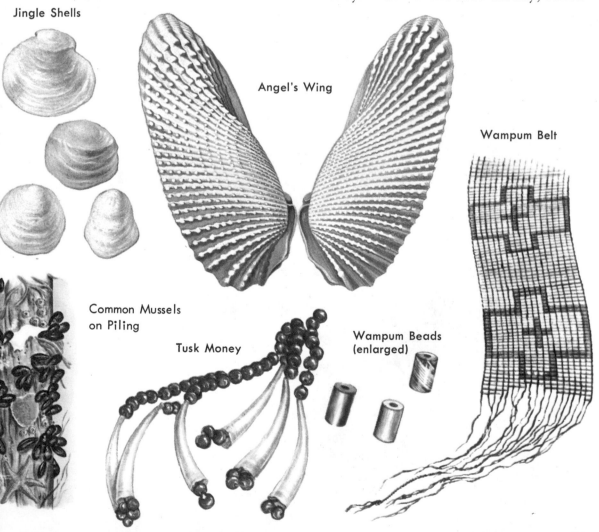

Jingle Shells

Angel's Wing

Wampum Belt

Common Mussels on Piling

Tusk Money

Wampum Beads (enlarged)

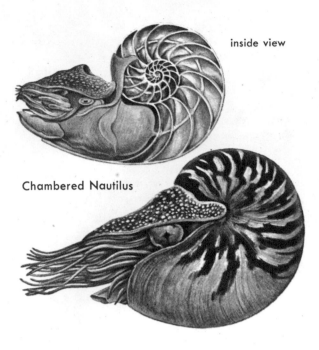

inside view

Chambered Nautilus

were the most highly developed animals in the sea. They have lost that high rank to fish and whales but, even so, they are still numerically strong. All the animals pictured on these two pages are cephalopods. These same animals might look quite different in another picture. All of them can change colour rapidly. They may be red, yellow, brown, or greenish one minute and the next be striped or white or rainbow-coloured.

In place of a foot a cephalopod has a number of arms which surround its head. These arms are helpful in gathering food, and they are, as a rule, equipped with suckers. The cephalopods, like the snails, have a long, rasping tongue, or radula. On their heads they have the best eyes to be found among animals without backbones.

The beautiful shell of a chambered nautilus is made up of many rooms, or chambers. When the nautilus is young, its shell only has one chamber. As the animal grows larger, it adds one chamber after another. Finally it has a house of many different chambers, but it only

wampum, was made from the shell of the clam.

The cephalopods—the 'head-footed' animals—make up a third of the main groups of molluscs. At times during the earth's long history the cephalopods

Octopus

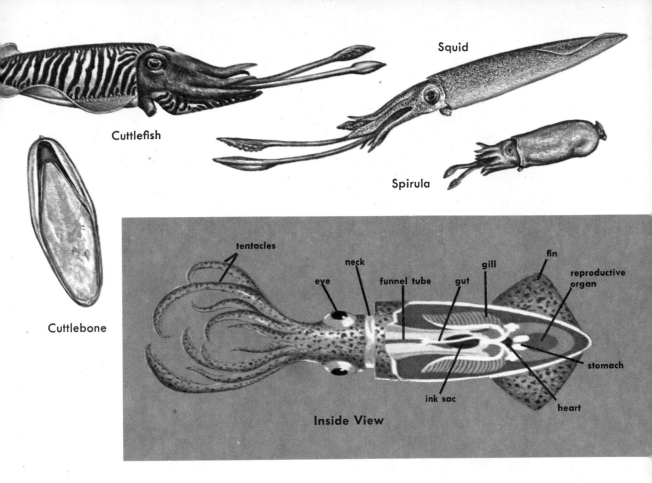

Cuttlefish

Squid

Spirula

Cuttlebone

Inside View

tentacles

neck

eye

funnel tube

gut

gill

fin

reproductive organ

ink sac

stomach

heart

lives in the last chamber it has built.

Squids are sometimes called 'sea arrows' because of their shape. With its fins a squid can swim forwards or backwards, make quick changes in direction, and even hover in one place. It also makes use of a form of jet propulsion. Underneath its head it has a funnel tube, or siphon, that it can point backwards, forwards, or to either side. Squirting water out of this funnel in one direction shoots the squid in the opposite direction.

Two of a squid's arms are much longer than the other eight. When a squid is chasing a fish to eat, it darts forward. It catches the fish with its two long arms and pulls it back far enough for the other eight arms to hold while it eats the fish.

In escaping from an enemy, a squid usually darts backwards. It has another good trick that helps it to escape: it squirts out a cloud of brown ink. The ink hides the squid and gives it a chance to escape.

The squids along our seashores are less than two feet long. But there are giant squids nearly 50 feet long. Their bodies measure from 15 to 18 feet and their long grasping arms stretch out for 30 feet more. Their suckers are as big as teacups.

The squids have no external shells. Buried in its body a squid has only a bit of horny shell known as the 'pen'. The cuttlefish has a similar remnant inside it, called cuttlebone, which is often bought by people for their pet birds.

Except for the chambered nautilus, the tiny spirula is the only living cephalopod with an external shell. Like the giant squid, it is at home deep in the sea.

The well-known octopus has not even a remnant of a shell. Octopuses are sometimes called devilfish. The biggest measure 12 feet with arms spread out, but most are much smaller. The danger to divers from octopuses is not nearly so great as most of us imagine. They seldom attack people.

85

Spider Crab

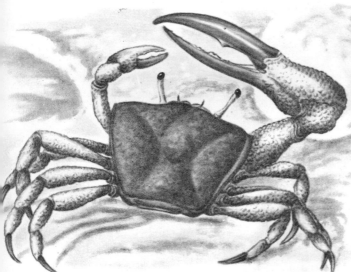

Crabs, lobsters and shrimps are closely related animals of the seashore. They are all crustaceans. The crustaceans make up one of the groups of arthropods.

Crustaceans are noted for their horny crust, or armour, which is something quite different from the shells of molluscs. This crust cannot stretch, and as the animals grow in size so they systematically shed one crust and grow a new, larger one.

Crustaceans are also noted for their large claws, which are used for catching food and for defence against enemies like the octopus. Note also that they all have the same number of legs, and eyes which

Fiddler Crab

Shrimp

Blue Crab

Hermit Crab

protrude rather curiously on stalks. They all breathe with gills, like fishes.

One of the main distinctions between crabs on the one hand and lobsters and shrimps on the other, is that crabs have short 'tails', or abdomens, curled up beneath them. Lobsters and shrimps have stretched-out abdomens.

In this respect the so-called hermit crab is more like a lobster or a shrimp. The really interesting thing about hermit crabs is that although they are a member of the crustacean group they do not grow any proper protective crust, or shell, over their abdomen. Instead they find an empty snail shell of exactly the

Lobster

right size and take possession of it.

Barnacles are strange crustaceans. Early in their lives they give up swimming about and anchor themselves in one place. A barnacle builds a shell around itself that holds it a prisoner for the rest of its life. It kicks food into its mouth with its feathery legs.

Barnacles are not important as a source of food, but other crustaceans, such as lobsters, crabs and shrimps, are eaten by the millions every year.

Some of the tiniest of the crustaceans are even more important to us than those we prize as food. They form an important part of plankton, the 'sea soup' that provides food, directly or indirectly, for most of the fish of the sea. We depend far more on saltwater fish for food than on lobsters, shrimps and crabs.

Surprisingly enough, small red crustaceans called krill are the chief food of some of the biggest whales. Krill are often found in such huge numbers that they make the sea water look like tomato soup.

Other small crustaceans are common along the ocean's shores. Sea slaters search for food among the seaweeds. Pill bugs creep over the sand and mud, curling up into tight balls if anything disturbs them. Wharf lice scurry about in wet piling. The small crustaceans of the seashore far outnumber the larger crustaceans.

The horseshoe, or king crab, like the hermit crab, is not a true crab. In fact, the horseshoe crab, although it is an arthropod, is not a crustacean at all. This animal is often called a living fossil, for it has existed almost unchanged for 175 million years. When young it looks much like the trilobites that dominated the animal kingdom 500 million years ago.

Starfish are the best known of the

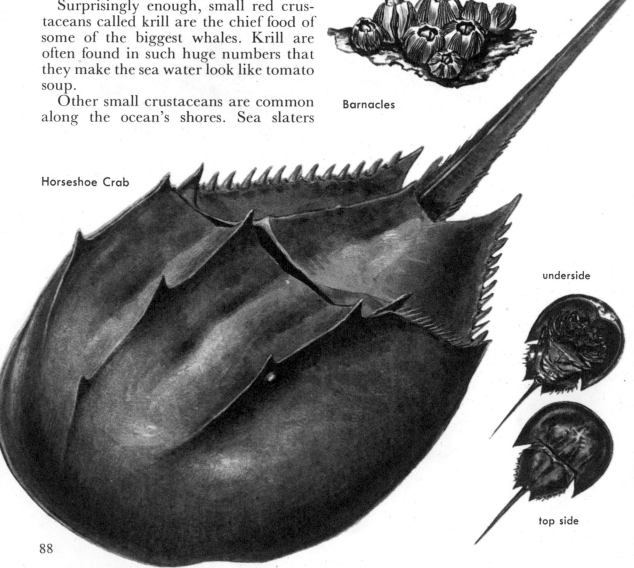

Barnacles

Horseshoe Crab

underside

top side

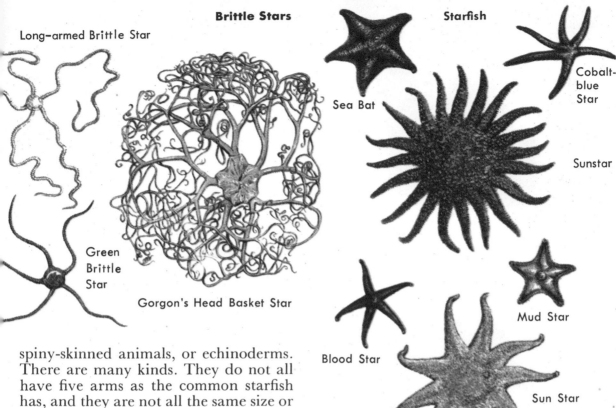

Brittle Stars

Long-armed Brittle Star

Green Brittle Star

Gorgon's Head Basket Star

Starfish

Sea Bat

Cobalt-blue Star

Sunstar

Blood Star

Mud Star

Sun Star

spiny-skinned animals, or echinoderms. There are many kinds. They do not all have five arms as the common starfish has, and they are not all the same size or colour. But they are all alike enough to be easy to recognise.

The echinoderms differ from all other animals in having inside their bodies a system of water canals connected with tube-feet which, as a rule, end in suction discs. Tube-feet are helpful for moving about and keeping clean. In bright sunlight an echinoderm may even use its tube-feet to hold up pebbles or seaweeds as parasols.

Tube-feet also help to catch prey. A starfish, let us suppose, comes upon an oyster. With its suction discs it fastens its arms tight to both parts of the shell, placing its mouth where the shell will open. Using all its might the starfish makes the oyster shell open a tiny crack. A tiny crack is all the starfish needs, for it has a strange way of eating. It turns its stomach inside out and slips it into the oyster shell through the crack. Its stomach stays there until the oyster is digested.

Brittle stars, though not true starfish, are very closely related. Only the gorgon's head basket star, with its many branched, snakelike arms, is noticeably different in appearance.

Starfish Eating Oyster

Common Starfish

Sand Potato

You might not guess from their looks that the animals pictured on these two pages are also close relatives of the starfish. However, they are all echinoderms. The sand potato lives on the sandy sea bed in rather sheltered places. It moves about on its tube-feet. If it is turned over, it turns a somersault to get right side up again. A sand potato's spines are short. They make the little animal look as if it were made of velvet.

Many people who have never seen a live sand potato have seen its skeleton. The skeleton is made of lime. It gives the creature its distinctive appearance.

The sea urchin has a limy skeleton, too. A sea urchin's skeleton is beautifully shaped and may have very attractive colouring. It is the sea urchin, with its prickly spines, that gives the whole group of echinoderms their name. Some sea urchins with long, sharp spines are called hatpin urchins.

Of course, the sea cucumber is not a vegetable nor the sea lily a flower. These animals, too, were named from their shape.

Although the sea cucumber is an echinoderm, it has a tough, leathery skin rather than a spiny one. Its mouth is surrounded by branched tentacles. The animal feeds itself with its tentacles. It rubs them around in the mud and cleans them off in its mouth one by one. Tiny bits of plant and animal material in the mud are its food.

Sea Urchin

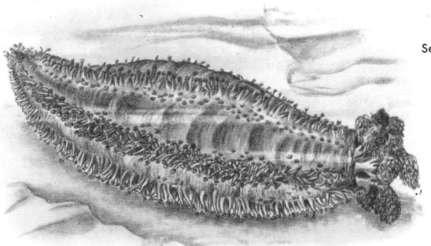

Sea Cucumber

A sea cucumber has a strange way of protecting itself from its enemies. From an opening opposite its mouth it throws out a mass of sticky pink and white threads that so entangle the attacker that it cannot move. A sea cucumber can even turn itself almost inside out and throw its breathing and reproductive organs at an enemy.

The sea cucumber cannot, however, pull the threads or organs in again. It must get along without them until it can grow new ones. Many of the lower animals are able to replace a part that has been lost or injured. A lobster, for example, can grow a new claw, a starfish a new arm, and a flatworm a whole new head.

The sea lily, like its near relatives in the age of the trilobites, anchors itself to rocks and stays in one place. It must wait for food to come to it. Its tube-feet are on the branching arms of the 'flower'. Particles of food picked up from the water by the tube-feet are swept into the sea-lily's mouth.

Except for the sea cucumber's, which move about in a flopped-over position, echinoderms have no front or back. A sea urchin, for example, may move forwards with any part of its body in front. It is built on what might be called a wheel plan rather than on a two-sided plan. All the markings on its skeleton go out from the centre like the spokes of a wheel. All adult echinoderms are built on this plan. Even the sea cucumber, as you will realise if you can picture it in an upright position, mouth down, is much like a stretched-out sea urchin.

Strangely enough, young echinoderms are not built on a wheel plan. They are two-sided, like most other animals. They are much like the young of the simplest of the chordates, the big group to which all the animals with backbones belong.

Many animals of the seashore have rather close relatives that live in the fresh water of ponds and streams. There are, for example, freshwater crabs, clams, snails, and shrimps. But there are no land forms, either. All echinoderms live in the sea.

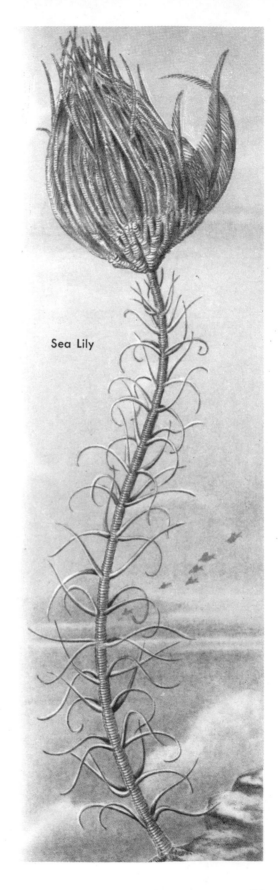

Sea Lily

Insects

In the world today there are so many species of insects that some people think the period in which we are living ought to be called the Age of Insects instead of the Age of Man. Over three-quarters of all the species of animals are species of insects. At least 750,000 species of insects are known and the list is growing.

It is not easy to get an idea of what so large a number means. Suppose the scientific names of all the species of insects were printed on a strip of paper, one below another in type like this. The strip of paper would be over two miles long! Suppose you set out to learn about insects by studying a different one every day. To finish, you would have to live more than 2,000 years!

Suppose, as another way of trying to get an idea of what 750,000 means, you were to imagine a parade of all the species of animal going by every minute, day and night. The whole parade would last for nearly two years. It would take a year and a half for just the insects to go by.

There are not only many species of insects; there are also many insects in a species. A single tree may have 20 million plant aphids on it. A swarm of gnats may be made of hundreds of thousands of gnats. At times there are plagues of locusts. If all the people on the earth were scattered evenly over the land, there would be about 60 people for every square mile. If the insects were scattered evenly, for every square mile there would probably be at least 25 million! Insects may outnumber people more than a million to one.

The insects form one division—the largest—of the arthropods. Sometimes insects are called hexapods. 'Hexapod' means 'six-footed'. The name is a good one, for all insects have six legs. Their common name comes from the word 'incised', which means 'divided'. An insect's body is divided into three parts— the head, thorax and abdomen. You can see the three parts clearly in an ant. Notice in the picture that the legs are in pairs and that they all come from the thorax.

Woodcricket   Long-horn Grasshopper

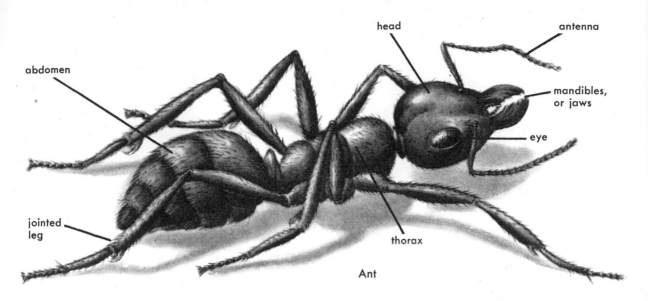

abdomen

head

antenna

mandibles, or jaws

eye

jointed leg

thorax

Ant

In addition to having three pairs of legs and three body regions, all insects are alike in having one pair of feelers, or antennae. They all have a covering of a remarkable substance called chitin. They therefore have a skeleton of a sort outside their bodies, just as many animals of the seashore do. In fact, the outside skeleton of crabs and their relatives is also made of chitin. Chitin is flexible, waterproof and very light and strong.

Most insects have compound eyes— eyes made up of many facets. Most of them, moreover, have wings. The ant pictured was chosen to show the parts of an insect because it has no wings to hide the three body regions. Some ants, how-ever, do have wings. In all but a few species of ants, some individuals have wings, even though most do not. The ant in the picture is one of those without wings.

An insect, as a rule, has two pairs of wings. The butterfly's show clearly. All the winged insects pictured below have two pairs, even though, except for the flying grasshopper, only one pair shows. They hide the other pair. Some species of stick insects also have two pairs of wings, but the one shown has none.

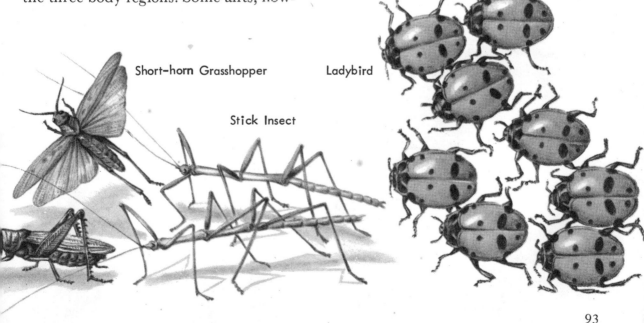

Short-horn Grasshopper

Ladybird

Stick Insect

Family Tree of Arthropods

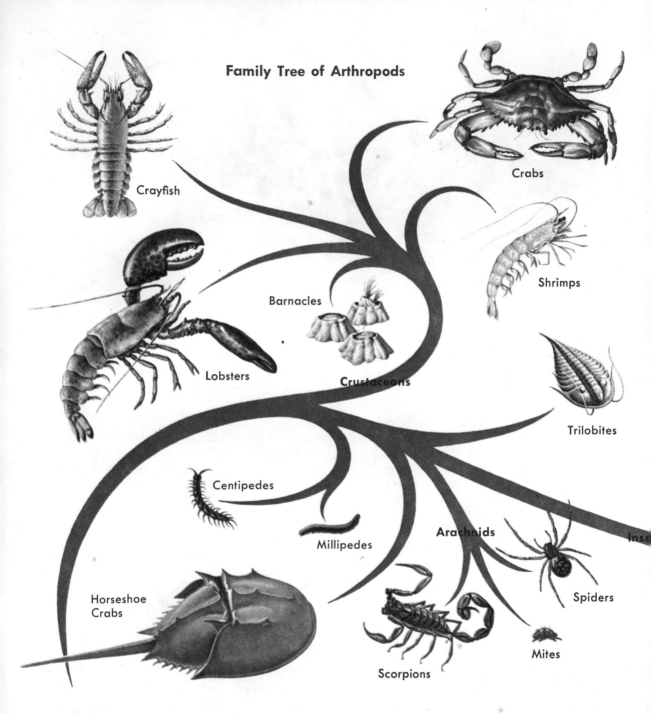

Crayfish

Crabs

Lobsters

Barnacles

Shrimps

Crustaceans

Trilobites

Centipedes

Millipedes

Arachnids

Inse

Spiders

Horseshoe Crabs

Scorpions

Mites

Insects live in a larger number of habitats than any other group of animals. Almost everywhere in the world has a large insect population. The seashore and the mountains, the forests and the fields, the hot lands near the equator and the cold lands near the poles, all have their insect populations. Insects teem in every pond and stream. They are not common in salt water lakes but even there, there are some. Hardly any insects, however, live in or on the ocean.

The tree chart shows many of the insects' arthropod relations, as well as fourteen of the more than twenty-five orders of insects. On one branch, you notice, are the ancient trilobites. Unlike them and many of the insects' other relations, insects are air-breathers. Even those that breathe in water when they are larvae are air-breathers as adults.

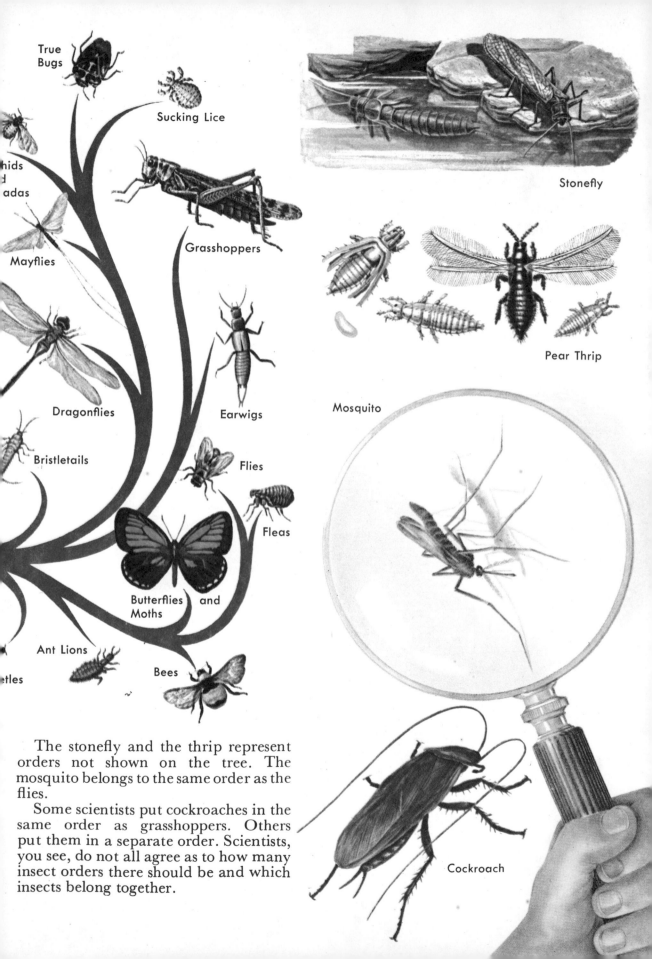

True Bugs

Sucking Lice

hids and adas

Grasshoppers

Mayflies

Dragonflies

Earwigs

Bristletails

Flies

Fleas

Butterflies and Moths

Ant Lions

Bees

tles

Stonefly

Pear Thrip

Mosquito

Cockroach

The stonefly and the thrip represent orders not shown on the tree. The mosquito belongs to the same order as the flies.

Some scientists put cockroaches in the same order as grasshoppers. Others put them in a separate order. Scientists, you see, do not all agree as to how many insect orders there should be and which insects belong together.

The scientific names of most orders of insects end in 'ptera'. This ending means 'wings'. Their wings are a big help in identifying insects.

The scientists' name for the moths and butterflies is Lepidoptera. The name means 'scaly wings'. The wings of all moths and butterflies are covered with tiny scales that look like powder when they are rubbed off. The separate scales are too small to be seen clearly without a microscope.

Both the mud dauber wasps and the honeybees are Hymenoptera—the 'membrane-winged' insects. The giant water bug is a member of the Hemiptera, the 'half wings'. This order gets its name from the front wings of the insects in it. The wings are half leathery and half gauzy.

The name for the order which includes the flies, gnats, and mosquitoes is Diptera. 'Diptera' means 'two wings'. The beetles are the Coleoptera, or 'sheath wings'. There are over a dozen more orders with names that end in 'ptera'. The chart on page 369 lists some of them.

Every insect, to whatever order it belongs, needs oxygen and food. Insects are like all other animals in this way.

The insects have a system of tubes which carry air to all parts of their bodies. Air enters through tiny openings called *spiracles*. Some insects, for at least a part of their lives, have special breathing devices which fit their particular way of living. The mosquito larvae, for instance, live in water and breathe through tubes that extend to the water's surface.

As you would guess, not all the thousands and thousands of species of insects eat the same materials. The food of the four insects pictured here gives some idea of the variety of things insects eat.

The water bug lives on small water animals. It captures tadpoles, snails, other insects and even small fish.

Giant
Water
Bug

Honeybees

The mud dauber, which is a kind of wasp, is a meat-eater when it is immature but becomes a vegetarian later. Its larvae eat spiders. Mud daubers build a nest of mud. In each room of her nest a female mud dauber packs a spider or two and then lays an egg. When the young wasp comes out of the egg its spider food is ready. The adult wasps live on nectar, the sweet juice found in many flowers.

Adult honeybees only eat honey. The larvae are fed on a mixture of pollen and honey. Pollen is the yellow powder that is found on the stamens of flowers.

When young, the Camberwell Beauty butterfly eats the leaves of elm, poplar, or willow trees. When fully grown it, too, lives on nectar. Clearly, a giant water bug would starve on the food a Camberwell Beauty eats.

But the story of these four insects and what they eat is only a tiny part of the whole story of insects and their food. The food of the hundreds of thousands of species of insects includes almost every variety of plant and animal material.

There is a race between people and insects for every bit of food that is grown. In a big field of corn there is a good deal of food. But insects may get to the corn first and eat so much that there is little of it left for people. They may be busy eating the young ears while people are waiting for them to ripen. Every 'wormy' apple or tomato, every 'buggy' bunch of broccoli and every jar of jam with wasps flying all round it means a race won by insects.

Each part of a tree provides food for some species of insect. Some insects drink the sap of the tree. Others eat the leaves, the bark, the young twigs, or the roots. After the tree has been cut down, there are other insects ready to eat both the green and the dried timber.

In the same way, several different species of insect may be eating a pea plant at the same time. There are insects that eat the young pods where the peas are, others that suck the sap of the plant, and still others that nibble on its leaves or its roots or bore into its stalks.

Camberwell Beauty Butterfly

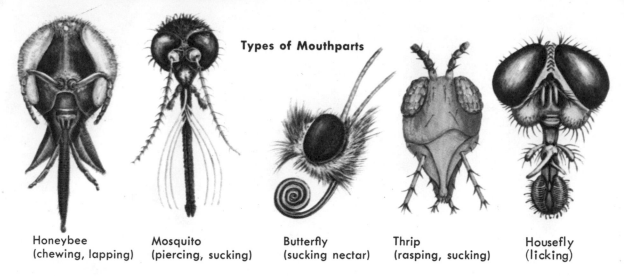

Types of Mouthparts

Honeybee
(chewing, lapping)

Mosquito
(piercing, sucking)

Butterfly
(sucking nectar)

Thrip
(rasping, sucking)

Housefly
(licking)

Fur, woollen goods, and blood—these are a few of the other things insects eat. Some people spend a lot of money every year putting their furs and woollen clothing in cold storage so that clothes moths will not damage them. No one needs to be told that mosquitoes suck blood. Many people do not know, however, that only the adult female mosquito lives on blood. The male mosquito lives on plant juices. Larval mosquitoes live on tiny water plants and animals. Anyone who has a dog or cat knows how carefully these pets have to be guarded against lice and fleas, which are also bloodsuckers. The ox louse is a cattle pest. Too many ox lice on an animal do serious harm.

Some insects live part of their lives inside the bodies of other insects. An insect may, for example, lay its eggs inside the body of a caterpillar. When the eggs hatch the immature insects eat the caterpillar's body for their food.

Some meat-eating insects often attack dangerous prey. The picture below shows the tarantula hawk wasp, one of the largest wasps, about to attack a tarantula, a poisonous spider much bigger than itself.

Some insects are cannibals. They eat one another. It is not at all unusual for a female praying mantis to eat her mate. The lacewing fly lays its eggs in a special way. It keeps the first lacewing larvae that hatch, from eating either the remaining eggs or younger larvae as they are just hatching. Each egg is put on the end of a little thread-like stalk so that it is not too close to any other egg. You can see some stalked eggs on one of the leaves in the picture at the bottom of the next page.

Their mouthparts adapt different insects to eat different kinds of food. The grasshopper, which eats leaves, has biting

Ox Louse

Tarantula Hawk Wasp and Tarantula

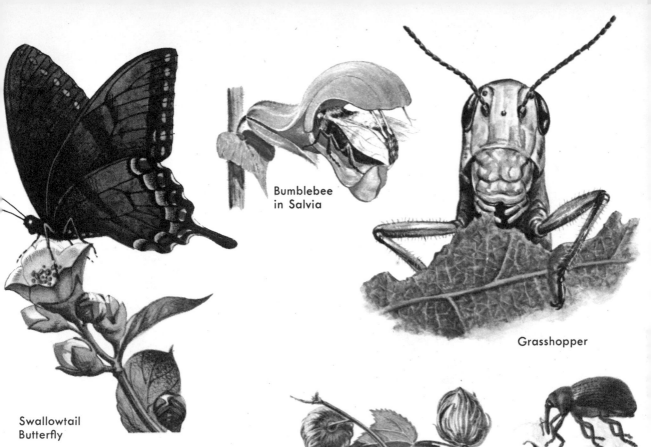

Bumblebee
in Salvia

Grasshopper

Swallowtail
Butterfly

mouthparts. Its jaws grind up the plant material bitten off. The mouthparts of a grasshopper would not help a butterfly or a bumblebee to gather nectar. In the same way, a housefly's licking mouthparts would be no good for a giant water bug or a lacewing. Neither would those of a pear thrip. The water bug and the lacewing have piercing mouthparts. Notice the snout of the cotton boll weevil. With it the weevil can pierce the buds of cotton flowers or the bolls filled with cotton and eat out the inside. The female weevil gets not only her food, but also a place for her eggs in this way.

The fact that some insects eat different food when they are immature than when they are adult suggests that these insects change greatly as they grow up. They do. Learning to recognise the insects around us is far more complicated than it would be if there were not so many larval insects bearing almost no resemblance to adults of the same species. You would probably recognise an immature water bug or grasshopper from knowing the adult, but certainly not a larval beetle, wasp, bee, or butterfly.

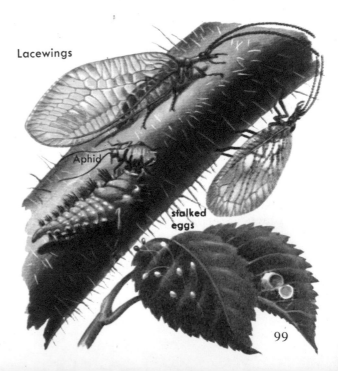

Cotton Boll Weevil

Lacewings

Aphid

stalked
eggs

99

This beautiful moth, the cecropia, is one of the silk moths. The pictures on the next page help to tell its life history.

The female cecropia lays her eggs on the leaf of some plant, perhaps an apple or cherry tree. The eggs hatch into tiny black caterpillars, or *larvae*. A cecropia caterpillar does not look in the least like a fully grown moth. It shows no signs of wings or antennae. It has six short legs close to its head, but it also has several false legs for crawling along. Its body

is clearly divided into many parts, or segments. The caterpillar's skin is studded with many little bumps called tubercles.

Each caterpillar, or larva, begins at once to eat the leaves of the plant the eggs were laid on. It grows fast and is soon too big for its skin. The skin has to be shed. Shedding one skin and growing another is called moulting.

The black skin splits down the back, and out comes the caterpillar with a dull

eggs

orange skin. The caterpillar keeps on eating and growing and is soon so big that it has to shed its orange skin.

The caterpillar's third skin is yellow. Some of its tubercles are brightly coloured. By the time it is yellow, the caterpillar is more than an inch long, but it is not nearly full sized yet. It sheds its skin twice more. After each of these moults, it has green with blue, red and yellow tubercles. In the final stage, it is much bigger than in any of the others.

Of course, the caterpillar has to breathe while it is growing. It breathes just as adult insects do—through spiracles. Almost every segment of its body has a pair of spiracles.

A fully grown cecropia caterpillar is more than three inches long. After it reaches full size, the caterpillar stops eating. It begins winding around and around its body a long thread of silk it spins from its mouth. At last the caterpillar is so well wrapped up that it cannot be seen. The larva has spun its cocoon, and then changes into a *pupa,* by moulting again.

The silken case the caterpillar spins is a cocoon. The caterpillar, as it makes its cocoon, firmly fastens it to a small branch or twig. At one end of the cocoon there is a weak spot, or door, through which the moth can push its way when it is ready. It is amazing that every cecropia caterpillar 'knows' just how to spin its cocoon with a door. It inherits its way of making a cocoon, just as it inherits its legs, its spiracles, and its beautiful colours.

The pupa stage of a cecropia is often called its resting stage. But really great changes are taking place inside the pupal case. The pupa is changing into an adult moth.

A cecropia usually spends the whole winter in its cocoon. In the spring the adult moth pushes its way out. When it first emerges, its big wings are crumpled and moist. But soon the moth pumps liquid into its wing veins so that they spread out and they are dry.

By the time it comes out of its cocoon a cecropia's life is almost over. It eats nothing at all. Shortly it finds a mate. After the eggs are laid, the moths die.

The life history of the cecropia can be readily told in just four words: egg, larva, pupa, adult. Many kinds of insects go through these same four stages. We say that these insects show *complete metamorphosis.* 'Metamorphosis' means 'change'.

Life History of Cecropia Moth

Cocoon, containing pupa

larvae

Grasshopper

A grasshopper has a pair of antennae, as all insects have. It has compound eyes, as most insects do. Between its compound eyes it has three simple eyes. This insect also has a way of finding out what is going on around it that few insects have— it has ears. A grasshopper's ears are hidden under its wings.

Grasshoppers do not have voice boxes of any kind in their throats, but the sound grasshoppers make is well known. A grasshopper makes this sound either by rubbing its two front wings together or by rubbing a leg and a wing together.

Grasshoppers have jaws strong enough to chew even tough leaves. They eat tender leaves when they can get them, but they do eat older tougher leaves when there are no tender leaves available. When a grasshopper is eating a leaf, it usually holds the leaf between its two front feet.

A grasshopper has two habits that anyone who watches grasshoppers soon learns to know. It keeps itself well groomed by cleaning itself often. It 'washes' its face with its front legs. It cleans each antenna by holding it down on the ground with one foot and then pulling it out from under the foot. It cleans its legs by rubbing them together.

Its second habit is less pleasant. At times it spits out a brown liquid often spoken of as 'tobacco juice'. Probably the juice helps protect this insect from birds that might relish a grasshopper dinner.

The grasshopper in the picture is a short-horned grasshopper because it has short antennae. There are long-horned grasshoppers, too, such as those shown on page 92.

The grasshopper and dragonfly are good examples of insects that do not have four stages in their life history. They go through only three—egg, nymph, and adult.

With her egg-laying organ—called an ovipositor—a female grasshopper lays a cluster of white eggs in a hole she makes in the ground, or in a piece of rotten wood.

Little grasshoppers that look much like their parents hatch from the eggs. There are two big differences between these young grasshoppers, or grasshopper nymphs, and their parents. They are much smaller, and they have no wings.

As each nymph grows, it moults five or six times. When, after a few weeks, it sheds its skin for the last time, it is fully grown and has two pairs of strong wings. Many people are surprised to find that a grasshopper has two pairs of wings. Only one pair shows unless the grasshopper is flying. The second pair is folded up under the pair that shows.

Even as a nymph, a grasshopper has hind legs that are much longer and stronger than its four other legs. These back legs are excellent for jumping.

Grasshopper Nymphs

Dragonflies are also called 'darters'. They have this nickname because they can fly very fast and they dart about among the waterside plants.

These insects begin their lives in the water of a pond or stream. The female lays her eggs in the water. In some species she simply drops them into the water. In other species she attaches them to the leaves of a water plant.

The eggs hatch into nymphs which, unlike grasshopper nymphs, do not look at all like their parents. You would probably never guess from seeing a dragonfly nymph crawling in the water that it would grow up to be one of the handsomest of insects.

The most remarkable part of a dragonfly nymph is its lower lip. This lip is long and, strange as it sounds, jointed. The larval insect hides among the water plants. When something it might eat swims or floats by, out goes the creature's long lip. Then back comes the lip with the food.

The dragonfly nymph grows and moults just as the grasshopper nymph does. But it grows rather slowly. It remains in the water for two or three years.

After the two or three years underwater, the dragonfly nymph climbs up above the surface. It sheds its skin for the last time, spreads its silvery new wings, and flies away a fully-grown dragonfly. In the picture the empty discarded skin is clinging to a water plant.

The adult dragonfly is remarkable not only for the beauty of its wings, but also for its huge eyes. Almost all insects have compound eyes, but the dragonfly has especially large ones. Each eye may

Dragonfly

be made up of as many as 30,000 facets, like tiny eyes. A dragonfly does not lose its appetite when it emerges as an adult. It darts through the air catching insects as it flies. Its front legs serve as a basket for trapping insect prey, usually flies, gnats and mosquitoes.

Many other insects have life histories much like those of the grasshopper and the dragonfly. They show *incomplete metamorphosis*. Some of them change rather gradually to their adult form as the grasshopper does. Some seem to change suddenly as the dragonfly does. None of these insects has a stage that corresponds to the pupa of the insects with complete metamorphosis.

Dragonfly Nymphs

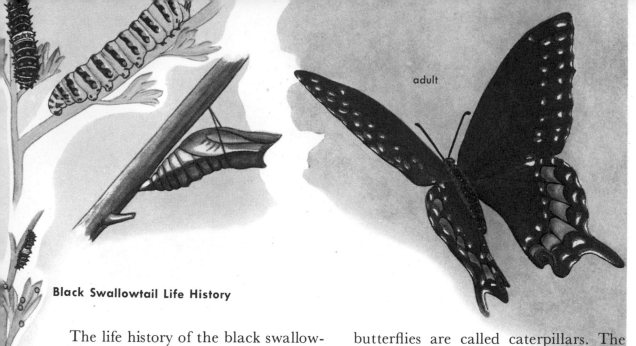

adult

Black Swallowtail Life History

The life history of the black swallowtail butterfly is very much like that of the cecropia moth. In fact, all butterflies and all moths go through the four stages of egg, larva, pupa and adult. Wasps, ants, bees, flies, mosquitoes and beetles are other insects with four stages in their life cycle.

We have different common names for the larvae of different kinds of insects. As you know, the larvae of moths and

Periodical Cicada Life History

butterflies are called caterpillars. The larvae of many beetles are called grubs. The larvae of flies are maggots, and those of mosquitoes are wrigglers or wigglers or wiggle-tails. The larvae of caddisflies live in lakes and ponds. In some species the larvae build cases from pieces of twigs. Other species, like those in the picture, make their cases from gravel and small shells.

The larvae of some species have special common names of their own. The larva of the cankerworm moth, for example, is called a measuring worm, an inchworm, or a looper. You can see how it gets these names. The caterpillar of the garden tiger moth is the well-known woolly bear. It is so hairy that it deserves the name. The orange puppy is the caterpillar of the giant swallowtail. Its looks and smell probably help to protect it from predators. The bag the caterpillar of the bagworm moth lives in, and later uses as its cocoon, is seen much more often than the moth itself. The bag, of course, gives the moth its name.

The pupal stage of butterflies is also sometimes called the chrysalis. In moths this stage does not have another name, it is just called the pupa. The chrysalis of the monarch butterfly is beautiful, as the picture shows. It is sometimes described as a 'green house with golden nails'. The cocoon of the luna moth looks like a ball of dead leaves.

After the insects that show complete metamorphosis reach the final stage, they do not grow. Any fly one sees flying about is as large as it will ever be. In the same way, as soon as a moth, butterfly, beetle, bee, or wasp has wings, it has reached its full size.

The periodical cicada is only found in the warmer parts of the United States of America and Mexico. It has a life history very much like that of the dragonfly. It is also called the seventeen-year locust. The nymph spends seventeen years under the ground, sucking juices from the roots of plants. Then it crawls out of the ground and climbs up a tree or post. The nymph sheds its skin and emerges as a gauzy-winged insect.

Some insects are born alive. With some flies and mayflies, for instance, the eggs hatch inside the body of the female and the larvae are born. Some generations of aphids, or plant lice, are females that instead of laying eggs give birth to aphids much like themselves. But such life histories as these are not common among insects.

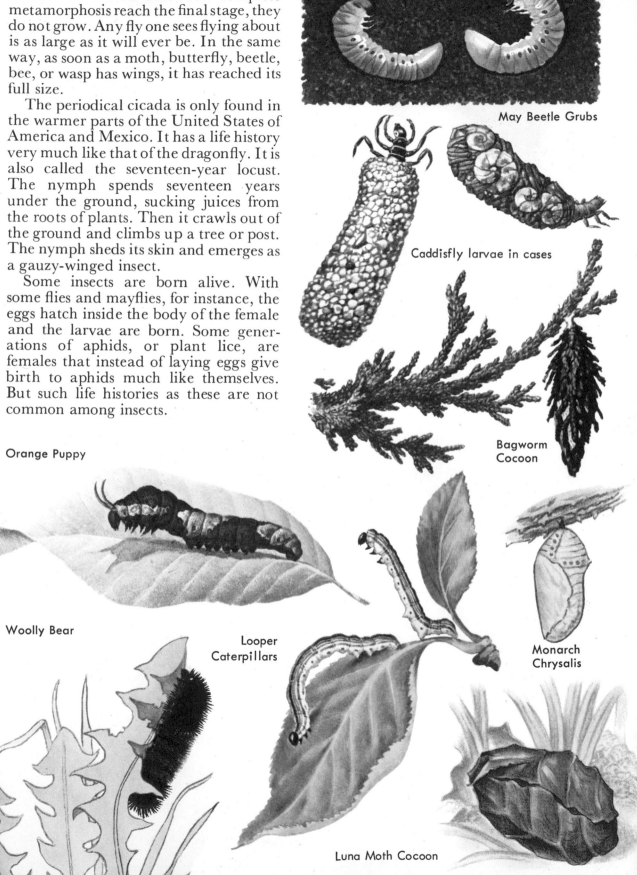

May Beetle Grubs

Caddisfly larvae in cases

Bagworm Cocoon

Orange Puppy

Woolly Bear

Looper Caterpillars

Monarch Chrysalis

Luna Moth Cocoon

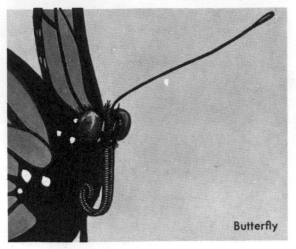
Butterfly

Moth

The scaly-winged insects—the moths and butterflies—are well known to most people. Almost everyone can call some by name.

Moths outnumber butterflies, so far as species are concerned, many times over. But moths fly by night as a rule and are not so likely to be seen, while butterflies flit about in the daytime. So most of us are better acquainted with butterflies than with moths.

There are several ways of telling whether a scaly-winged insect is a butterfly or a moth. Moths have rather thick bodies and big heads; butterflies as a rule have more slender bodies and smaller heads. Notice how slim the body of the

cloudless sulphur, a butterfly, is in comparison with the body of the silkworm moth. Moths usually rest with their wings held horizontally or in the position adopted by the widow underwing and the carpenter moth. Butterflies, when they alight, usually fold their wings together so that they make a kind of sail above them. More helpful as a way of telling moths from butterflies are the antennae. Butterflies have clubbed antennae. The antennae of moths may look like feathers, as those of the silkworm moth and the cecropia do. They may, on the other hand, be plain. Unfortunately for this moth-or-butterfly rule, there are a few moths with antennae clubbed like a butterfly's.

The skippers are a group of rather small butterflies. There is some doubt if they should really be called butterflies as

male

female

Cloudless Sulphur Butterflies

106

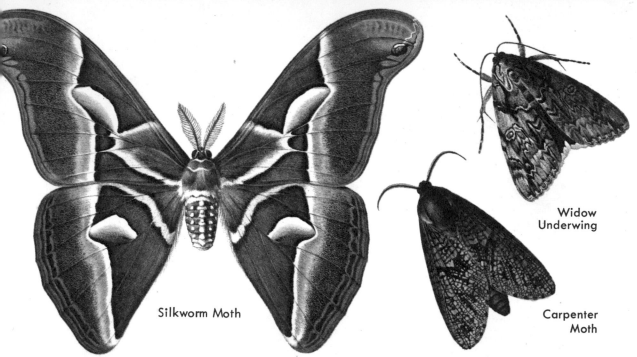

Silkworm Moth

Widow Underwing

Carpenter Moth

they show many of the features of moths. They have, for example, rather stout bodies and big heads. Their pupae are much like those of moths. But skippers fly about in the daytime like butterflies, and their antennae are clubbed.

The smallest skipper has a wing span of less than half an inch. There are moths only one-third as big. In contrast, some moths measure a foot across. And there are giant butterflies measuring almost as much with wings spread out.

Skippers

Small Skipper

Silver-spotted Skipper

Hoary-edged Skipper

Large Skipper

Great Purple Hairstreak

Pretty butterflies are found all over the world. The ones illustrated here are some well-known species.

Monarchs, as they are called in North America, are known as Wanderers in Australia. This species is found in many of the warmer parts of the world. They migrate long distances. Sometimes a few of the North American Monarchs are blown across the Atlantic Ocean to Europe.

Small tortoiseshells and red admirals are common butterflies in Europe. When the small tortoiseshell folds its wings it seems to vanish from sight as the lower surfaces of the wings are a very dull colour.

The zebra butterfly comes from South America. There are many species of very brightly coloured butterflies in South America.

The under surfaces of the wings of many butterflies have quite different colours from those seen on the upper side. Butterflies fold their wings over their bodies when they are at rest. The dull coloured under surfaces are all that can be seen. In that position butterflies are much less noticeable to birds and other animals that might eat them.

The comma is named after the comma shaped mark on the underside of its wings. All the blue butterflies are very small; most of them have a wingspan of less than one inch. Coppers are small butterflies too. But some of the species shown here are very large. The cairns birdwing is large enough to be mistaken for a small bird.

Most moths fly about at night, so they are not so brightly coloured as butterflies. Most people only see moths flying round the light in a room after dark. The moths have come in through the open window, attracted by the light. They can be seen and heard bumping into the light. Light

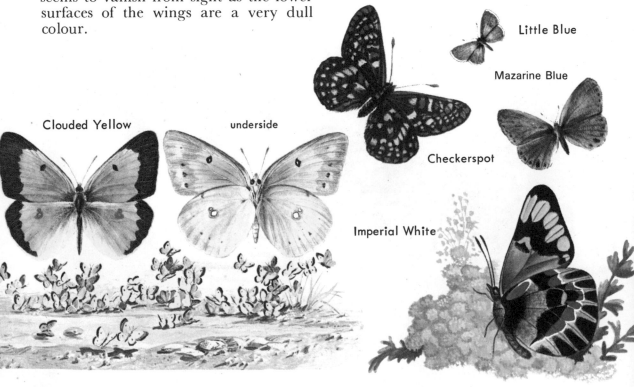

Little Blue

Mazarine Blue

Checkerspot

Clouded Yellow

underside

Imperial White

Monarch or Wanderer   Regal Fritillary

White Admiral

Red Admiral

Comma

Cairns Birdwing

Small Copper

Short Tailed Blue

Purplish Copper

Large Copper

Zebra

Silver Studded Blue

109

traps are set up by scientists when they want to catch moths to study. A fine net is suspended between two trees and a powerful light set up nearby. The moths fly into the net attracted by the light.

Many species of moths are very small, but the ones shown here are some of the largest and most beautiful in the world.

Hawk moths are found all over the world, and there are many species. Hummingbird moths are hawk moths. They are so called because they can hover over flowers while they are feeding on the nectar. Their wings beat very fast too, like a hummingbird.

There are many species of tiger moths too. All of them are readily attracted to light. Their wings are often brightly coloured.

Prominents are also easily attracted to light. The great prominent is one of the largest of this family of large moths.

Owlet moths, like the black witch, are so called because their large eyes shine in the dark. The little forester moth is closely related to the owlet moths.

Eight-spotted
Forester

Imperial

Isabella

Garden Tiger

Great Prominent

Bee Hawkmoth

Five-spotted Hawkmoth

Striped Hawkmoth

Luna

Emperor Gum Moth

Great
Owlet

111

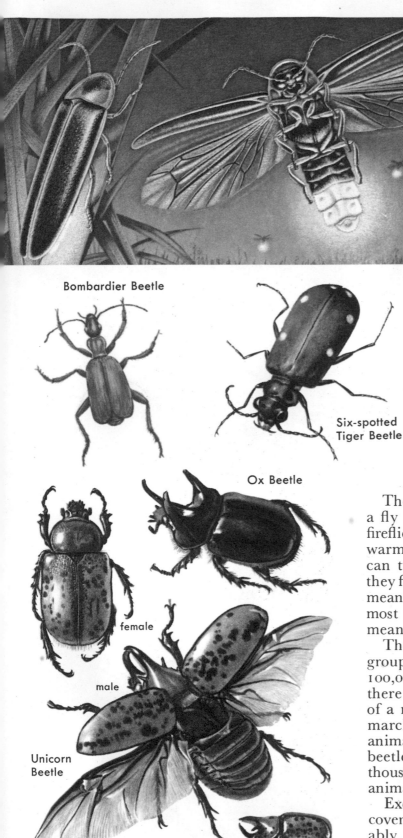

Firefly

Bombardier Beetle

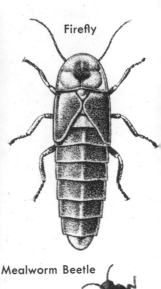

Six-spotted Tiger Beetle

Mealworm Beetle

Purple Tiger Beetle

Ox Beetle

female

male

Unicorn Beetle

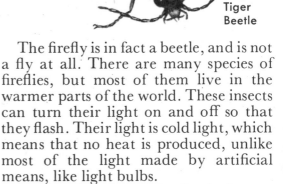

The firefly is in fact a beetle, and is not a fly at all. There are many species of fireflies, but most of them live in the warmer parts of the world. These insects can turn their light on and off so that they flash. Their light is cold light, which means that no heat is produced, unlike most of the light made by artificial means, like light bulbs.

The beetles make up by far the largest group of insects. There are at least 100,000 species. Scientists think that there are probably more than a quarter of a million. If all the animals were to march two by two in a parade, every animal with a backbone could have a beetle partner and there would be thousands of beetles left to pair up with animals without backbones.

Except when flying, a beetle is well covered by its hard front wings. Probably, beetles are successful partly because of that armour and partly because they

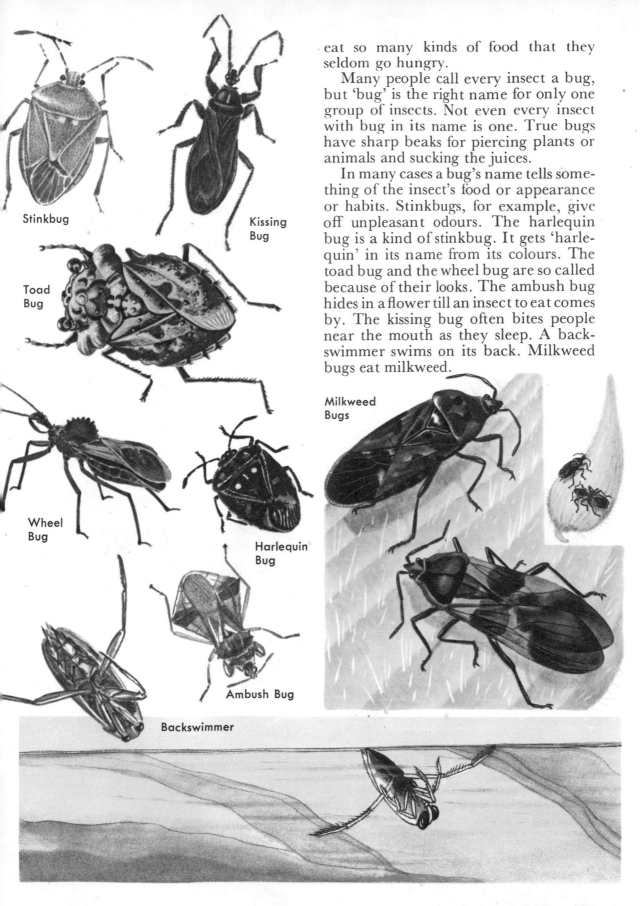

Stinkbug

Kissing Bug

Toad Bug

Wheel Bug

Harlequin Bug

Ambush Bug

Backswimmer

Milkweed Bugs

eat so many kinds of food that they seldom go hungry.

Many people call every insect a bug, but 'bug' is the right name for only one group of insects. Not even every insect with bug in its name is one. True bugs have sharp beaks for piercing plants or animals and sucking the juices.

In many cases a bug's name tells something of the insect's food or appearance or habits. Stinkbugs, for example, give off unpleasant odours. The harlequin bug is a kind of stinkbug. It gets 'harlequin' in its name from its colours. The toad bug and the wheel bug are so called because of their looks. The ambush bug hides in a flower till an insect to eat comes by. The kissing bug often bites people near the mouth as they sleep. A backswimmer swims on its back. Milkweed bugs eat milkweed.

Honeybee in Apple Blossom

The tomato worm does a great deal of damage by eating the leaves of tomato and tobacco plants. It is one of the insects that we count as our enemies.

There are a great many harmful insects. A common term for them is insect pests. They harm us in different ways. Many of them are our enemies simply because they eat food that we want for ourselves or keep plants from producing food we need. There are crop pests, orchard pests, garden pests and insects that eat stored food. Some insects do great harm to our garden trees and forests. Some ruin buildings we have built, and others clothes we have made. The most dangerous of the insect pests are those that carry disease.

So many insects harm us that many people think of all insects as our enemies. To them simply saying, 'It's a bug,' is a legitimate excuse for killing any insect on sight. But we have good friends among the insects, too.

Many insects help by visiting flowers and carrying pollen from one flower to another. By carrying pollen they help seeds and fruits to form. Without insect pollen-carriers, we would have no apples, no peaches, no clover seed—the list would be long.

The earth would lose much of its beauty if the pollen-carrying insects were to disappear. For if no seeds were formed, most flowering plants would soon die out. The bumblebees are very important to many plants as they pollinate them. Honeybees also carry pollen from one flower to another.

We get valuable products from some insects. Honey and silk are probably the two most important. Honey, of course, is made by honeybees. Silk comes from the cocoons spun by the caterpillars of the silkworm moth. Shellac, used in varnishes, is made from secretions of the lac insects. And some insects furnish useful drugs.

Some insects help us by eating insect pests. Ladybirds, for instance, eat plant lice. The beetles called caterpillar hunters, both as larvae and adults, search out

Bumblebees

Silkworm Moth and cocoons

and destroy the caterpillars of various moths harmful to trees.

There are some important insect scavengers. Dung beetles are among them. They eat up much dead animal matter and waste.

Some insects have high food value. Ants gorged with honeydew, the sweet secretion of plant lice and scale insects, are prized in Mexico. Grasshoppers, water boatmen, termites, and stinkbugs are other insects eaten in different parts of the world. Indirectly, insects provide us with lots of food by serving as food for the freshwater fishes we eat.

A number of insects help us to fight weeds. When the prickly pear cactus was first introduced into Australia, it spread rapidly and was soon a troublesome weed. As a way of fighting this weed, insects that feed on it were shipped to Australia. It was the cactus moth, sent there from Argentina, that finally brought the cactus under control.

Some insects are good guinea pigs for science. One kind of fruit fly has been much used in the study of heredity.

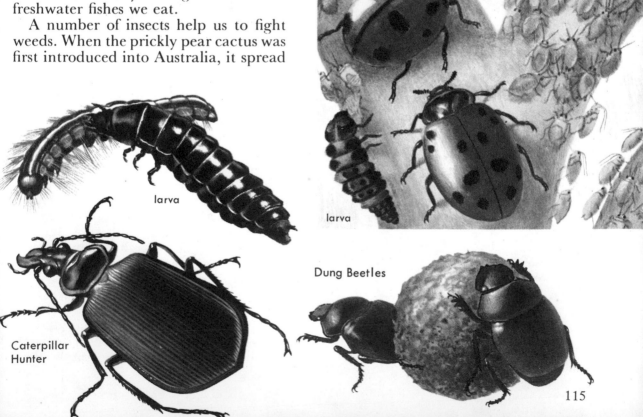

Ladybirds

larva

larva

Caterpillar Hunter

Dung Beetles

115

Praying Mantis

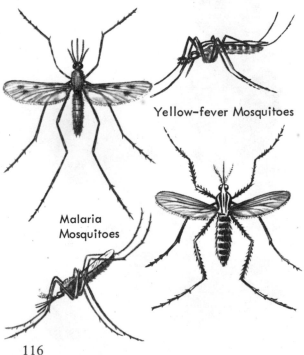

Yellow-fever Mosquitoes

Malaria Mosquitoes

The praying mantis is a large insect that eats other insects, so it is a very useful animal. All the other insects shown on this page are harmful, in one way or another.

Of course, the insects that are our friends do not deserve any credit for being helpful. Neither do those that harm us deserve any blame for the damage they do. The insects are simply living their own lives. It happens that in living their lives some of them make things we want or help us in other ways. It happens that others, in living their lives, interfere with ours.

There were no insect pests and no insect friends before man lived on earth. During the Coal Age, for example, there were giant cockroaches. But they were not pests, for there were no people for them to interfere with. The first honeybees were not friends, for there were no people for them to help. When we think of insects as being friends or enemies, we are being selfish. We are thinking only of ourselves and how the insects help or harm us.

But we cannot afford to be unselfish in thinking of insects. They are our greatest rivals. To hold our own against them we have to carry on a never-ending battle.

High on the list of insect enemies are mosquitoes of certain kinds. Malaria and yellow fever are two of the diseases they carry. The common housefly is not only a nuisance, but also a danger because it carries typhoid and tuberculosis germs. The tsetse fly has spread over four and a half million square miles in Africa, carrying sleeping sickness with it. Fleas and body lice both carry typhus. Fleas also carry bubonic plague, the dreaded Black Death of the Middle Ages.

The insects pictured on this page attack plants. They are all serious pests.

The cabbage-white butterfly, when it is a caterpillar, eats cabbage. It is one of our few enemies among the butterflies. Most butterflies are helpful, or at least not harmful. We have a great many more enemies among the moths.

The codling moth is often called the apple worm. This insect is to blame for many of our wormy apples.

Japanese beetles are not at all particular about their food. They destroy the leaves, blossoms, and fruit of nearly 300 different species of plants.

The gypsy moth is fairly common and an enemy of woodland and trees. Its caterpillars eat the leaves of coniferous and other types of trees. They were taken to the United States by a scientist in the last century. Some of the moths escaped into a nearby wood. Since that time thay have spread and 'done damage to many millions of trees. In Britain there are birds that feed on the caterpillars, but in America no bird fed on them, so the gypsy moth was able to spread very quickly.

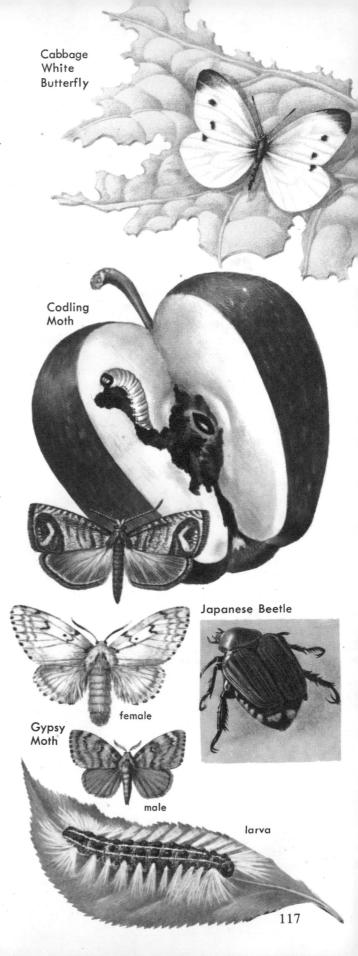

Cabbage White Butterfly

Codling Moth

Japanese Beetle

Gypsy Moth

female

male

larva

These insects also attack plants. The harm some of them do comes more from plant diseases they spread than from damage they themselves do. Cucumber beetles, for example, carry a disease from vine to vine.

Like the cucumber beetle and the pine sawyer several other insects are named after the plants they attack. Of those that are not so named, the tussock moth caterpillar attacks garden trees as does the flat-headed borer beetle. The tarnished plant bug feeds on a great variety of plants including strawberries, fruit trees and peonies. Army moth caterpillars destroy valuable crops like cotton and grain.

It goes without saying that many ways of fighting insect pests have been worked out. But fighting them is not easy. One problem is to get rid of them without killing helpful insects at the same time. And we do not wish to harm the plants the pests are on, or the other animals— including ourselves—that may eat the plants.

We can set traps for some kinds of insects. A band of sticky gum around a tree acts as a trap for caterpillars that try to climb the tree. It is a common way of protecting trees from the tussock moth. There are light traps that attract some night-flying insects. Trenches filled with oil have been used to trap other pests. But we have to know a great deal about an insect before we can set a good trap for it. The army worm, the larva of a moth, gets its name because it moves in great armies from one field to another. An oil-filled trench is a good trap for marching army worms. It would be of no use in fighting mosquitoes.

Removing breeding places is an excellent way of fighting some insects. It makes better sense to try to keep them from multiplying than to kill them after they are at work against us. Many swamps have been drained as a way of getting rid of mosquitoes. Clearing away piles of rubbish and manure takes away the chief breeding places of the common housefly.

The most widely used way of fighting

Army Worm

insects is with chemicals. The chemicals are of two kinds: stomach poisons and contact poisons. Some are both kinds in one. Some, for example, kill insects on contact when they are first sprayed on plants. Later, after they have been absorbed by the plants, they act as stomach poisons to insects that chew or bore into the plants or suck the juices.

Contact poisons may do their work by stopping up an insect's spiracles. They may eat their way through the chitin into the insect's body.

Unfortunately, insects build up resistance to chemicals used in fighting them. DDT, when it was first used, was thought to be the final answer to many of our insect problems. It is used to kill insects of many kinds. But now there are strains of these insects that are not affected by it. We have to keep on developing new insecticides.

We can use germ warfare against some caterpillar pests—the tomato worm, the cabbage worm, and the caterpillar of the gypsy moth among others. Plants the caterpillars eat are treated with a spray containing disease germs that kill the caterpillars.

A region in which there is a serious insect pest is sometimes quarantined to keep the pest from spreading. Nothing that might carry the pest can be carried or transported from the region.

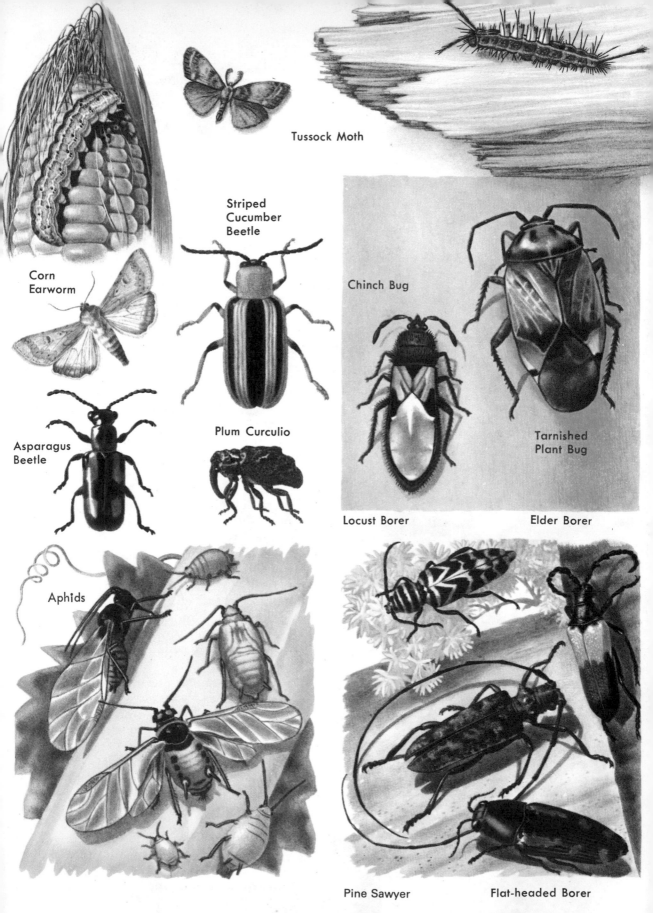

Tussock Moth

Corn
Earworm

Striped
Cucumber
Beetle

Chinch Bug

Tarnished
Plant Bug

Asparagus
Beetle

Plum Curculio

Locust Borer

Elder Borer

Aphids

Pine Sawyer

Flat-headed Borer

119

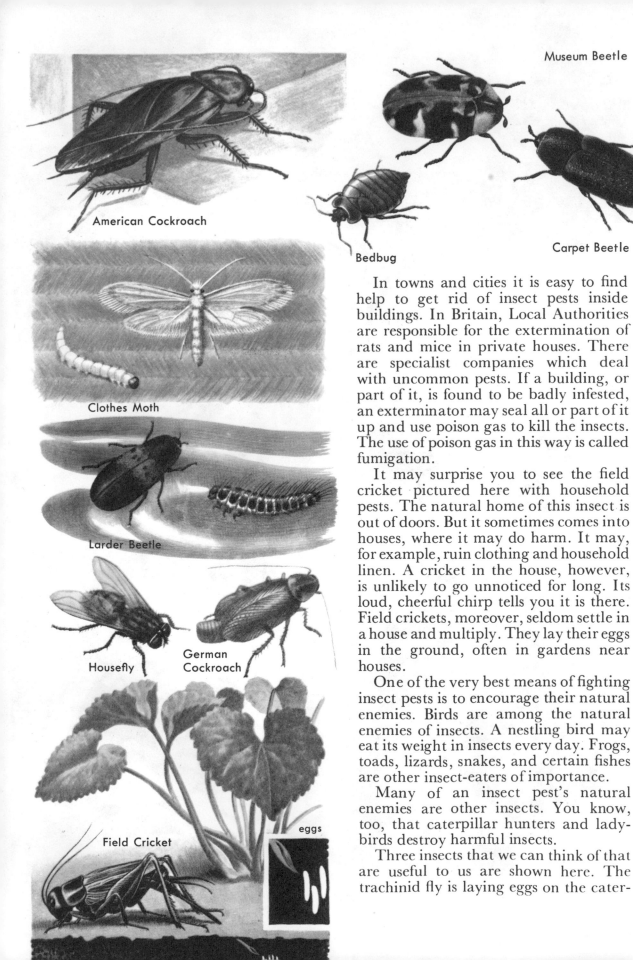

Museum Beetle

American Cockroach

Bedbug

Carpet Beetle

Clothes Moth

Larder Beetle

Housefly

German Cockroach

Field Cricket

eggs

In towns and cities it is easy to find help to get rid of insect pests inside buildings. In Britain, Local Authorities are responsible for the extermination of rats and mice in private houses. There are specialist companies which deal with uncommon pests. If a building, or part of it, is found to be badly infested, an exterminator may seal all or part of it up and use poison gas to kill the insects. The use of poison gas in this way is called fumigation.

It may surprise you to see the field cricket pictured here with household pests. The natural home of this insect is out of doors. But it sometimes comes into houses, where it may do harm. It may, for example, ruin clothing and household linen. A cricket in the house, however, is unlikely to go unnoticed for long. Its loud, cheerful chirp tells you it is there. Field crickets, moreover, seldom settle in a house and multiply. They lay their eggs in the ground, often in gardens near houses.

One of the very best means of fighting insect pests is to encourage their natural enemies. Birds are among the natural enemies of insects. A nestling bird may eat its weight in insects every day. Frogs, toads, lizards, snakes, and certain fishes are other insect-eaters of importance.

Many of an insect pest's natural enemies are other insects. You know, too, that caterpillar hunters and lady-birds destroy harmful insects.

Three insects that we can think of that are useful to us are shown here. The trachinid fly is laying eggs on the cater-

Harvester Butterfly

pupa

larva

American
Chameleon

pillar of a gypsy moth. Ichneumon wasps
are insects that destroy other harmful
insects by laying their eggs in the bodies
of the larvae. The caterpillar of the
harvester butterfly eats aphids.

Developing plants and animals that
can better stand the attacks of insects is
another hopeful way of fighting insect
pests. Changing crops often in a field—
crop rotation—is still another way. But
the problem of holding our own against
our insect enemies is so big that every
once in a while someone asks the
question, 'Will the insects win?'

Toad

Tachinid Fly

Ichneumon
Wasp

Wren

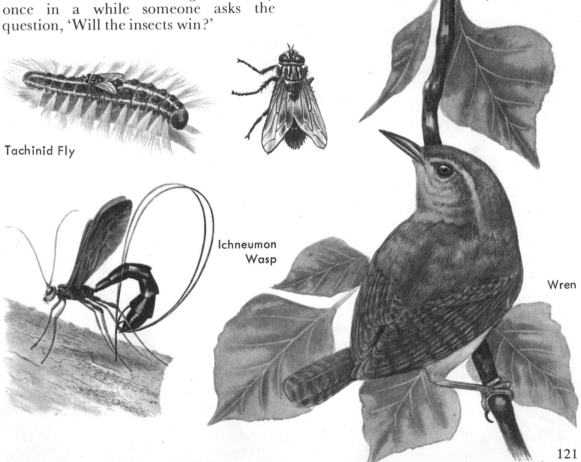

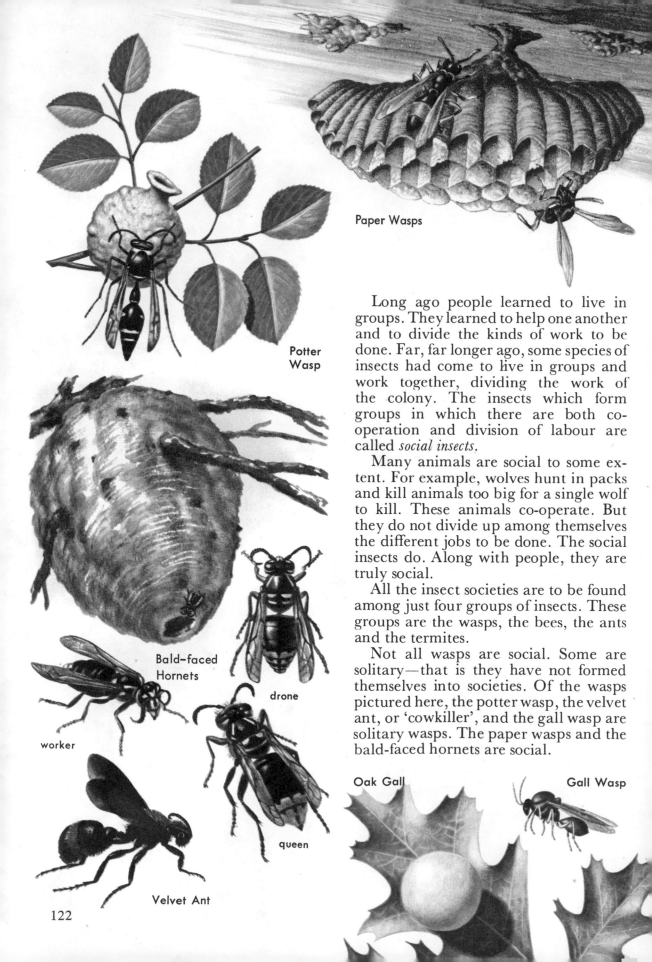

Paper Wasps

Potter Wasp

Bald-faced Hornets

worker

drone

queen

Velvet Ant

Oak Gall

Gall Wasp

Long ago people learned to live in groups. They learned to help one another and to divide the kinds of work to be done. Far, far longer ago, some species of insects had come to live in groups and work together, dividing the work of the colony. The insects which form groups in which there are both co-operation and division of labour are called *social insects*.

Many animals are social to some extent. For example, wolves hunt in packs and kill animals too big for a single wolf to kill. These animals co-operate. But they do not divide up among themselves the different jobs to be done. The social insects do. Along with people, they are truly social.

All the insect societies are to be found among just four groups of insects. These groups are the wasps, the bees, the ants and the termites.

Not all wasps are social. Some are solitary—that is they have not formed themselves into societies. Of the wasps pictured here, the potter wasp, the velvet ant, or 'cowkiller', and the gall wasp are solitary wasps. The paper wasps and the bald-faced hornets are social.

122

The colonies of the paper wasp are small. A colony is made up of the queen —a female that lays eggs—a few male wasps, or drones, and a number of worker wasps. The workers are females that do not lay eggs. They find food and take care of the queen and the larvae that hatch from her eggs. The different kinds of individuals in an insect society are called *castes*. There are three castes in a society of paper wasps.

There are the same three castes in a nest of bald-faced hornets. But there are usually several thousand wasps in each nest.

Even a colony of bald-faced hornets is small beside a colony, or hive, of honeybees. In a beehive there may be 80,000 bees.

In a honeybee hive there are the same three castes as in a wasp nest—the queen, the drones and the worker females. In a wasp colony only the queen lives through the winter. But many honeybee workers, as well as the queen, do. They live on the honey they have stored up.

The making of honey is complicated. It involves several processes—hunting for flowers, gathering nectar from them, building a comb, filling it with honey made from the nectar, and capping the cells to seal the honey in. There are many housekeeping chores to be done in a hive, too. Among them are taking care of the queen bee, keeping the hive clean, ventilating it by fanning fresh air in, feeding the larval bees, and mending any cracks that appear in the hive. Worker bees also protect the hive from intruders. They have good weapons— stings. But if a worker has to sting an enemy, she is giving up her life for the group. For she cannot pull out her sting, and without it she dies.

Bumblebees are social, too, but their societies are simple. There are seldom more than 500 workers. Only queen bumblebees live through the winter. As with the wasps, some bees are solitary.

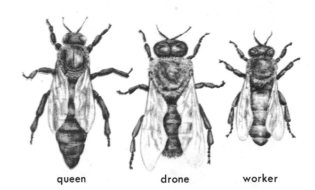

queen   drone   worker

Honeybees

Ants

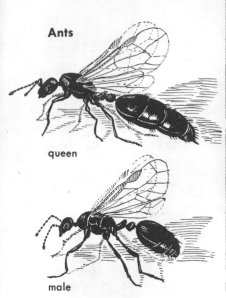

queen

male

worker

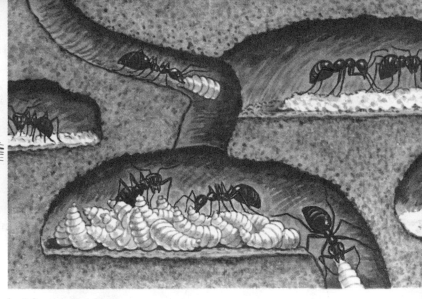

Inside an Ant Nest

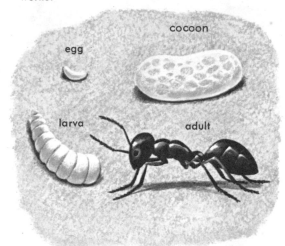

egg

cocoon

larva

adult

All ants are social. Some live in rather simple societies. But some ant societies are almost unbelievably complex. In many there are several castes of workers. In some there is a special caste called soldiers. As one would guess, their work is to protect the colony from attack. They have especially powerful jaws.

Among the most remarkable ant societies are those of the army ants and the leaf-cutter, or parasol, ants. Both have soldier castes and other workers of several sizes.

Army ants eat other insects. They move slowly about in large armies searching for food beneath the litter on the floor of a forest. If the trail is rough, worker ants make it smooth by filling in the hollows with their own bodies. Where there is a gap in the trail, workers hang on to one another to form a bridge

Parasol Ants

over the gap. When an army stops to rest, workers may even form themselves into a nest of many rooms. As soon as the army is ready to move on, the walls fall apart to become the separate workers that formed them.

Parasol ants raise underground gardens of fungus plants much like tiny mushrooms. They cut up leaves and bring them to their gardens as food for the fungus plants.

Some ants have domesticated animals, among them ant 'cows'. Ant cows are aphids. The ants take care of the aphids and protect them from enemies. The aphids in turn give off a sweet juice, honeydew, when the ants stroke them with their antennae. The ants eat the honeydew.

All termites, too, are social. Termite castes differ in one way from the castes of wasps, bees, and ants. All the workers among the wasps, bees, and ants are females. There are both male and female workers among the termites.

The biggest colonies of termites make even the biggest colonies of the other social insects seem small. A single termite colony may have several million workers in it. A termite queen has been known to lay from 8,000 to 10,000 eggs in one day. It is not surprising that such an egg-laying machine has a large body.

In some ways an insect society is far ahead of a community of people. Every individual that is old enough to work has work to do: there is no unemployment. Each one knows exactly how to carry on its work without having to be taught how. They all live together happily and there is no quarrelling between members of the group.

Termites or White Ants

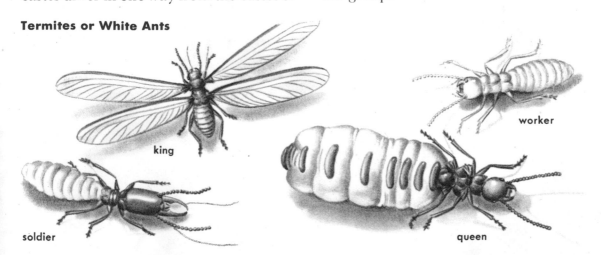

king

worker

soldier

queen

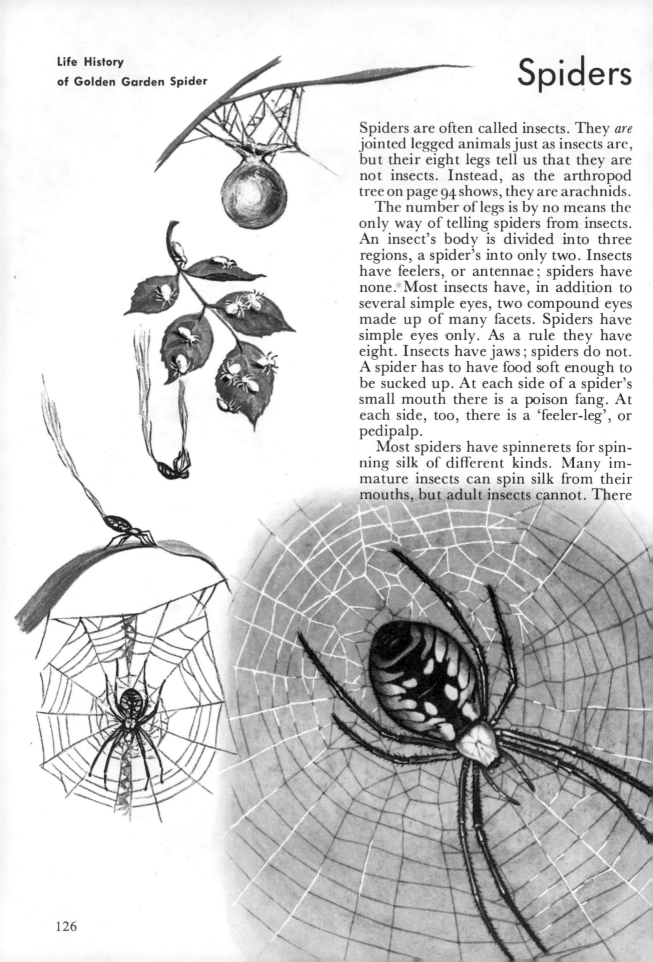

Spiders

Spiders are often called insects. They *are* jointed legged animals just as insects are, but their eight legs tell us that they are not insects. Instead, as the arthropod tree on page 94 shows, they are arachnids.

The number of legs is by no means the only way of telling spiders from insects. An insect's body is divided into three regions, a spider's into only two. Insects have feelers, or antennae; spiders have none. Most insects have, in addition to several simple eyes, two compound eyes made up of many facets. Spiders have simple eyes only. As a rule they have eight. Insects have jaws; spiders do not. A spider has to have food soft enough to be sucked up. At each side of a spider's small mouth there is a poison fang. At each side, too, there is a 'feeler-leg', or pedipalp.

Most spiders have spinnerets for spinning silk of different kinds. Many immature insects can spin silk from their mouths, but adult insects cannot. There is still another obvious way in which spiders differ from insects: no spiders have wings.

Spiders hatch from eggs. A female spider may lay more than a thousand eggs at a time. In many cases she spins a silken sac for them. When little spiders hatch, they look like fully-grown spiders except that they are smaller and are very pale. There is never any food stored up for the young spiders. They may turn cannibal and eat one another.

There are thousands of species of spiders. They differ greatly in size. The large hairy spiders called tarantulas are many times as big as the little crab spiders. Spiders differ in colour and shape, too.

Spiders are scattered far and wide over the earth. The warm lands near the equator have the greatest number of species. But there are many that live where it is cold, some even in the far north or on mountain tops. An explorer found jumping spiders high up on Mount Everest, 22,000 feet above sea level. Some spiders are more often found in buildings than out of doors. The common house spider—the spider to blame for most of our cobwebs—is one of them.

Most spiders are land animals. But there are some water spiders. The fresh-water spider carries air down to a silken sac under the water so that it can breathe there. For all spiders are air-breathers. They do not, however, all breathe the same way. Some have air tubes inside their bodies. Some have book lungs, air sacs filled with thin flaps of skin. Many spiders have both air tubes and book lungs.

Wolf Spider

Black Widow

Trapdoor Spider

Tarantula

Jumping Spider

Crab Spider

Construction of an Orb Web

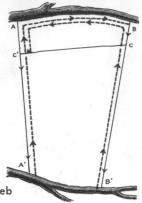

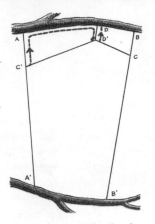

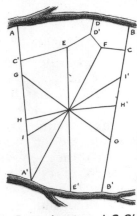

The spider begins the web by dropping thread from A on top branch to A' on bottom branch. Then it climbs back up that thread, along the branch to B, and drops down to B'. It returns along this thread and starts a new thread at C. It trails this thread as it climbs on up and across the branch and down thread A-A' to C'.

2 The spider climbs back up to the branch and drops a new thread at D. This is secured around thread C-C' and pulled tight.

3 From the thread C-C', the spider drops to the lower branch for the first radial thread, then weaves the other radial lines.

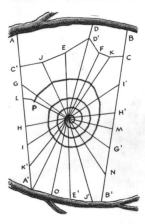

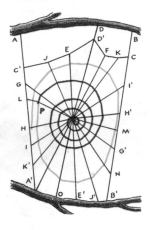

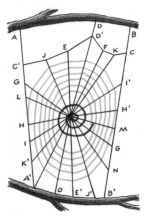

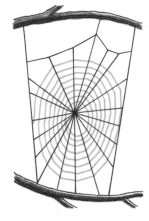

4 After completing the radial thread system, the spider begins the primary spiral (shown in red). Neither of these is sticky.

5 The viscid, or sticky, threads follow (blue), working from the outside and in toward the center of the web.

6 As the spider nears the center of the web, it cuts away the primary spiral, replacing it with the viscid thread.

7 In the finished web, the primary thread has been removed, leaving the heavy supporting framework and the spiral of sticky thread.

'Arachnid' comes from the name of a girl in a Greek myth, Arachne. The goddess Athena, the myth tells, changed Arachne to a spider and condemned her to spinning and weaving silk all her life. Actually, being able to spin and weave silk is an enormous help to spiders. Spider silk is a marvellous material. It is fine, smooth, and very strong. With it, as you know, many spiders make silk egg cases. Almost everywhere it goes, a spider plays out a fine thread of silk that serves as a 'lifeline' on which it can retreat if there is danger ahead. Immature spiders spin many threads that together catch the wind and act as balloons to carry the spiders to new homes. But spiders chiefly spin their webs to catch their food.

Different spiders follow different patterns in building webs. Trapdoor spiders spin tube-shaped webs in holes dug in the ground, complete with trap-door lids. Many spiders build orb, or wheel-shaped, webs. Building such a web is not simple, as the chart above shows.

Spiders only eat the juices of living animals. Insects are the commonest spider food. But large spiders near water may eat tadpoles or even small fish. One big tarantula is called the bird-eating spider because it is big and strong enough to capture small birds. Their poison fangs, as well as their webs, help spiders to get food.

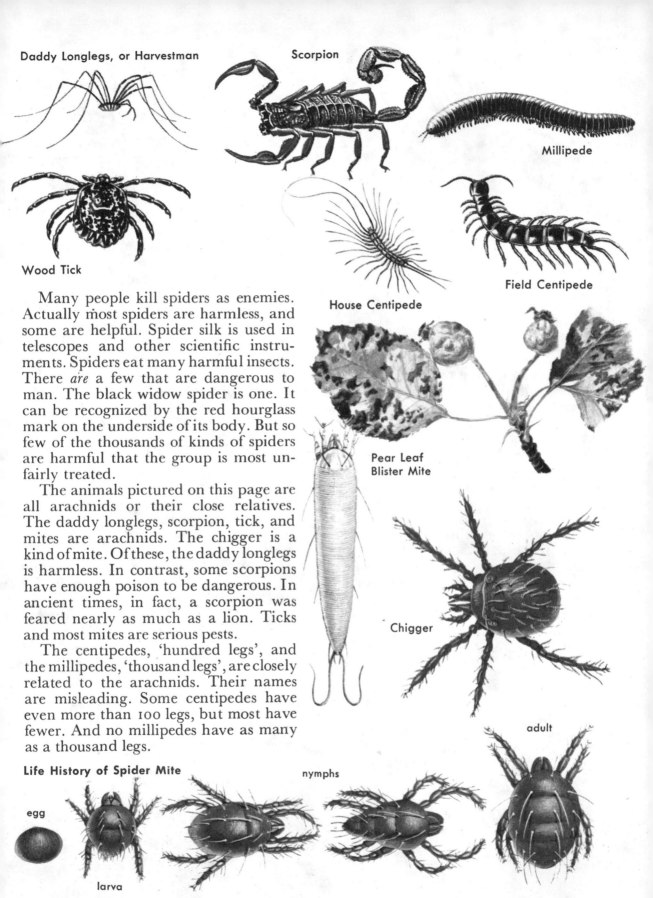

Daddy Longlegs, or Harvestman

Scorpion

Millipede

Wood Tick

House Centipede

Field Centipede

Many people kill spiders as enemies. Actually most spiders are harmless, and some are helpful. Spider silk is used in telescopes and other scientific instruments. Spiders eat many harmful insects. There *are* a few that are dangerous to man. The black widow spider is one. It can be recognized by the red hourglass mark on the underside of its body. But so few of the thousands of kinds of spiders are harmful that the group is most unfairly treated.

The animals pictured on this page are all arachnids or their close relatives. The daddy longlegs, scorpion, tick, and mites are arachnids. The chigger is a kind of mite. Of these, the daddy longlegs is harmless. In contrast, some scorpions have enough poison to be dangerous. In ancient times, in fact, a scorpion was feared nearly as much as a lion. Ticks and most mites are serious pests.

The centipedes, 'hundred legs', and the millipedes, 'thousand legs', are closely related to the arachnids. Their names are misleading. Some centipedes have even more than 100 legs, but most have fewer. And no millipedes have as many as a thousand legs.

Pear Leaf Blister Mite

Chigger

Life History of Spider Mite

egg

larva

nymphs

adult

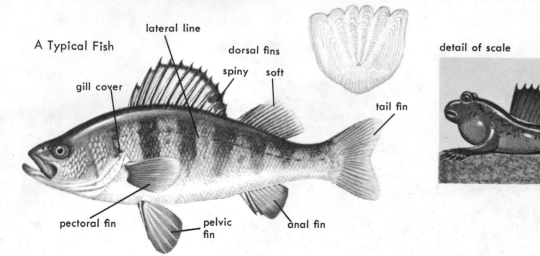

A Typical Fish

gill cover

lateral line

dorsal fins

spiny   soft

tail fin

pectoral fin

pelvic fin

anal fin

detail of scale

Mudskipper

Fishes

To many people any animal that lives in water all its life is a fish. For this reason names with the word 'fish' in them have been given to many water animals that are not really fish. Jellyfish, starfish, crayfish, and cuttlefish are not true fish. Neither are oysters, clams, and the other animals called shellfish. All these 'fish' are invertebrates (i.e. they have no backbone). Even a backboned animal with 'fish' in its name may still not be a fish. For example, one kind of whale is known as a blackfish, although all whales are mammals.

Even though there are many 'fish' that are not fish at all, there is still a great variety among the true fishes. A typical fish has two pairs of fins which correspond to the legs of a four-legged animal (pec-

toral fins and pelvic fins), unpaired fins on its back (dorsal fins) under its body near the tail (anal fin) and on the tail itself. Just behind the fish's head are its gills covers. They protect the gills with which it breathes. Most fishes have a streamlined shape and have scales that overlap one another like tiles on a roof.

The saying 'as lost as a fish out of water' is a good one; all fishes are water animals. But a few fishes, while they are not adapted for living on land can take short excursions out of water. The flying fishes, for example, can leap from the water and sail through the air for hundreds of feet. The mudskipper stays in shore when the tide moves out and skips about in the mud. It can be out of water a long time and gets enough oxygen if its gills and part of its body—as a rule its underside and tail—stay wet.

In contrast with most fishes, the sea horse swims head up. It also has a tail very different from the tails of other

Coelacanth

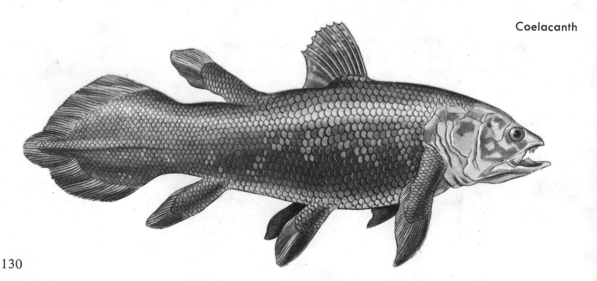

fishes. Its tail can be twisted around the
stem of a plant. The sea horse differs from
most fishes in still another way: the male
fish has a pouch on its stomach in which
it carries the eggs the female lays.

Notice how very different the fins of
the coelacanth are from those of the
typical fish shown on the other page. This
fish is truly a living fossil, for it is very
much like its lobefin ancestors that lived
back in the Age of Fish. Until 1938
scientists had thought that the lobefins
disappeared at about the same time that
the dinosaurs did. But in 1938 a living
coelacanth was caught off the south-east
coast of Africa. Since then others have
been found.

The long-nose gar is another living
fossil. It has remained almost unchanged
for millions of years living in the lakes and
streams of North America. Its scales,
instead of overlapping, fit together like
tiles on a wall.

Flying Fishes

Longnose Gar

Sea Horse

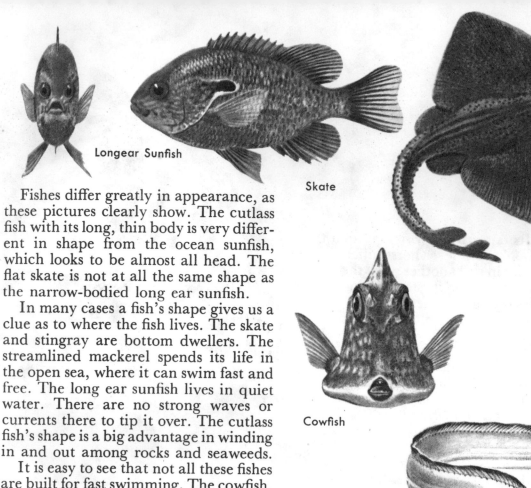

Longear Sunfish

Skate

Cowfish

Cutlass Fish

Fishes differ greatly in appearance, as these pictures clearly show. The cutlass fish with its long, thin body is very different in shape from the ocean sunfish, which looks to be almost all head. The flat skate is not at all the same shape as the narrow-bodied long ear sunfish.

In many cases a fish's shape gives us a clue as to where the fish lives. The skate and stingray are bottom dwellers. The streamlined mackerel spends its life in the open sea, where it can swim fast and free. The long ear sunfish lives in quiet water. There are no strong waves or currents there to tip it over. The cutlass fish's shape is a big advantage in winding in and out among rocks and seaweeds.

It is easy to see that not all these fishes are built for fast swimming. The cowfish, the porcupine fish, and the stargazer lack the streamlining that makes for speed.

Some of these fishes have ways of protecting themselves that make it unnecessary for them to swim fast to escape enemies. The porcupine fish blows itself up so that it makes too big and prickly a mouthful for an enemy to swallow. The stargazer has electric organs on its head that give a strong electric shock to an attacker. The stingray can sting an enemy with a poison spine on the top of its whiplike tail.

Weapons, however, are not limited to the fishes that are not fast swimmers. The ocean surgeon carries a sharp 'knife' on each side of its body just in front of the tail. Its knives are hinged like jack-knives so that they can be 'open' or hidden. The knives of surgeonfish are immovable,

Porcupine Fish

Mackerel

but there may be several of them on each side, all very sharp. The sword of a swordfish has been known to pierce the thick wooden hulls of small boats. Its sword not only protects the fish but also helps it to get food.

A person who keeps fish as pets is likely to think of them as being very quiet animals. Some of them are, but others are very noisy at times. During the Second World War underwater devices were developed to detect engines of submarines by the sounds they picked up. Very often however the noise of the submarine was drowned by the noise made by the fish. The grunts get their name from the grunting noise these fishes make. They make these sounds by grinding their teeth together. The air bladder inside their bodies acts as a resonator making the noise louder.

Croakers and sea robins are other noisy fishes, but they do not make their sounds by grinding their teeth. Instead, they snap muscles attached to the air bladder. The muscles act like the strings of a guitar, and the air bladder acts like the box of the guitar. Sea robins play their 'guitars' so well that they are among the noisiest of fishes. Of the croakers, those called drums make the loudest clatter.

White Grunt

Bluestriped Grunt

electric organs

Stargazer

Ocean Surgeon

Stingray

Swordfish

Ocean Sunfish

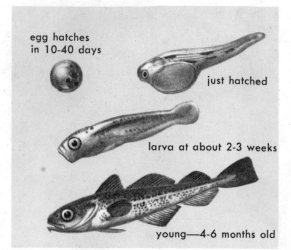

egg hatches in 10-40 days

just hatched

larva at about 2-3 weeks

young—4-6 months old

The story of the cod is a typical fish life history. A female cod lays many eggs at a time, thousands or even millions. An egg hatches into a tiny fish, called a fry, that still has, in a yolk sac on its underside, some food left from the supply stored in the egg. By the time this food is used up, the young cod is able to forage for itself. Without any great changes like those which moths and butterflies go through in their lives, the young cod grows to be an adult.

female

male

Mosquito Fish

Life History of the Cod

The cod takes no care of its eggs. Some fishes, however, do. A number of them even build nests for their eggs. Male sticklebacks make their nests of water plants. After a female stickleback or bluegill has laid her eggs in the nest, the male stands guard until the eggs hatch.

Sea catfish use their mouths as nests for their eggs. After the female lays her eggs in the water, the male picks them up in his mouth. He carries the eggs about for a month or so before they hatch and the fry for two weeks afterwards. All this time he has to go without food.

The little mosquito fish protects its eggs in quite a different way. The female keeps the eggs inside her body until the young fish develop from them. Then the

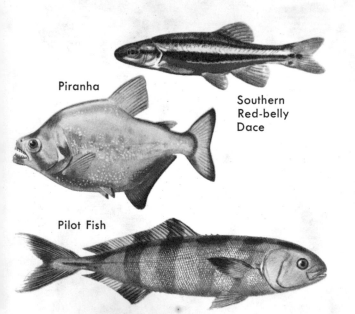

Piranha

Southern Red-belly Dace

Pilot Fish

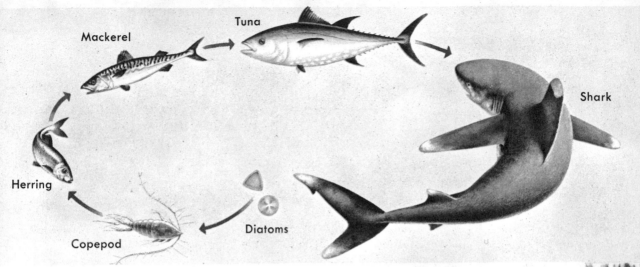

Mackerel

Tuna

Shark

Herring

Copepod

Diatoms

young mosquito fish are born alive. There are many other fish that are born alive.

As a rule the fishes that do not take care of their eggs produce more at a time than the fishes that do. You can see why. Little fish are such good food for larger fishes and other water animals that a young fish has little chance of growing up.

Even grown-up fishes are in constant danger of being eaten. Every fish is fair prey to other, usually bigger, fishes and other animals. These in turn are food for still other meat-eaters. The diagram at the bottom of the page shows an important food chain in the sea. Notice that it begins with green plants. Every food chain, both on land and in the sea, begins with plants. The fishes in this chain are all meat-eaters. But some fishes eat plants.

The food habits of the five fishes at the right differ considerably from one another. The little killifish eats mosquito larva. The clown fish lives among the poisonous tentacles of sea anemones and steals food gathered in by the tentacles. The dace eats plants and small crustaceans. The piranha—the terror of South American rivers is bloodthirsty. Even a horse that wanders into a stream where piranhas are numerous may be torn to shreds in just a few minutes. A pilot fish follows sharks and ships about and eats any scraps of food it can find.

Common Killifish

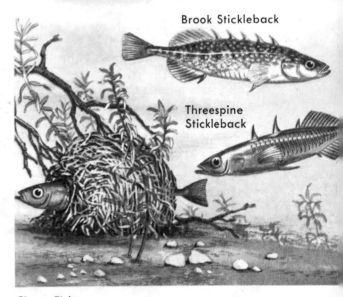

Brook Stickleback

Threespine Stickleback

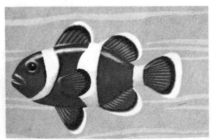

Clown Fish

135

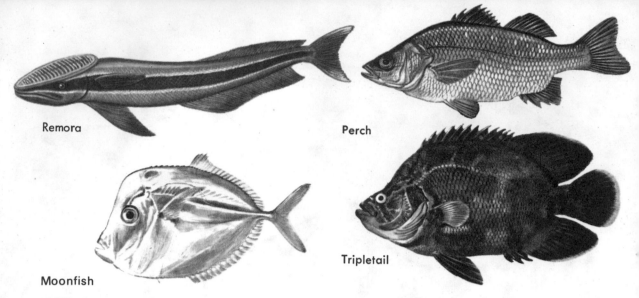

Remora

Perch

Moonfish

Tripletail

Their sense of taste helps some fishes find food. A catfish has taste buds scattered all over its skin. This fish can taste its food even before it eats it. But this plan for tasting is not common.

Many fishes have a keen sense of smell. They find food by tracing its odour. In only a very few cases are a fish's nostrils of any use in breathing.

Some fishes have, hanging down from their 'chins', sensitive whiskers, or barbels, that help them find food by tasting or by feeling. The sketches at the lower left show some of the ways barbels vary.

Many fishes have a line of special cells along their sides that let them feel move-ments in the water. The lateral line shows clearly on the four fishes pictured at the top of the page.

Fishes have ears with which they hear sounds in the water, but their ears do not show. A fish's ears are deep in its head.

Probably most fishes depend at least partly on seeing to find their food. Almost all of them have eyes with one eye on each side of the head. The hammerhead shark's eyes are at the ends of its strange 'hammer'. Most fishes can see very little of the same thing with both eyes at the same time. But there are exceptions. When they are grown up, the flatfishes, of which the flounder is one, swim on

Flounder

Barbels

Hammerhead Shark

136

their sides and have both eyes on the upper side. Their eyes are always open. Only a few fishes have eyelids. The hammerhead shark is one that does.

Being able to see may lead some fish into danger. The large anglerfish is so called because it has a 'fishing rod' in its head. It lies in the bottom, half covered in sand waiting for a fish to come along. A fish swimming near is attracted by the lure and comes closer, sometimes near enough for the anglerfish to swallow it without moving. Deep down in the sea it is very dark. The anglerfish living there have a lantern at the end of their fishing rod. Many deep sea fish are partly luminous, some have light producing cells on the sides of their bodies. This light may help them to find food.

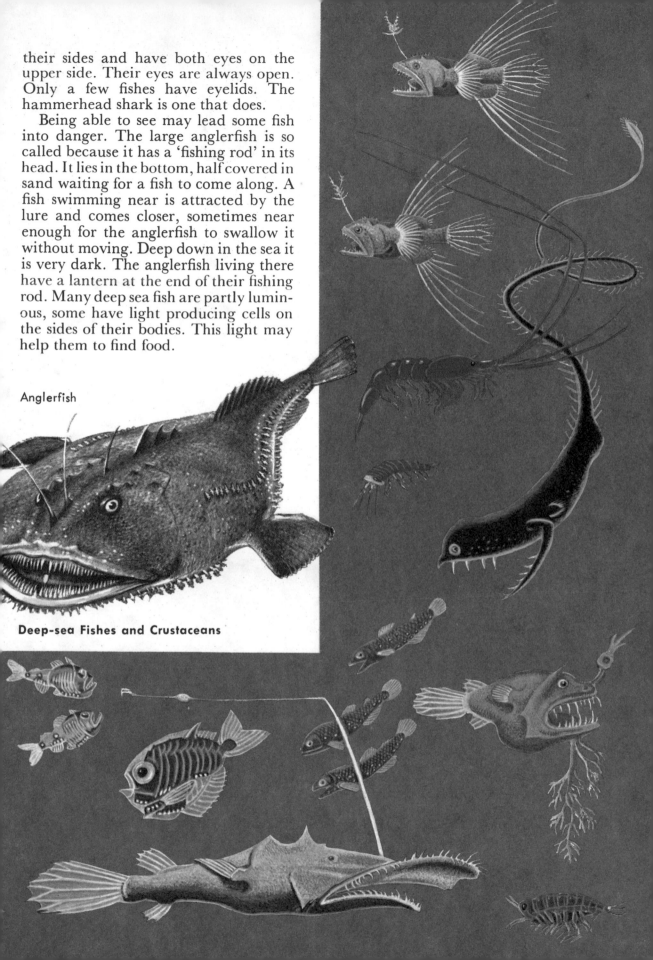

Anglerfish

Deep-sea Fishes and Crustaceans

Common
Perch

Catfish

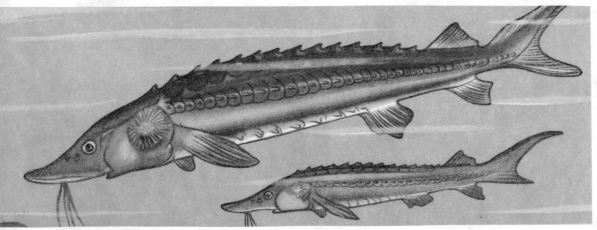

Lake
Sturgeon

'He can swim like a fish' is high praise for a swimmer, for most fishes are wonderfully built for swimming. Their finned tails make good propellers for pushing their streamlined bodies forward. Their other fins help them guide themselves and keep their balance. Their air bladders make it easy for most fishes to go up or down quite easily. In order to sink, a fish expels some of the air from its air bladder. To rise, it forces more air in. Some sharks use their stomachs the same way. Sharks have no air bladder.

Except perhaps for the eel, the fishes pictured on these two pages are easily recognizable as fishes. But they can be distinguished from one another. And they would never all be found in the same area of water. The perch, lake sturgeon and catfish are freshwater fishes. The cod

Pilchard

Eels

Cod

and haddock are saltwater fishes. The eel lives most of its life in fresh water, but it spends part of it in salt water.

The perch is a very common fresh water fish. It is found in lakes as well as in rivers. It is a typical fish, just as the cod and the pilchard are, but the eel, the lake sturgeon and the catfish are not typical fish. The lake sturgeon is a reminder of the fishes of ancient times. Like the gar and the coelacanth, it differs very little from its ancestors of millions of years ago. Its scales are bony plates. In contrast, the catfish, has no scales at all. The eel, as you see is rather snakelike. It has scales, but they are buried so deep in the skin that they are very hard to see.

The cod, pilchard and sturgeon are well known as food fishes. Of them the cod is by far the most important. It has

Herring

Red-fish

Pompano

Yellowtail

Anchovy

Japanese Mackerel

Spanish Mackerel

Tomcod

Pollack

Haddock

dark p

golden p

made the Atlantic near Newfoundland one of the great fishing regions of the world. Eels, too, are good fishes and are either eaten smoked or as jellied eels or are made into a pie. Sturgeons are also famous for the caviar made from their eggs, or roe. The pilchards are also good to eat. Small pilchards are sometimes called sardines. Most pilchards and sardines are eaten when they have been tinned.

All the fishes pictured here are also good food fishes. Those on this page are saltwater fishes. Those on the opposite page live in fresh water.

The herring ranks first so far as the number caught is concerned. In fact, the herrings are the world's leading food fishes. Every year millions are taken. They are easy to catch because they swim in great schools, or shoals. One school is likely to have from half a million to three million fish in it. The herring is so important a source of food that battles have

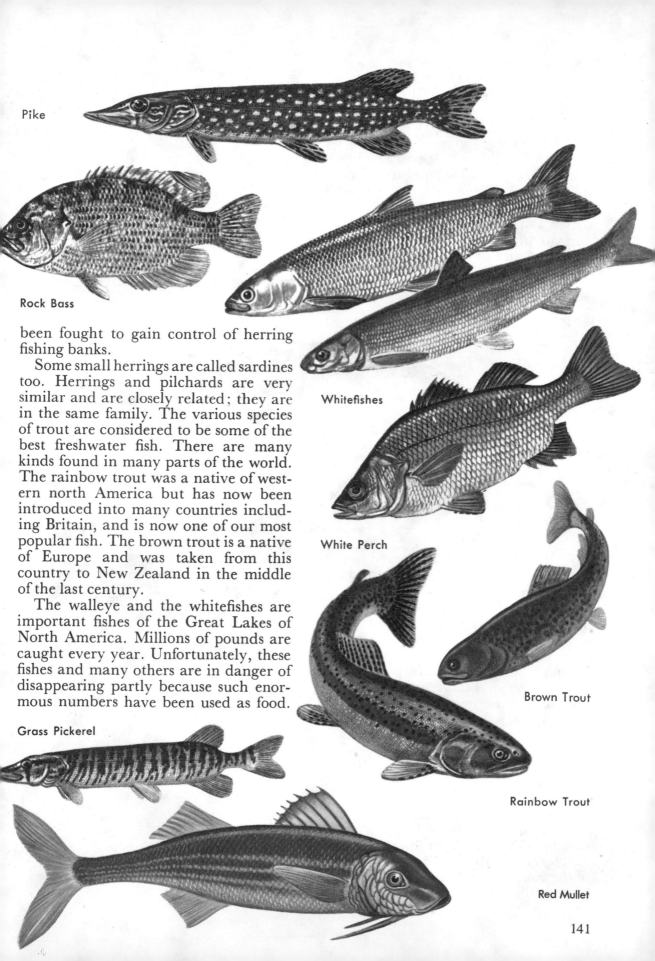

Pike

Rock Bass

Whitefishes

White Perch

Brown Trout

Rainbow Trout

Grass Pickerel

Red Mullet

been fought to gain control of herring fishing banks.

Some small herrings are called sardines too. Herrings and pilchards are very similar and are closely related; they are in the same family. The various species of trout are considered to be some of the best freshwater fish. There are many kinds found in many parts of the world. The rainbow trout was a native of western north America but has now been introduced into many countries including Britain, and is now one of our most popular fish. The brown trout is a native of Europe and was taken from this country to New Zealand in the middle of the last century.

The walleye and the whitefishes are important fishes of the Great Lakes of North America. Millions of pounds are caught every year. Unfortunately, these fishes and many others are in danger of disappearing partly because such enormous numbers have been used as food.

141

Some fishes are called game, or sport, fish. They are fishes that fishermen think are fun to catch because they put up a fight to avoid being landed. As a rule fish swim about as fast as a man walks. When hooked, however, some of them put on tremendous bursts of speeds. Some of them, moreover, show amazing strength and stamina. These three fish are well known sporting fish. Two of them, the tarpon and the sailfish live in warm seas. The salmon however, lives part of its life in the sea and part in fresh water. It is caught when it swims up rivers to spawn.

The tarpon is a large fish. Tarpon weighing from 50 to 100 pounds are fairly common, and some weigh in at

Tarpon

Salmon

more than 300 pounds. A hooked tarpon may reach a speed of 30 miles an hour trying to escape.

Sailfish, too, are large game fish, but they never get to be the size of the largest tarpon. Even though not so large as a tarpon, a sailfish is faster. In short bursts it can go 60 miles an hour.

The salmon is large for a freshwater fish. A big one may weigh twenty-five pounds. But a fisherman is very lucky to find one more than twelve pounds in weight.

Among the largest of the saltwater game fish are some relatives of the sailfish —the marlins and the swordfish. The average weight for a blue marlin is 300 pounds, and 800-pound ones have been caught. The swordfish reaches 1,200. Still larger are the bluefin tuna and some of the sharks. Although not in the same class with these giants of the sea, the

Sailfish

freshwater game fish afford inland fishermen plenty of sport.

The fishes pictured on this page give people a great deal of pleasure too, but of a different kind. They are tiny tropical fish suitable for living in aquariums. Four—the guppy, mollie, platy, and swordtail—are relatives of the mosquito fish and their young are born alive. The other four lay eggs. One of these, the neon tetra, is a close relative of the bloodthirsty piranha.

One problem in keeping baby fishes is to keep the adult fish from eating the young ones. The aquarium must have plenty of plants to afford hiding places. There is a similar problem in keeping some egg-laying tropical fish. The parents may eat the eggs. The Siamese fighting fish on the other hand, takes good care of its eggs and young. The father fish makes a nest of bubbles on the surface of the water. When the eggs are laid he carries them on to the bubble nest and watches over them until after the babies hatch and use up the food of their yolk sacs.

Siamese fighting fish get their name from the fighting of the males. They mainly fight to get a mate. For centuries the people of the Far East have bet on the outcome of these fights.

Seeing that the water is warm enough during the winter months and providing the right kind of food are important in keeping tropical fish. One of the easiest to care for is the guppy. Of all these fishes, it is the most popular.

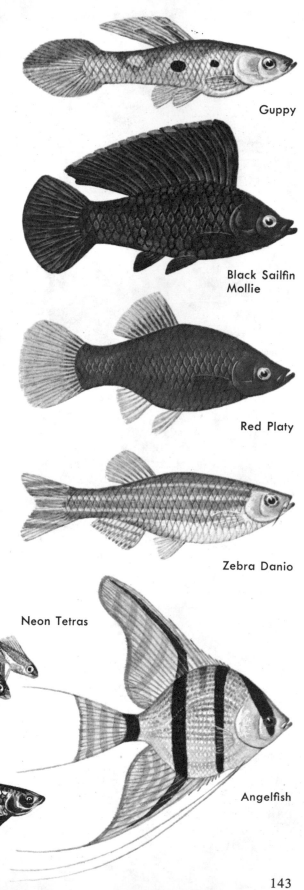

Guppy

Black Sailfin Mollie

Red Platy

Zebra Danio

Neon Tetras

Swordtail

Siamese Fighting Fish

Angelfish

Four Common Aquarium Plants

When aquarium is half full, add plants and decorations. Using newspaper, as before, fill aquarium.

Net

Do not fill a bowl aquarium to the top.

Pouring water onto a newspaper keeps the sand from being stirred up.

The goldfish is by far the most popular of all our aquarium fishes. Goldfish may be bought in a great variety of colours. You may choose goldfish with bulging 'pop eyes' and with long, flowing tails. You may have them with conspicuous scales or with scales so thin that they are nearly invisible. There are even goldfish with thick, round scales that look like pearls. Some, moreover, have eyes turned upwards and others have short bodies and 'lion' or 'buffalo' heads. The pictures show several of the many varieties. The story of the goldfish is a story of man's ability to change some animals, by careful selection and breeding over the years to suit his purposes.

All the goldfish of today are descendants of the wild goldfish that lives in the streams of China and Japan. This wild goldfish is not an especially pretty fish. It is usually dull greenish-brown, and it has small fins and a rather short tail.

The Chinese found out more than fifteen centuries ago that it is easy to keep goldfish in small ponds and aquariums. Many species of fish do not do well in captivity, but the goldfish does. The Chinese who kept goldfish noticed that not all the goldfish were alike in colour.

Occasionally they found a fish that had the dark pigment left out of its skin in places. In those places the skin was yellowish, or gold.

The Chinese goldfish breeders watched carefully for fish with a gold colour. They chose these fish as breeding stock and took good care of them and their eggs. Some of the fish that came from the eggs had more gold colour than their parents.

The breeders kept on choosing and mating the fish that were best. In time they had fish that were all gold.

A thousand years after the Chinese began raising goldfish, the Japanese, too, were breeding them. Breeders in both countries found that they could produce not only fish that were gold all over and fish part gold, part brownish-green, but also goldfish of other colours. They could have black goldfish, silver goldfish, white goldfish, and goldfish mottled like a tortoise-shell cat.

The breeders discovered, too, that colour was not the only thing they could change. They could also change the eyes, the scales, and the shape of the body.

Now goldfish are kept in many parts of the world. Thousands of goldfish of different colours and shapes are bred

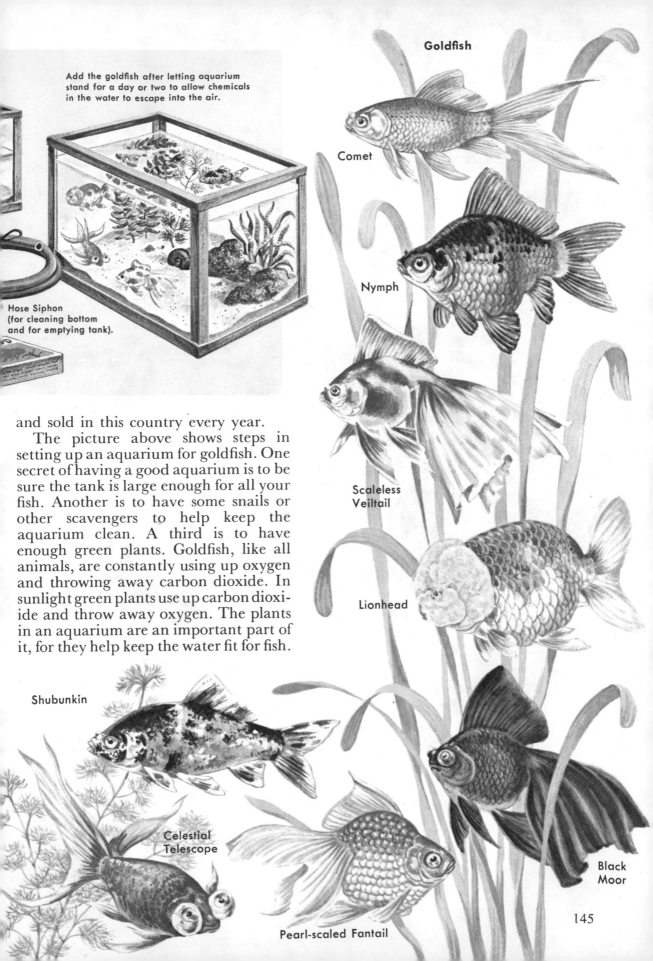

Add the goldfish after letting aquarium stand for a day or two to allow chemicals in the water to escape into the air.

Hose Siphon (for cleaning bottom and for emptying tank).

Goldfish

Comet

Nymph

Scaleless Veiltail

Lionhead

and sold in this country every year.

The picture above shows steps in setting up an aquarium for goldfish. One secret of having a good aquarium is to be sure the tank is large enough for all your fish. Another is to have some snails or other scavengers to help keep the aquarium clean. A third is to have enough green plants. Goldfish, like all animals, are constantly using up oxygen and throwing away carbon dioxide. In sunlight green plants use up carbon dioxide and throw away oxygen. The plants in an aquarium are an important part of it, for they help keep the water fit for fish.

Shubunkin

Celestial Telescope

Black Moor

Pearl-scaled Fantail

145

Amphibians

The frog and toad are the best known amphibians. They are sometimes spoken of as the tailless amphibians since, when they are adults, they have no tails. In addition to frog and toad, there are two other groups of amphibians: caecilians, and salamanders and newts.

Although most amphibians are able to live on land for part of their lives, most of them are unable to stand extreme dryness. They have no protecting scales or fur or feathers. A few, by using water stored in the body, can live where there is no rain for months or even years at a time, but most amphibians must stay close to water or moist places. An amphibian spends part of its life in fresh water. There are no amphibians of any kind that live in the sea.

Like fish, all amphibians are cold-blooded. Those that live in regions that have cold winters, as many of them do, protect themselves from the cold by hibernating.

Most amphibians lay their eggs in water. With those that lay eggs out of water, the early stages, as a rule, are passed inside the egg. A very few—some caecilians and salamanders and a toad—give birth to their young.

Amphibians vary greatly in size. They range from tiny frogs less than a inch long to the five foot giant salamander of Japan.

But even this salamander is not much of a giant compared with *Eryops* and some other large amphibians of the past.

The life story of the common frog is a typical amphibian life history. It shows how the amphibians got their name. frog lays her eggs or spawn in the water near the edge of a pond or a quiet stream. Each egg is surrounded by a layer of clear, tough jelly. The jelly holds the eggs together. There are so many eggs that they form a 'pancake'.

As soon as they are laid, the eggs begin to develop. Each egg elongates till it is bean-shaped. One end is larger than the other. The larger end will become the head, the smaller end the tail.

In about a week the eggs hatch. A tiny tadpole wriggles out of each jelly covering. The tadpole is less than half an inch long. There is a tiny bump where each eye should be, and below the place where its mouth will form it has a sucker so that the baby tadpole can cling on to the jelly it has just left behind. Its tail looks like a fish's tail.

Very soon tiny fringes appear at the sides of its head. These are its gills. A tadpole is truly a water animal.

By the time it is a day old, the tadpole can swim a little. But whenever it finds a stick or a plant it holds on with its sucker and rests for a while.

Bullfrog

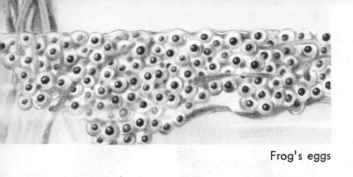

Frog's eggs

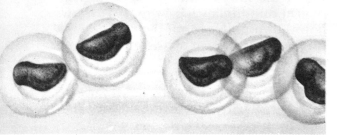

Eggs (magnified)

New-hatched tadpole

Tadpole with hind legs

Tadpole with all four legs

Young frog with remnant of tail

In two or three days the tadpole has eyes and a mouth. Now it can see where it is going, and it can nibble tiny plants off the stones and sticks in the water. The tadpole's body soon bulges out so that it is much bigger in proportion to the tail. Its sucker disappears, and skin grows over its gills and hides them. To breathe, the tadpole gulps water into its mouth. The water goes past its gills and out through a little hole, the breathing pore, on the left side of the tadpole's body.

The tadpole eats a great deal—mostly tiny green water plants. Sometimes it gets scraps of food left by the bigger animals that share the pond or stream.

In time two legs begin growing out from near the base of the tadpole's tail. Later two front legs appear. The left one pushes its way out first and is soon followed by the right leg. The tadpole is now a four-legged animal. But it still has a long tail.

Other changes are going on in the tadpole. Lungs are developing. The tadpole's mouth is changing, too. It is getting wider, and a long, sticky tongue is forming inside. While its mouth is changing, the tadpole cannot eat. It lives on its tail. Gradually the tail shrinks as the food in it is used up. Before all the food has gone the little frog takes excursions on land. With its tongue it now catches insects. It has become a meat-eater at the same time that it has become an air breather.

Finally the last stub of its tadpole tail disappears. The young frog has the shape it will keep for the rest of its life. It grows so fast that it has to shed its skin several times.

At last the frog is an adult. It is ready to mate and start many thousands of new frogs on their way. By this time it has developed a voice, if it is a male frog, and its croaking mingles with the voices of its neighbours in the breeding pond or stream.

Almost all frogs have the same type of life cycle, wherever they live in the world.

In tropical countries a frog grows very fast and it only takes a few weeks for a newly laid egg to become an adult frog. In cold countries several years may be needed before a tadpole becomes an adult frog.

The life history of a frog is not nearly so safe as it might seem from looking at the pictures. Actually very few of the eggs a female lays grow up into frogs and produce eggs of their own. Tadpoles have many enemies. They provide food for small fish, water beetles and even bigger tadpoles living in the same pond. When they have become adult frogs there are still many predatory animals that like to eat frogs. For example, some birds, hedgehogs and otters like to eat them.

The edible frog shown at the bottom of the page is another type of frog that is found in this country. It was not always found here as it is a native of the continent of Europe and was introduced to Britain. As you might expect from its name, this frog is caught and eaten. Many frogs are eaten in France and other European countries where they are thought of as a great delicacy. The meat has a tender, delicate flavour and it is served quickly browned in butter, with lemon and parsley. The edible frog is not the only type of frog that is eaten. In fact, it is not eaten as often as the common frog. Only the large hind legs are eaten, because the rest of the frog does not have much meat on it.

Frogs have big strong hind legs so that they can jump or swim out of danger. Some species of frogs can jump a very long way for their size. Most frogs can jump about six to nine times their own length. The leopard frog is the champion of North America. It can jump about thirteen times its own body length. However, it is not the champion of all the frogs. That honour goes to a very small African frog that can jump over forty-five times its own length.

Edible Frog

149

Leopard Frog

We call all the tailless amphibians frogs or toads, but these names in many cases do not mean much. There are several groups of tailless amphibians, and in each some are commonly called toads and others frogs. Many of these animals, in fact, have both a frog and a toad name. 'Frog' and 'toad' have separate meanings only when they are used for the frogs and toads of two well-known families—the Ranidae, or true frogs, and the Bufonidae, or true toads. It is easy to tell frogs and toads apart.

True frogs have soft, moist, smooth skins. True toads have tough, dry skins covered by little bumps that are often spoken of as warts. Frogs are slender; toads have broad bodies. Toads, with their short legs, are clumsy looking. Frogs are far more graceful. They are faster, too. Frogs have more conspicuous eardrums. Toads have large poison glands just behind the eyes. Frogs have small teeth in their upper jaw; toads have none. The two frogs and the toad on this page and the common toad on the next show some of the differences between frogs and toads.

The warts on toads are not like the warts people sometimes have. They are small glands. When an enemy comes near, the glands give off an irritating fluid that is highly poisonous to some animals.

The life of most toads, however, is very much like that of a frog.

Few true toads and frogs take any care of their eggs. Some of the other tailless amphibians, however, have strange ways

Marsh Frog

Fowler's Toad

Life History of a Toad

Toad

Midwife Toad

of doing so. The female midwife toad lays her eggs in long strings which the male puts around his body. He hides in a hole in the ground or under a stone by day. At night he comes out of hiding and lets the eggs soak for a while in a pool of water or in dew. In a month or so, when the eggs are ready to hatch, he goes into a pond or stream. The tadpoles hatch out in the water, where they will live until they have four legs.

The Surinam toad spends most of its time in the water. As the female toad lays her eggs, the male puts them on her back. Her skin swells and covers them so that each egg is in a separate pocket. There the eggs develop into tadpoles. The tadpoles stay in the pockets till they are little four-legged toads. Then each pocket opens up and the toadlets wriggle out and swim away.

Surinam Toad

Toad croaking

Green Tree Frog

The croaking and trilling of toads and frogs are familiar sounds. The loudest singing comes from males with vocal sacs. When the sacs are filled with air they serve as sounding boxes for the noises made by the vocal cords. A frog or toad can even sing underwater. The little green tree frog does most of its singing in the rain. A very few frogs and toads are voiceless. The bell toad is one of them. Even if it had a voice, it would never be heard above the roar of the water in the cold mountain streams where it lives.

All frogs and toads are meat-eaters. When they are eating such a tasty morsel as an earthworm, they may use their front feet to help push it into their mouths. Their tongues are a big help in catching insects. Most have tongues fastened at the front of the mouth, not at the back as ours are. A toad or frog can flip out its tongue a long way. It will only strike at animals that are moving. It does not, therefore, eat dead animals.

When a toad or frog swallows its food it blinks. Doing so helps it to push food from its mouth into its stomach, for closing its bulging eyes means pulling them downwards. Frogs and toads have big appetites. A toad may eat 50 insect larvas at a single meal. Many of the insects and other animals toads and frogs eat are harmful to us. The marine toad, for example, eats quantities of sugar beetles. It is shipped from its home in tropical

Toad eating

Three-striped Poison Frog

Fire-bellied Toad

America to sugar-producing areas in many other regions to fight this pest.

The three-striped poison frog produces a poison that is used by South American natives on their poison arrows. Of course, its poison is a good protection. The pickerel frog also protects itself with poison. The fire-bellied toad frightens its enemies by throwing its head up so that the bright red spots on its under-surface show. Most toads and frogs depend on hiding, jumping away, or blowing themselves up to protect themselves. Many find it easy to hide because their colours blend into their surroundings.

Toads and frogs differ greatly in size. The ten inch goliath is a giant beside the inch-long greenhouse frog. The smallest frogs measure less than half an inch.

Bell Toad

Corroboree Frog

Goliath Frog

Greenhouse Frog

Marine Toad

153

Salamander Eggs and Larva

Mudpuppy

One of these pictures shows a caecilian. The others all show salamanders.

Salamanders are fairly common. As adults they have both legs and tails. Caecilians are chiefly found in tropical regions. They look like oversized earthworms.

Even people who live in the regions where there are caecilians seldom see them. The caecilians spend their lives in underground burrows. Their eyes are small and in most cases useless. They have feelers which they can use in place of eyes to find their way about their dark homes. Most caecilians are less than a foot long, but a giant species found in

Colombia may measure over four feet. They are all meat-eaters.

Caecilians differ from other amphibians in another way besides lack of legs. Most of them have scales buried in their skin.

The young of some caecilians are born alive. Others lay eggs, but when the larvae hatch out most of them have lost their gills and are already breathing air. The picture shows two gilled larvae taken from eggs before the time of hatching.

The salamanders and newts are not nearly so well known as the toads and frogs. For one thing they live in out-of-the-way places. Many live under fallen leaves on forest floors. Some spend all their lives in water. A few live in trees, and some make their homes in caves. The cave-dwelling salamanders are nearly or entirely blind.

Another reason why we are less aware of salamanders in this country is because they do none of the singing and croaking that toads and frogs do, although a few can 'bark' or scream. Newts can make a squeaking noise, too.

Most salamanders and newts hatch from eggs laid in the water and follow the usual frog-toad plan of growing up. The mudpuppy follows a different plan. It never becomes an air-breathing animal. A mudpuppy lives underwater all its life and keeps its fringe of gills. Most salamanders have external gills—when they have just hatched from the egg. They lose them as tadpoles do and grow lungs, so that they can breathe air on land.

Red Salamander

Purple Salamander

Young Red Salamander

Sticky Caecilian

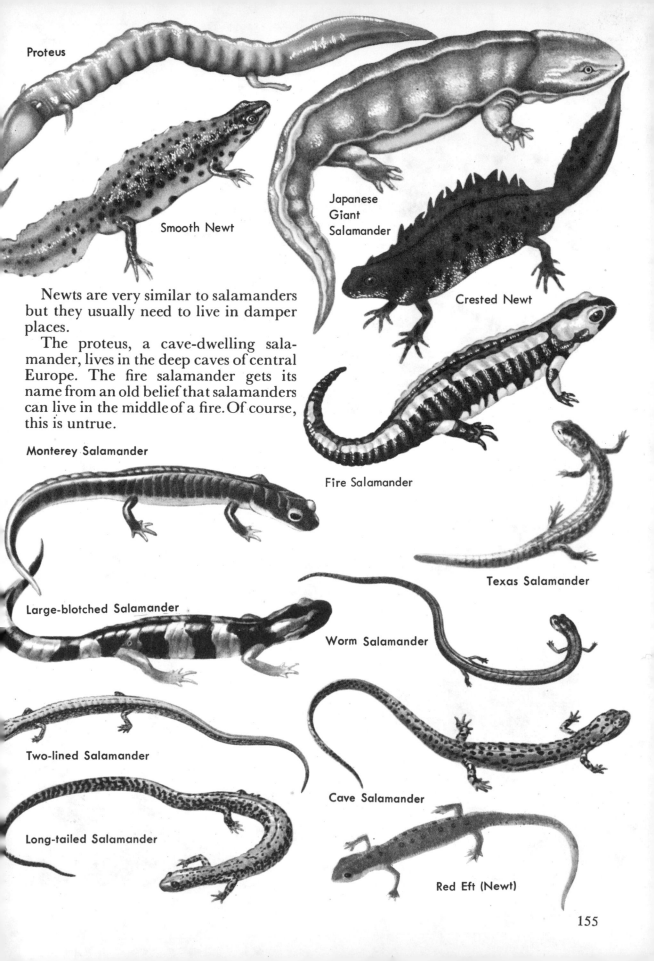

Proteus

Smooth Newt

Japanese Giant Salamander

Crested Newt

Newts are very similar to salamanders but they usually need to live in damper places.

The proteus, a cave-dwelling salamander, lives in the deep caves of central Europe. The fire salamander gets its name from an old belief that salamanders can live in the middle of a fire. Of course, this is untrue.

Fire Salamander

Texas Salamander

Monterey Salamander

Large-blotched Salamander

Worm Salamander

Two-lined Salamander

Cave Salamander

Long-tailed Salamander

Red Eft (Newt)

Reptiles

The great days of the reptiles are over. They ended millions of years ago, when the last dinosaurs died. But there are still over 5,000 species. The reptiles of today are divided into four groups: the turtles, the alligators and crocodiles, the lizards and snakes, and, all by itself, the tuatara.

Turtles can be distinguished from other reptiles by their shells, as no other reptiles have them. There are freshwater turtles, sea turtles, and land turtles.

The turtles shown here are all freshwater turtles. They spend part of their life in water and part out of it. Since they breathe with lungs, as all reptiles do, they must be out of the water or at the surface when they breathe.

As the pictures show, terrapins hatch from eggs. All turtles and terrapins do. The eggs, like those of other reptiles are laid on land. The parent terrapins take no care of the eggs or of the little terrapins that hatch from them in the autumn. A newly hatched terrapin looks very much like its parents except for size.

Soon after it is hatched, the little terrapin makes its way to water. There it swims about, coming up to breathe and at times climbing up on a rock or log to

Musk Turtle

European Pond Turtle

Snake-necked Turtle

Snapping Turtle

sun itself. The baby terrapin does not have to look for food, for inside it, there is still enough yolk left over from the egg it hatched out from to last until spring. It spends the winter in the mud at the bottom of the pond or stream where it is living.

Terrapins are often kept as pets. Mud turtles as you would guess, live in ponds and streams with muddy bottoms. Musk turtles owe their name to their smell. One of their nicknames is 'stinkpot'.

The snapping turtle snaps at anything that disturbs it. It has no teeth—no turtles do—but its jaws are sharp enough to bite off a finger. Baby snappers, instead of hatching in the autumn, may winter inside the eggs and hatch in the spring.

Young Snapping Turtles

Box Turtle

The turtles called tortoises are all land turtles. So is the box turtle. Surprisingly enough, the box turtle, even though it lives on land, belongs to the freshwater turtle family that includes the slider and the painted turtle.

Tortoises are famous for their slow movements—everyone has heard the fable of the hare and the tortoise. They are also famous for their long lives. Giant tortoises may live to be over 100 years old. They rank at the top of the animal kingdom for length of life. Also these big land turtles of remote islands may weigh over 500 pounds.

The hawksbill, leatherback, and green turtles all live in the sea. Their legs are paddles. Sea turtles have to come on land to lay their eggs. Green turtles sometimes come out, too, to sun themselves.

Tortoiseshell, once much used for combs and spectacles frames, comes from the shell of the hawksbill. Green turtles are often caught for food. A fully grown one gives a great deal of food, for it may weigh 400 pounds. The eggs, too, are eaten. The leatherback's shell is covered with very tough skin. This turtle is not as big as some of the sea turtles of long ago, but it may be eight feet long and weigh more than half a ton. By weight, the leatherback is the biggest reptile found anywhere in the world today.

Gopher Tortoise

Hawksbill Turtle

Green Turtle

Leatherback Turtle

Giant Tortoise

African Crocodile

The tuatara only lives on some small islands near New Zealand. This little reptile is another living fossil. It has been on the earth since before the days of the dinosaurs.

The tuatara lives in burrows in the ground. Usually it does not make its own burrow but lives in one made by a bird, a shearwater. The shearwater and the tuatara share the burrow.

The tuatara is carefully guarded by the government of New Zealand. People do not want this creature to become extinct.

Although the largest alligator or crocodile is not as bulky as the largest leatherback, so far as average size goes, the alligators and crocodiles are the largest reptiles. The longest may measure 24 feet and the smallest about four. They look much alike. On each side of its mouth, however, a crocodile has a long, lower tooth which shows outside the upper teeth when its jaws are shut, and its snout is notched for the two teeth. A third member of this group, the gavial of India,

can be recognized by its long, thin snout.

Alligators and crocodiles spend most of their time in the water. They have webbed feet but do not use them in swimming. They swim with their tails. In water, flaps of skin protect their ears. On land an alligator or a crocodile usually lies sprawled on its belly, but it can lift itself up on its stout legs and run fast when it needs to.

The nostrils and eyes of an alligator or a crocodile stand up from its face. The reptiles can float with only their eyes and nostrils above water. They are almost hidden underwater and yet can breathe and see what is happening up on the bank or shore.

Most alligators and crocodiles live in warm waters near the equator. They cannot stand cold weather. The American alligator lives the farthest north.

Alligators and crocodiles eat fish and many other kinds of animals. If their catch is too big to swallow whole, they can wring off the part held in their jaws by spinning themselves around fast.

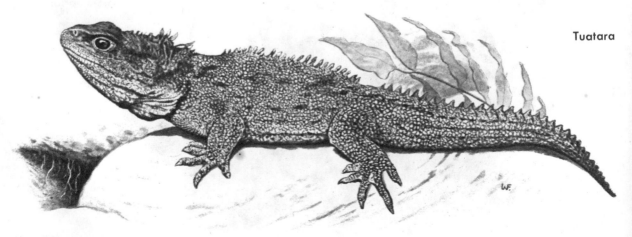

Tuatara

Life History of an Alligator

All alligators and crocodiles hatch from eggs. The female reptile lays her eggs in a nest on land. The alligator makes a nest of mud and plants. Heat from the sun and from rotting plants keeps the eggs warm. When the little alligators are ready to hatch, they make a piping noise. The mother, who has stayed nearby, then uncovers the nest. A young alligator has a point—the 'egg tooth' on its head that helps it to break out of its hard shell.

Alligators and crocodiles have a very tough skin that is used to make beautiful leather for bags and shoes. So many of these big reptiles have been killed for their skins that there is danger that they will all disappear. Now both the American alligator and the American crocodile are protected by law.

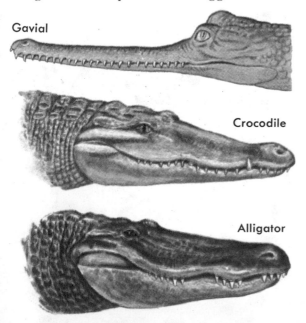

Gavial

Crocodile

Alligator

161

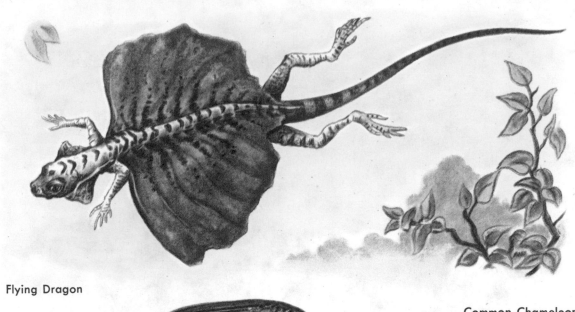

Flying Dragon

Common Chameleon

Glass Snake

Collared
Lizard

Skink

There are lizards of many different sizes, colours and shapes. The skink is the shape we think of as the typical lizard shape. It is a small lizard. The flying dragon is about the same size and shape. But its wings, which are simply folds of skin that act as parachutes, make it look much like a big butterfly when it 'flies'.

Most lizards run or crawl on four short legs, but some can get up on their hind legs and run or leap. The collared lizard does. Some lizards have no legs. The glass snake, in spite of its looks and name, is not a snake, but a legless lizard.

Lizards eat food ranging in size from tiny insects to wild pigs. Some have remarkable tongues. The chameleon can shoot its tongue out a long distance to catch an insect. The tip of its tongue is very sticky.

Not all lizards are meat-eaters. The marine iguana eats seaweed. Crested iguanas thrive on cactus.

A big marine iguana may be five feet long, but it is by no means the world's largest lizard. Some of the monitor lizards of southern Asia may be twice as long and weigh 300 pounds.

The glass snake, like other lizards, has a remarkable way of escaping from its enemies. If it is in danger, it simply breaks off its tail and runs away without it. Soon it grows a new, but shorter tail. Some lizards use their tails as whips to lash enemies away, and only break off their tails as a last resort. The frilled lizard

Frilled Lizard

erects its frill, like an umbrella. It can also bite and lash out with its tail. The armadillo lizard protects itself by rolling up with its tail in its mouth. It is as safe from its enemies as a closed-up box turtle. This tiny lizard looks flat enough to have been put through a wringer.

A few lizards are poisonous such as the Gila Monster. But on the whole lizards are our friends. They help by eating insect pests and harmful mammals.

Most lizards hatch from eggs just as turtles, alligators, and crocodiles do. But the young of some lizards are born alive.

Marine Iguana

Crested Iguana

Armadillo Lizard

163

Bandy Bandy

Boa Constrictor

Hog-nosed
Snake

There are about 2,500 species of lizards and almost as many snakes. Some snakes are much larger than others. The Indian python, for example, is a giant beside a bandy bandy. But all snakes are about the same shape. The only other reptiles that look like them are the legless lizards.

Since they have no legs, snakes cannot move in the way that most other reptiles move. One way snakes move is by slightly lifting groups of the underside scales and moving them forward before putting them down. The snake's body flows forward in a straight line. A faster and more common way is to wriggle along. The snake pushes the curves in its body against tiny ridges of sand or soil made by the curves. Some desert snakes throw loops of their bodies forward to move themselves along in a hurry. The trail left is not a continuous one but a series of parallel tracks at an angle to the direction the snake has gone. In addition to moving on the ground, snakes can swim, and many are good climbers or burrowers. The hognosed snake is a burrower.

Bull Snake

Indian Python

All snakes have skins covered with scales. As you can see, their colouring and the patterns the colours make may be beautiful. Snakes have the reputation of being slimy and unpleasant to touch. They are not; their scales are dry.

Snakes have many teeth, but they do not use them for chewing. Their teeth point backwards towards their throats. They have long, slender tongues that are forked near the the ends. The tongue may be black, red and black, yellow, green, or even some other colour. A snake uses its tongue for feeling and to help it smell. The tongue, as it touches things, picks up particles and brings them to the mouth where the snake smells them. Its tongue helps the snake to find food and avoid enemies. It can dart in and out with remarkable speed.

Most snakes lay eggs. Some snakes, however, bear their young alive.

All snakes are meat-eaters, and they all swallow their food whole. Many of them eat animals that look much too big to be swallowed by a snake. The secret is that a snake's jaws are fastened together in such a way that the snake can open its mouth very wide indeed. A snake's skin, moreover, stretches like rubber. One big swallow may provide it with enough food to last for weeks.

As its grows, a snake has to shed its skin. Crawling out of its old skin is not easy.

The boa constrictor is not a poisonous snake. The only way it can kill its prey is to squeeze it to death. Most of its food consists of small mammals like rats. The boa constrictor throws a coil of its body round its prey and then squeezes hard, so that the prey cannot breathe. Boa constrictors can be kept as pets. They only need feeding once a week.

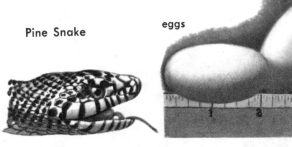

Pine Snake   eggs

Snake Shedding

Poison Fangs

Bushmaster

Many people are so afraid of snakes that they kill every snake they can. But most snakes do us no harm, and some are helpful. A few snakes, however, are dangerous. The dangerous ones, for the most part, are those with poison fangs. When these snakes bite an animal, poisón runs through their fangs into the animal. The snakes pictured here are among the most poisonous snakes in the world. The four shown below are found in the United States.

The water moccasin, nicknamed the 'cottonmouth', the copperhead, and the eastern diamondback, which is a rattlesnake, belong to a group of snakes called pit vipers because of the pits between their eyes and their nostrils. The eastern diamondback is the largest of America's poisonous snakes. Like all rattlesnakes—except for very young ones—it has a warning rattle at the end of its tail.

A coral snake's fangs are much shorter than those of the pit vipers. They do not, fortunately, go through heavy cloth or shoe leather. The cobras of the Old World are among this snake's many relatives.

The Indian cobra can be blamed for a great many of the deaths from snakebite in India. Another cobra, the king cobra of south-eastern Asia, is the largest of all

Tiger Snake

Tic-polonga

Indian Cobra

Gaboon Viper

Black Mamba

Fer-de-lance

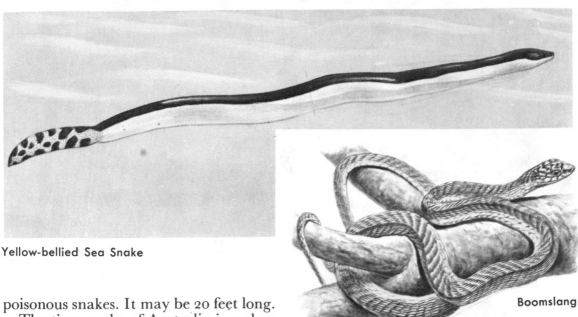

Yellow-bellied Sea Snake

Boomslang

poisonous snakes. It may be 20 feet long.

The tiger snake of Australia is a close relative of the cobra. A fully-grown one has enough poison to kill 400 people. The mamba of Africa is another cobra relative.

South America can claim the largest poisonous snake of the Americas—the bushmaster. It may grow to be 12 feet long. Like the diamondback, the bushmaster is a pit viper. Another dangerous pit viper of South America is the fer-de-lance.

The Gaboon viper of Africa belongs to the family of snakes called true vipers. Its poison fangs may be an inch and a half

long. India's tic-polonga is another true viper.

The boomslang of the African bush is the only one of the so-called rear-fanged snakes that is dangerous. As a rule it is mild tempered, but its poison is deadly.

Most snakes spend all, or at least most, of their time on land. But in the warm regions of the Pacific there are sea snakes, and they are very poisonous.

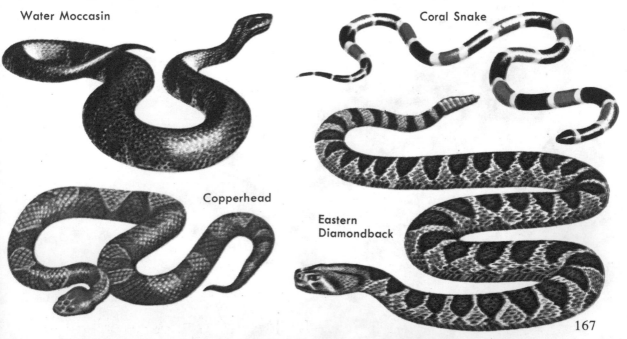

Water Moccasin

Coral Snake

Copperhead

Eastern Diamondback

Chimney Swift

Birds

Almost all the animals that fly are in two great groups; animals with backbones and animals without backbones. The two groups are, of course, the insects and the birds. In the days of the dinosaurs the birds had backboned rivals in the air, the flying reptiles. But times have changed. Today, the only vertebrates besides the birds that can fly are bats, and birds outnumber bats ten times over.

Scientists have tried to find out how fast birds fly by timing some of them. The robin's speed is about 30 miles an hour. The swift can fly twice as fast.

A bird's wings are one of the important ways in which they are equipped for flying. A flying fish can soar through the air for a long way. A flying dragon lizard can glide from tree to tree. But only creatures with true wings can really fly.

A typical bird's wings are powered by strong muscles. On the breastbone there is a projection called a keel to which the chief wing muscles are fastened. The wing feathers do much to make a bird's wings into wonderful flying machines.

A bird's light weight is a help in flying. A swift weighs less than a mouse or lizard

American Robin's Nest and Eggs

European Robin

or toad of the same size. One reason why a bird is so light is that, as with the flying reptiles of long ago, many of its bones are hollow and filled with air. Connected with its lungs a bird also has air sacs scattered throughout its body. The air sacs act like tiny hot-air balloons.

A streamlined body is another help in flying.

Many birds use their power of flight to spend part of the year in one region and the rest of it in another. Robins, like many other birds, spend the winter here. But others only come to Britain during the summer, like the swifts. The swifts fly to Africa at the end of the summer and spend the winter there. Then each spring they leave Africa again and fly back to Europe. Some birds that live in the far north in the summer come to Britain in the winter.

Kiwi

because air is trapped between them, feathers serve this purpose very well.

Just as there are some flying vertebrates that are not birds, there are a few birds that cannot fly. Far back in the record of birds on earth, there have been flightless birds. *Hesperornis* you may remember, was an early one. Among the flightless birds of today are those pictured on these two pages. Still another, the emu, is pictured on page 176.

With no tail, no wings that show, a rounded back, and short, thick legs, the kiwi is a strange-looking bird. Even

Besides being a great help in flying, feathers are excellent protection for a bird's body. They shed water because they are kept oily and because the parts of each feather, as well as the feathers themselves, are very cleverly fitted together.

Feathers, moreover, help to keep a bird's body warm. Since birds are warm-blooded animals, it is important for them to have a covering that will keep the heat of their bodies from escaping. Largely

Ostrich

Penguins

Jackass   Magellan   Little   Gentoo   Adelie   Rockhopper

though its legs are short, it lumbers along fast. Its long curved bill is good for pulling worms out of the ground. The kiwi is only found in New Zealand.

The ostrich, a native of Africa, is the largest living bird. This giant bird is about eight feet tall and runs faster than a horse. With each step it can cover 25 feet. In their habitat, ostriches often travel about in groups of 30 or more.

The cassowary is a bird of Australia and New Guinea. It is almost as tall as an ostrich. No one should find it hard, however, to tell the two birds apart. A cassowary has no beautiful plumes like those of an ostrich. And it has a strange crest on its head. The bare skin of its head and neck, moreover, is brightly coloured. Hanging down from the throats of some cassowaries are folds of skin called wattles.

The rhea is a bird of the South American grasslands. It is about three feet shorter than an ostrich, and, in spite of its broad look, not so heavy. Its weight of 50 pounds, however, is greater than that of any other bird of the Americas. Its feathers make good feather dusters.

Many people think, when they see a penguin or a picture of one, that these birds have fur instead of feathers. Penguin feathers really are furlike. They make a good covering for the birds, many of which live on the icy shores of Antarctica and nearby islands. There are 15 different species of penguins, but all of them are alike in standing upright and in having paddle-like wings.

Rhea   Cassowary

Ruby-throated Hummingbird

Without any exceptions, birds hatch from eggs. Birds' eggs all have hard shells very much like the shell of a common hen's egg. But they vary greatly in size. An ostrich egg is about six inches long. A hummingbird's egg, in contrast, is only as big as a pea. As a rule the eggs are laid in nests built by one or both of the parents.

Some nests are wonderfully made. The ruby-throated hummingbird builds a

Mallee Fowl

beautiful little nest about the size of half a walnut. The nest is lined with soft plant down and covered on the outside with moss, cobwebs, and lichens.

The mallee fowl makes a nest that is very different from that made by most birds. It lays its eggs in a wide deep hole it has dug. The eggs are covered with soil and dead leaves and the heat formed by the rotting leaves hatches the eggs. When the chicks hatch they have to dig their way out of the nest. They have to look for their own food and can fly at once, without having to learn.

Birds were living on the earth millions of years before the first humans. Obviously they could not build their nests near to houses. But many birds prefer to do so now. The robin is one of them. This bird will build its nest in an old tin can or even in the pocket of a discarded coat. It will also accept a man-made nest-box. Many other species of birds will use nest-boxes too. Sometimes they have to be a special shape. Woodpeckers prefer log-shaped nest boxes. All nest-boxes must be put up in suitable places. The young birds must not get too hot, too cold or too wet.

Doves have been living in dovecots for

Nest-box

hundreds of years. Some old houses have dovecots built into the side of the house.

Each kind of bird has its own special kind of nest. A hummingbird never builds a nest like a wren's, or the other way around. A bird inherits its way of nest building. It does not have to be taught how to build the nest, just as a bee does not have to be taught how to gather nectar and make honey, a spider does not have to be taught how to spin its web, and a human being does not have to be taught how to walk upright.

Birds' eggs, in order to hatch, have to be kept at a fairly steady temperature. As a rule the female bird sits on the eggs to keep them warm. With some kinds of birds the male shares or takes over this duty. Many male birds are much brighter in colour than their mates. It is often an advantage, if the female does the sitting on the eggs, for her to be dull coloured. She does not show up so clearly and attract the attention of enemies.

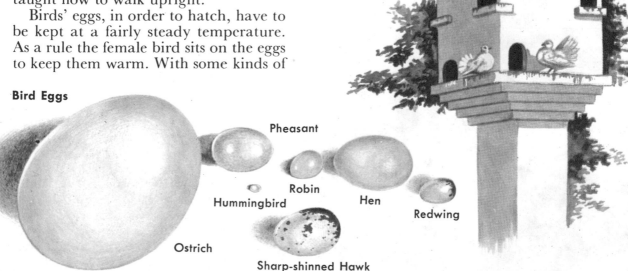

Dovecot

Bird Eggs

Pheasant

Robin

Hummingbird

Hen

Redwing

Ostrich

Sharp-shinned Hawk

New-hatched
Mockingbirds

Golden Eagle
and Nestlings

The time that a bird's eggs must be kept warm, or incubated, before they hatch is different for different birds. A robin's eggs must be incubated for 12 or 13 days. A hen must sit on her eggs for about 21 days. The incubation time for an ostrich egg is twice as long, and that for the egg of a wandering albatross about twice as long again. The tiny egg of a hummingbird hatches in 14 or 15 days.

Many birds, like the young in the picture above are almost naked when they are hatched. They are so weak that they cannot stand up. Their eyes are shut, just as a new-born kitten's eyes are. Their mouths are big, and their bills are rather soft. Such baby birds need to be kept warm and protected and well fed.

Nestling birds like these eat an amazing amount of food for their size. Since they are warm blooded, they have to eat not only enough to grow but also enough to help keep themselves warm. At night the mother bird, as a rule, protects them with her own feathers to keep them from getting cold. Many little birds seem to be hungry all the time they are awake. A young bird, in fact, may eat its weight in food every day. A record kept of four baby robins showed that these little robins ate 16 earthworms in an hour— more than five feet of earthworm altogether. It keeps both parents busy from daybreak to dark finding enough food for a nestful of baby robins.

Some adult birds first swallow the food they get for the baby birds, then they pump it up out of their stomachs into the wide-open mouths of the babies in a more easily digestible form.

Baby birds grow fast. Even if they are naked when they are hatched, they are soon covered with soft downy feathers. Then bigger, stouter feathers begin to grow.

While baby birds are still in the nest, they are often called nestlings. Young robins stay in their nest for 13 days or so. Little golden eagle nestlings like those in the picture have to stay in their nest for almost three months, for the nest is likely to be at the top of a steep cliff. The nest itself may be several feet tall. A pair of golden eagles often uses the same nesting place year after year. Each year the eagles add more sticks to their nest.

Young birds like those pictured on this page are called fledglings. The mother and father birds may continue to bring them food for days, weeks, or even months.

Notice that the tails of all the fledglings in the pictures are short. Their tails must grow before the young birds can fly well and take over from their parents the job of getting food for themselves.

The common cuckoo lays its eggs in the nests of other species of birds. The young cuckoo hatches first and throws out the other eggs in the nest. Often the fledgling cuckoo is much bigger than its foster parents. They have to work very hard to feed the young one with insects and other small animals.

Warbler Fledglings

Robin Fledglings

Common Cuckoo and foster parent

Emu and Young

after coming out of the egg. As a rule such birds stay in the egg longer than other birds of the same size. They have more time to grow there. In the eggs they hatch from, there is enough food to nourish the baby birds for the extra time.

The emu and the woodcock are land birds. Their babies run about on the ground. The swans and the Canada goose are waterfowl. Their babies spend much of the time swimming although they can walk on land.

The emu, a big flightless bird, lives on the dry plains of Australia. The eggs it lays are dark green and about five and a half inches long.

Emu eggs must be incubated for about 60 days. The male emu sits on the eggs, and for the first few days after hatching he broods the babies just as a hen broods her chicks. Their conspicuous stripes make baby emus easy to identify.

Even young woodcocks show some of the features that make adult woodcocks easy to tell from other birds. They have, for example, long bills with movable tips. A woodcock can push its bill into the ground and feel about with the movable tip for an earthworm. It can open, if need

The four kinds of young birds pictured here are not naked and helpless when they are hatched, as nestlings are. Instead, their eyes are bright and their bodies are covered with down. They are able to follow their parents about soon after their down is dry. As you see, these baby birds are much like little chicks.

Many other baby birds are like these in being able to fend for themselves soon

Swans

Black-necked

Trumpeter

Black

Mute

Woodcock Nestlings

be, only the tip. A woodcock's eyes, moreover, are set so far back that it can see all the way around its head. The woodcock is a bird of forests and wet meadows.

Baby swans and geese—and baby ducks, or ducklings, too—are very much alike. Young swans are called cygnets, and young geese goslings. The goslings of the Canada goose need their coats of down to keep them warm, for they spend this early part of their life in the far north.

Of course, the down with which all such baby birds are covered gives way to bigger feathers. Strangely enough these birds take rather a long time before they grow their feathers. The little birds hatched naked and helpless soon catch up with them. It is really no great wonder, for the little birds that are helpless when hatched are, as you know, stuffed with food. The down-covered birds do not eat so much in proportion to their size.

Canada Goose Nestlings

Ibises

Sacred

Scarlet

Glossy

White

There are about 8,600 species of birds altogether. Feathers easily distinguish them from other animals. Bills and wings are a help, too, in telling whether an animal is a bird. But although birds are similar enough to be distinguished easily from other animals, there are many differences among them. Birds range in size, for example, from the tiny hummingbird, which weighs less than a penny, to the ostrich, which may weigh 300 pounds. As you know, there have been in past ages birds even larger, but these bird giants are now extinct.

All birds have two legs, but the legs of one kind may be very different from those of another. Some are long, some short; some are strong, others weak; some are fastened farther back on the body than others.

The feet of birds are as different as their legs. Most birds have four toes. As a rule, three of the four toes point forwards and one points backwards. But some birds—the woodpecker for example— have two toes that point forwards and two that point backwards. Some birds have webbed feet. Some have spreading toes or toes with sharp, strong claws. Some have feet so weak that the birds can barely walk with them.

You already know that the wings of birds are not all alike. You know, too, that a bird's bill—the woodcock's for one —may be peculiar. Bird bills come in many different shapes. Some are long and slender, some short and stout. Some are curved, some straight. Some end in sharp points and some are blunt. Bills are much more than mere mouths. They are also hands and tools. If you can imagine building a house and getting dinner with

Green Woodpecker

Zebra Finch

your hands tied behind your back, you can get an idea of how important to a bird its bill is.

A fully grown bird has several kinds of feathers—as a rule downy feathers, body feathers, and wing and tail flight feathers. It may have others, too, that serve special purposes. One bird's feathers may be very different in shape from another's. Notice the woodpecker's sharp-pointed tail feathers.

The common names of birds often tell us something about the colour of the bird. They show what a wide range there is among birds. We have, for example, the scarlet ibis, the golden whistler, the yellowhammer, the green catbird, the blue tit, the blackbird and the zebra finch.

Many differences in birds are related to the places where they live. Webbed feet help water birds to swim. Long legs help shore birds to wade. Strong legs like a robin's and a blackbird's are good for hopping or walking about on the ground. Woodpeckers dig their nests in tree trunks. Their pointed tail feathers act as braces as the birds work. A woodpecker's sharp, strong bill is a good digging tool.

body feather

down feather

primary flight feather

secondary flight feather

tail feather

body feather

Feathers

Feet of Birds

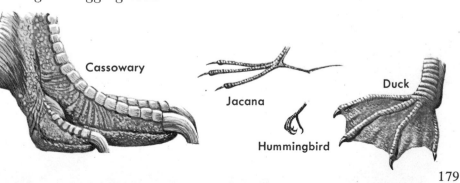

Cassowary

Jacana

Duck

Woodpecker

Hummingbird

179

Northern Shrike

A northern shrike would soon be very hungry if it had nothing to eat but the food a yellowhammer eats. A cuckoo could neither catch nor eat the food of a puffin. A frogmouth would not do at all well on the food of a tree sparrow. Most birds have their own food or foods. Many of the differences between birds are caused by the kinds of food they live on.

Frogmouth

The northern shrike is sometimes called the butcher-bird. It gets this nickname because it often hangs up its 'meat' just as a butcher hangs meat up on hooks in his market. A shrike's meat mainly consists of mice and big insects such as grasshoppers. The hooks it hangs its meat on are the thorns of a bush or tree or the barbs of a barbed-wire fence. Some people think, when they see the food it has hung up, that a shrike kills other animals just for the fun of it. Probably, however, hanging up some of the mammals and insects it catches is just a way of storing up food for a rainy day.

The frogmouth mainly feeds on insects and spiders but it may also catch small mice. It waits on a branch until suitable prey comes near, then it darts off to catch it. Feeding on small animals, the frogmouth needs only a very small bill. During the day it perches along a branch and is very hard to see.

The cuckoo eats insects, but it does not catch them in the air. It eats many hairy caterpillars, a food most birds avoid, as well as other insects.

Yellow-billed Cuckoo

Goshawk

Peregrine Falcon

Sparrow Hawk

House Sparrow

Yellowhammer

Puffins

All hawks are meat-eaters. The smallest hawks can only catch insects, mice, and other little animals. Large hawks may catch mammals as big as rabbits and fast-flying birds as large as themselves. Catching such prey means that the hawk must fly very fast. The peregrine falcon is thought to be the fastest bird. It sometimes reaches a speed of 175 miles an hour. It feeds on pigeons and sea birds.

The yellowhammer and the sparrow for the most part eat seeds. As they gather the seeds, they catch some insects, too. But they could live on seeds alone. Their stout bills are good for cracking small seeds. These two birds are built very differently from hawks. Since the seeds they eat, unlike animals, cannot move and run away, there is no need for fast flight to get food. To gather seeds, moreover, there is no need for the hooked beaks and strong claws of the hawks.

Puffins are fish-eaters. One of the puffins in the picture, you notice, has several small fish hanging from its bill. A puffin that goes out to sea on a fishing expedition may bring back as many as twenty fish for the 'pufflings' in its nest.

Some birds live on a wide variety of food. The robin, for example, eats earthworms, blackberries, cherries, and grubs among many other things.

Scientists have divided birds into more than twenty orders. The perching birds make up by far the largest order as more than half of all the thousands of species of birds are in it.

The birds pictured on these two pages belong to seven different orders. Although some of them are shown perching, they are not in the order of perching birds.

The kookaburra belongs to the same order as the kingfisher. The kookaburra is only found in Australia. Most of their food consists of snakes and lizards which it drops from a considerable height to kill. They are often called laughing jackasses because they make a noise that sounds like a man laughing.

Owls are placed in an order of their own. They are only active at night. Their eyesight is so keen that they are able to catch small animals like mice. Bright sunlight hurts their eyes. They also have very good hearing. Unlike many birds, owls do not make any noise when they are flying, so they are able to get very near to their prey without it running away.

A peacock is a male peafowl. With its beautiful train of feathers, it is one of the handsomest of all birds. It often raises this train of feathers into a great fan as it struts about. In the order with the peafowl are all the pheasants, quail, grouse, and partridges, as well as the turkeys and chickens.

The whip-poor-will is one of the goat-

Kookaburra

Barn Owl

Peacock

suckers. The nighthawk is another bird in this order. There is an old superstition that goatsuckers can milk goats. There is no truth in it. Actually they eat nothing but insects. The whip-poor-will gets its name from its call. The nighthawk looks like a hawk and flies about at dusk. The whip-poor-will calls incessantly as it flies.

The white stork is in an order that includes all the storks, herons, bitterns and flamingos. Many of the birds in this order are long-legged shore birds. The white stork is the bird, according to legend that brings new-born babies. This bird lives in central Europe and builds its nests on the roofs of houses.

Gulls are water birds. They are a common sight along the shores of lakes and seas. They are fish-eaters. In the same order with the gulls are the terns, sandpipers, auks, puffins, plovers, and jacanas.

In the order with the Canada goose are all the other geese, the ducks, and the swans. They are all water birds and good swimmers. They are also good fliers. Some of them can fly at 60 miles an hour.

Whip-poor-will

White Stork

Canada Goose

Gulls

Emperor Penguin

Great Northern Diver

Common Kingfisher

Wandering
Albatross

Gannet

Yellow-headed
Amazon Parrot

Coot

These birds represent eight orders of non-perching birds. The rails, cranes, and coots are all in the same order. The other birds are in seven different ones.

Penguins are in an order of their own, a very ancient one. The three foot tall emperor looks almost human as it walks about.

European kingfishers are not only found in Europe, they may be seen perching on a branch near a river in many parts of Asia too. Hornbills belong in this order too.

The wandering albatross has the greatest wing-span of any living bird. The distance from wing tip to wing tip is nearly twelve feet. This big bird spends most of its time far out at sea. It glides on the winds high above the water day after day. In the order with the albatrosses are the petrels and shearwaters. They, too, are sea birds that spend most of their lives miles from shore.

Divers, like penguins, are in an order by themselves. There are only four kinds. All are expert swimmers and divers. They are good fliers, too, but they have trouble taking off. The divers all live in the far north and are not very often seen in this country.

The gannet is a common bird of the North Atlantic coasts. It is not as spectacular as some of the other birds in the same order, for the order includes, the pelicans and the magnificent man-of-war, or frigate, birds. It also includes the boobies.

Parrots, too, form an order all their own, but there are many more kinds of parrots than there are kinds of loons or penguins. It is common knowledge that some parrots can be trained to talk. The yellow-headed Amazon parrot is a good talker. Some parrots are called cockatoos, others macaws, budgerigars, lovebirds, lories, or parakeets.

The osprey is found in many parts of the world. It is always seen near the sea or large lakes as it only feeds on fish. It is in the same order as the eagles, hawks and vultures. Birds of this order are often collectively called birds of prey as they all feed on meat or fish.

Corncrake

Osprey

Cranes

Crowned

Whooping

Sandhill

Demoiselle

Golden Oriole

The order that includes the cranes, coots and rails also includes the moorhens. All are birds of shores or swamplands.

The large order containing all the small perching birds is divided into many families. The finches, thrushes, tits, wrens, flycatchers, magpies and bowerbirds are all in this order. There are some families that are only found in certain parts of the world. One family of flycatchers is found in North and South America, while another family of flycatchers lives in most of the rest of the world. Bowerbirds are only seen in Australia, as are the lyrebirds. However, martins, crows, thrushes and finches live in many places.

Tits are members of a family of perching birds. They are common in Europe, Asia, Africa and North America. All the tits are small acrobatic birds. In winter they often visit bird-tables and feed off the crumbs placed there. Blue tits and great tits are some of the most common. Less well-known are the willow tits and long-tailed tits. In North America the tits are often called chickadees.

Bowerbirds are so called because many of the males build elaborate bowers. The bowers are only made to attract the females. The bowers are not nests. The females build the nest and lay their eggs in it. The golden bowerbird makes a bower that is shaped like a bell-tent. There is a small branch in the middle and the bird weaves twigs around the branch, so that a semi-circular shape is made. In front of the bower there is an open space. Here the male places brightly coloured flowers. The bower of the satin bowerbird is simpler. He builds a long narrow passage of twigs. The walls are decorated with brightly coloured muds which the male paints on the sides. Catbirds are in this family too. They do not build bowers, however. They are so called because the mewing calls they make sound rather like the mewing of a cat.

Blue Tit

Great Tit

Crestless Gardener

Satin Bowerbird

All the birds on this page are in the crow family. These are thought by some people to be the most intelligent of all the birds. They appear to have good memories. However, they are great thieves too. Jackdaws in particular will steal anything that is bright and shiny. Nutcrackers and jays for example, store nuts away during the summer and autumn, and in the winter can go straight to where the nuts are hidden. Magpies are also members of this family.

The carrion crow is a very common bird in the country, but it is easy to confuse it with the rook. Rooks are larger birds and have long feathers down their legs that look like trousers.

Ravens are not often seen as they nest on cliff tops and mountains. There are a few at the Tower of London, but these

Raven

Crow

European Jay

Spotted Flycatcher

Blackcap

Willie Wagtail

Eastern Kingbird

have their wings clipped so that they do not fly away. They do not build nests there and so fresh birds have to be brought in every now and then.

All the birds on this page are flycatchers. But they are divided into two families. The eastern kingbird and the scissor-tailed flycatcher are called tyrant flycatchers. There are many species of tyrant flycatchers in North and South America, but they do not live anywhere else. The willie-wagtail and the spotted flycatcher are members of the Old World flycatcher family. This family is found in many parts of the world, except the Americas. The willie-wagtail is a common Australian bird. The spotted flycatcher lives in Europe and Asia. Old World flycatchers also live in Africa. The birds of these two families have similarly shaped bills. These bills are good for catching insects. As well as flies, flycatchers eat many other kinds of insect.

Bullfinch

Greenfinch

Goldfinch

Gouldian Finch

Yellow Wagtail

Here are some more perching birds. They are in five different families. The bullfinch, greenfinch, the gouldian finch are all members of the very large finch family. Yellow wagtails are in another family. They are not closely related to the willie-wagtail. Lyre birds are in a family that is only found in Australia.

The goldfinch is a common bird in many parts of Britain. It can often be seen in gardens. The males have much brighter colours than the females. But in the autumn they moult and grow new feathers that are dull in colour, like the female. The females of most birds are duller in colour than the males. Goldfinches are very tiny birds. Like all the finches they are seed eaters.

Bullfinches are some of the largest of all the finches. The male bullfinches and gouldian finches are much brighter in colour than the females.

Lyre birds are so-called because the tail feathers, when displayed, look like a lyre. Lyres were common musical instruments in ancient Greece. The male displays his tail to attract the female.

Wagtails, like the yellow wagtail, often live near streams. They get their name because they wag the rear end of their bodies up and down.

The barred cuckoo shrike belongs to the cuckoo shrike family of Australia. It is not related to the cuckoos, which are placed in a family of their own. It has cuckoo as part of its name only because it flies like a cuckoo. It flies very straight but goes up and down as it flies. The cuckoo shrike is a common bird in large gardens and open grassy places.

Lyrebird

White-breasted Nuthatch

Barred Cuckooshrike

Some birds of other orders make pleasant sounds, but all the true bird songsters are perching birds. By no means every bird of this group, however, has a beautiful song. No one would call the starling, the crow, or the sparrow a good singer, although they are all perching birds.

Saying that someone sings like a lark is paying them a very great compliment. Larks do have very beautiful songs. Poems have been written about the songs of the skylark. This dull little bird has one of the most beautiful songs of all birds. The shorelark also has a pleasant song but it is much less famous.

Another very famous song bird is the nightingale. Some people think it has the finest song of all. Both the larks and the nightingale are in the large thrush family. Blackbirds are in this family. They are good singers too. They were originally only found in Europe and Asia, but the early settlers introduced them to New Zealand, to remind them of home. The common European robin and the American robin are also members of the thrush family. Birds called robins are found in many parts of the world, but not all of them are in the same family. Not all of them have red breasts either. Some Australian robins are yellow.

The Old World warblers are good singers too. Willow warblers are among the best in this family. This small dull bird is a common summer visitor to northern Europe. However, they are not seen very often as their dull colouring gives them very good camouflage among bushes. Blackcaps are Old World warblers too. Only the males have the distinctive black caps. The females have reddish-brown caps. Emu wrens are members of this family. Some of these Australian wrens are very brightly coloured. They are not related to the true wrens.

Shore Lark

Skylark

Blackbird

American Robin

Song Thrush

Nightingale

Emu Wren

Willow Warbler

193

House Martin

Welcome Swallow

Scientists have studied the food of birds carefully. Some birds are helpful and others are harmful because of the kinds of food they eat.

Birds help us by eating weed seeds, small harmful mammals such as field mice, dead animals, and insect pests. Weeds in a field or garden crowd the plants we are trying to grow and often take from the soil water and minerals the crop plants need. Field mice eat seeds and young plants. Dead animals would turn the earth into a great rubbish heap if there were no clean-up brigade. And insect pests, as you know, do harm to ordinary trees, fruit trees, crop plants, our tame animals, and even to ourselves.

Birds harm us by eating fruit, grain, and helpful insects. Some birds do harm, moreover, by eating the eggs of other birds and even small birds themselves. A few kinds of birds eat the buds of trees or drill into the trunks to get sap.

Of course, no bird is ever consciously helping us or harming us. We should not blame the birds that harm us any more than we should praise those that help us. They are simply eating the food they are suited to eat.

Not many birds have records that make them entirely helpful or entirely harmful. We have to weigh the good a bird does against the bad.

The birds pictured here are all beneficial. We count them as friends.

The house martin and the welcome swallow are friends. They feed almost entirely on insects. Among the insects they eat are many harmful ones. All the birds in the swallow and martin family are insect eaters. They are among the best liked of all birds. Their arrival in the countries where they nest heralds the beginning of spring. In the autumn they

Wren

migrate to warmer areas, such as Africa and southern Asia.

All wrens are insect eaters too, so they can be counted as friends. There are several families of wrens living in different parts of the world. One family lives mainly in North and South America, with only one species in Europe. All Australian wrens are in the Old World warbler family. Wrens all have short, rather fat bodies.

The grosbeak lives in the north of Europe. It is another useful bird. It eats insects that attack potatoes.

Many of the common birds that can be seen in gardens feed on insects. They not only eat the adult insects but they eat many larval insects too. Many species of birds are very fond of caterpillars. As you know, caterpillars often do a great deal of damage to the plants on which they live. Other small animals are eaten by birds too. Thrushes, for example, eat a lot of snails and slugs. These molluscs can cause a great many young plants to die. They are especially fond of lettuces and newly bedded out flowers. Birds that eat these animals really are friends of the gardener.

Rose-breasted Grosbeak

195

Griffon Vulture

Eider Duck

Of course, some birds are beneficial to us not because of the food they eat, but because they provide food for us. Centuries ago men found the meat of birds so good to eat that they began domesticating wild fowl of several kinds. We now raise millions of ducks, chickens, geese, and turkeys. Eggs, too, are important in our diet. There are still many wild game birds. Ducks, geese, quails, grouse, partridges, and pheasants are among them.

We use the feathers of some birds. Eider down, for instance, is used to fill eiderdowns and quilts.

Pheasant

The bird friends you have just read about all belong to the order of perching birds. But there are many helpful birds in other orders. We get a great deal of help in fighting rats and mice from the hawks, kites and owls. The vultures are the best bird scavengers as they eat the bodies of dead animals, and the cuckoos, nighthawks, swifts, and woodpeckers destroy vast numbers of insects.

Some birds have a bad reputation which they do not deserve. The red-tailed hawk is a good example. This hawk occasionally kills chickens when its usual food is scarce. But it catches so few chickens in proportion to the mice and insects it eats that its common name of chicken hawk is unfair.

Some perching birds, too, are valued for their feathers. Among them are the strange and colourful birds of paradise. To see one of them in its native home, you would have to go to northern Australia, New Guinea, or nearby small islands. Some birds of paradise live in mountain forests almost impossible to reach. Much of what scientists know about this family comes from studying birds of paradise in zoos.

All the birds of paradise pictured are male birds. Their wonderful display of feathers chiefly has to do with courtship.

For centuries bird of paradise plumes have been used as ornaments in New Guinea. The first sight of them in Europe was when Magellan's ship 'Victoria' came back to Spain in 1522 from its round-the-world trip with two bird of paradise skins brought as a gift to the king. They were so beautiful that the Spaniards said the birds must have come from paradise. The name 'bird of paradise' has been used ever since.

Quetzal

All these colourful birds, too, are natives of tropical regions. The beautiful quetzal is the national bird of Guatemala. One of the coins of that country is called a quetzal. To the early Indians of Middle America, quetzal plumes were a sign of royalty. And even recently quetzals were being killed in large numbers for their plumes. Now the bird is protected.

Most of the more than 300 kinds of hummingbirds live near the equator. Many, like these three, have very gay colours or ornate feathers.

Cockatoos are parrots of the Australia-New Guinea region. They can raise and lower their crests to suit their moods. These parrots are not such good talkers as the African grey parrot which is the best.

Tropical Hummingbirds

Cockatoos

Toco Toucan

Emerald Toucanet

Great Hornbill

Toucans are easy to recognize by their bills. With these enormous bills they gather fruit and catch insects, lizards, and even nestling birds to eat. The toco toucan is over two feet long, much longer than the emerald toucanet. Toucans clacking their bills make a great deal of noise.

The great hornbill deserves its name. It is five feet long and has a very strong, horny bill. This bird of Asia is famous not only for its size and strange appearance, but also for one of its habits. When the female is ready to lay her eggs, she climbs into a hole in a hollow tree. Then the entrance is walled up with mud, with only a narrow opening left. The mother bird stays walled in until the young birds that hatch from her eggs are ready to fly. While she is imprisoned, the male feeds his family through the small opening in the mud wall.

Dodo

Prairie Chicken

Great Auk

California Condor

Once the dodo was common on the tiny island of Mauritius in the Indian Ocean. But this bird has been extinct since 1681. Sailors that landed on the island had a great deal to do with making the dodo disappear. They killed many dodoes for meat. This large bird could not fly, and so could not escape from its hunters.

Another flightless bird now extinct because people killed too many is the great auk. This bird lived in the sea and nested on islands in the North Atlantic. Hunters trapped and killed the nesting birds for their meat and feathers. No great auks have been seen since 1844.

The passenger pigeon became extinct more recently, just over 150 years ago. There were many thousands in the forests of North America. Hunters killed them in huge numbers. The nestlings were especially valuable and were easier to catch, as the pigeons nested very close together. Gradually they became fewer in number and eventually died out completely.

When people saw that the passenger pigeon was disappearing, laws were passed to protect it. But they were too late. However, similar laws protecting other rare birds and animals, have been passed in many countries. It is to be hoped that these laws will prevent such a thing from happening again.

Prairie chickens, once common game birds from the western prairies of North America to the Atlantic coast, are now rare. One kind, the heath hen, has already gone.

Probably fewer than 50 of North America's largest bird, the California condor, are still alive. All that we know of, live in a wildlife sanctuary in the mountains of California. Leaving the condor undisturbed is the best hope of saving it.

The story of the trumpeter swan is an encouraging one. This big white bird is the largest waterfowl in the world. Every year large numbers used to be seen on their trips between their summer home in northern Canada and Alaska and their winter home in the southern half of

Trumpeter Swan

the United States. Hunters found the trumpeter an easy target. In 1933, in spite of a law to protect it, only 66 were counted. But now it is again increasing in numbers. By the last count there are nearly a thousand.

In recent years the draining of its swampland homes has threatened the roseate-spoonbill. Wildlife refuges now established to ensure it a place to live, may save this beautiful bird for us.

A bird that has been saved from almost certain extinction, in its natural home, is the Hawaian goose. About two hundred years ago there were several thousand alive. But as the forests were cut down they almost died out. A few birds were captured and bred in captivity. Now a few more have been released in Hawaii, in what remains of their natural habitat.

The kapapo is another very rare bird. It is the only member of the parrot family that cannot fly. As it is only active at night it is sometimes called the owl parrot. This bird only lives in the forests of New Zealand. It lays its eggs in a burrow, dug under the roots of a tree. It is virtually flightless and has been almost wiped out by predators that were brought to New Zealand by the early settlers.

Roseate Spoonbill

Eurasian Spoonbill

Mammals

Of the animals pictured on this page, the koala and platypus clearly are mammals. Their fur tells us that they are. The spiny anteater is also a mammal, but its stiff, sharp spines stop it from looking furry. Another name for this strange-looking animal is echidna.

The platypus and the spiny anteater belong to an order of mammals called *monotremes*. The monotremes differ from other mammals in that they lay eggs. All other mammals are born alive. After monotreme eggs have hatched, however, they are fed on milk from their mother just as other mammal babies are. Monotremes are found only in Australia and some nearby islands.

The platypus is also called the duck-billed platypus. When early settlers in Australia sent some platypus skins back to England, scientists thought it was a joke. They thought that the bills of ducks had been sewn on to the skins of some furry animal.

The platypus is like a duck not only in having a bill and laying eggs, but also in having webbed feet. Platypuses are very much at home in the water. They use their stout bills to dig worms and shellfish out of the mud at the bottom of streams and ponds. The animals live in long burrows dug in the banks. The female makes a nest of weeds at the far end of a burrow and lays two or three eggs. Young platypuses are undeveloped and very tiny when they hatch. The mother helps to hold them in place with her tail as they suckle

On their hind legs the males have poison spurs. The only other known poisonous mammals are shrews.

A female spiny anteater rolls up in a ball and lays her two eggs directly into a pouch on the underside of her body. When the young have hatched they stay in the pouch for several weeks. When they get to be too prickly, the mother pulls them out.

The spiny anteater is well built for living on ants. It has stout claws that are useful in tearing ants' nests apart, a long snout, and an even longer sticky tongue. There are other anteaters among the mammals, but none are at all closely related to the spiny anteater.

The koala is a pouched mammal, or

Koala

Duck-billed Platypus

Spiny Anteater

marsupial. Marsupials do not lay eggs. The young are born alive, but they, too, are undeveloped and very, very small. The mother carries them about—in most cases in a pouch on her underside—until they are well covered with fur and able to eat food other than milk. Even after a young marsupial is able to leave its mother's pouch it may climb back into the pouch when it needs protection.

Like all the monotremes, most marsupials live in the Australian region. The common opossum is the only North American marsupial, but some kinds of opossum live in South America. Unlike most other marsupials, opossums have many young at a time, often 12 or more, and sometimes as many as 18.

The marsupials are far and away the most common mammals native to Australia. There are many kinds. For a very, very long time they had the continent almost to themselves as far as mammals were concerned. Australia has been separated by the sea from the rest of the world since the Age of Reptiles. Few mammals were able to reach it on their own.

Of Australia's marsupials that are widely known, the koala is second only to the kangaroo. This little native 'bear'

Common Opossum

Australia

Koala

Glider

Kangaroo

Duck-billed Platypus

Kangaroo

lives in trees and mainly eats eucalyptus leaves. Only one or two young are born at a time. A young koala stays in its mother's pouch for about six months and then climbs on her back and rides pick-a-back for another year. Its rides must be exciting, for koalas, although they spend most of the day sleeping among the lower branches of trees, go hopping about in trees at night, often making jumps of several feet.

A young kangaroo's rides in its mother's pouch must be thrilling, too, when it is old enough to sit up and watch what is going on. Kangaroos are famous for the long leaps they make. The leaps often measure 20 feet. Kangaroos are grazers and browsers, mainly eating grass. Many of them live where plant foods are scarce. It is an advantage to be able to cover ground fast.

The honey possum, sugar glider, and Tasmanian devil are other marsupials of the Australian region. The Tasmanian devil is now only found in Tasmania.

The honey possum or 'honey mouse', and the sugar glider are close relatives of the koala. The honey possum is the same size as a mouse. It pushes its slender snout and long tongue into flowers and pumps nectar, pollen, and insects up into its mouth. Gliders, also known as flying phalangers, are very much larger than the honey possum. They cannot really

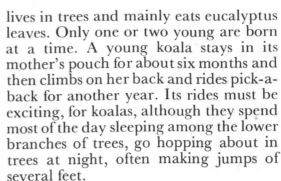

Honey Possum

Sugar Glider

Tasmanian Devil

House Mouse

fly—they can only glide. The sugar glider lives on nectar, leaves and flowers, insects, and the sap of trees.

The Tasmanian devil is about the size of a big house cat. The sounds it makes are as ugly as its looks. It is strong and fierce enough to kill animals far bigger than itself.

Among the other marsupials of Australia are 'pocket-mice', wombats, bandicoots, wallaroos and wallabies. The wallaroos and wallabies are members of the kangaroo family.

Scientists call all the mammals except monotremes and marsupials *placentals*. The house mouse, grey shrew and blue whale are all in this group. The young of placental mammals are kept inside the mother until they are much better developed than baby marsupials. Although the young at birth are not so tiny and helpless as new-born marsupials, they,

too, need care for weeks or months—in some cases even years—after they are born. It is easy to see that young mice need to be taken care of.

'As big as an elephant' is a common saying, but a blue whale is far larger. It is, so far as anyone knows, the largest animal that ever lived. The desert shrew is only three inches long including its tail. A blue whale may measure 100 feet! The light weight among the mammals is another tiny shrew—the pigmy. It would take more than 50 million pigmy shrews to weigh as much as one big blue whale.

A shrew is a bundle of energy. It is so active that every day it has to eat more than twice its weight in food, mainly insects. As you know, the blue whale lives in the sea. It mainly eats tiny crustaceans called krill. This whale does not have teeth. Instead, it has plates of whalebone. On the edges of the plates are long bristles which strain the little animals out of the water. A blue whale eats less in proportion to its size than a shrew, but imagine how many millions of krill it has to devour in one day!

Grey Shrew

Blue Whale

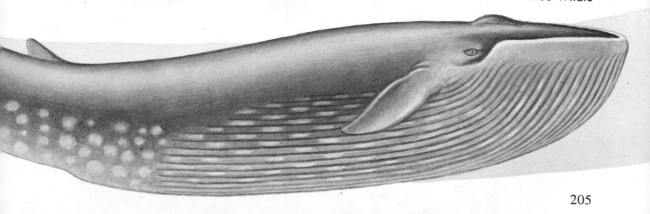

All the animals on these pages are mammals of the sea. The walrus and the seals are fin-footed mammals. They spend part of the time on land. Although the fin-footed mammals are great fish-eaters, they eat many other kinds of animals besides. The walrus mostly eats shellfish. Together with the clams it digs up with its long tusks it gets some sea-weed. The walrus and most kinds of seals live in cold waters.

In contrast the manatee, or sea cow, lives in tropical seas close to the shore and often in river estuaries and freshwater lagoons. This gentle beast only eats plants. A manatee has no hind legs. Probably seeing the homely but human-looking sea cow holding her baby in her flippers gave sailors the idea of mermaids.

Fur Seal

The killer whale, porpoise, and dolphin are all toothed whales. The killer, which is only about a third as long as the blue whale is one of the fiercest meat-eaters alive. With its huge, sharp teeth it catches seals and smaller whales and often bites great chunks out of bigger whales. It has an enormous appetite. Dolphins are extremely intelligent, friendly animals. They are very agile and graceful in the water and love to play near ships.

A sea otter often floats on its back. It sometimes uses its stomach as a lunch counter on which to spread out the crabs, clams and sea urchins it has caught as food. A mother sea otter sleeps on her back holding her baby with her forepaws. Sea Otters are only found in the Pacific Ocean, from Mexico northwards to Alaska.

Manatee

Killer Whale

Dall's Porpoise

Sea Otter

Harbour Seal

Dolphins

Common

Bottlenose

Spotted

Big-eared Bat

Hoary Bat

Pika

The mammals on these pages all live on land. They belong in four different orders.

Bats form an order all their own. They are the only mammals that can truly fly. There are many varieties. The bats of Europe mostly eat insects. In Asia and Africa fruit bats are common. In tropical America there are vampire bats that bite animals and suck the blood.

European Hare

European Rabbit

Anteaters   **Giant**

Pigmy

Lesser

Rabbits, hares and pikas form another order. It is easy to tell rabbits and hares from other mammals by their looks, but it is not so easy to tell rabbits and hares apart. Hares have much longer ears than rabbits and do not dig burrows; their young are born in nests, called forms, made out of grass.

The small round ears of pikas make them easy to tell from their rabbit-hare relatives. These little animals make a lifework of gathering and storing food. The pile up stacks of grass and other plants near the entrances to their rock-crevice homes. When it rains they rush their stores inside.

The three anteaters pictured here are in an order that also includes the sloths and armadillos. The giant anteater, as you can see, is an awkward-looking creature. The claws on its front feet are so long that they interfere with walking. But they are wonderful for ripping open nests of ants and termites. The anteater catches the insects with a sticky tongue 12 inches long. Its bushy tail makes a good sunshade or umbrella for the animal when it rests. The other two ant-eaters pictured live in trees just as sloths do. Their tails are able to coil round branches and they can hang from them.

Moles are seldom seen, for they live underground. They belong to the order

Mole

European Hedgehog

Common Tenrec

of *insectivores*, or insect-eaters, an order that includes the shrews and the hedgehogs. Like the shrews, moles eat almost every minute they are awake. Their food is mostly earthworms, but they eat any insect or other small animal they find.

A hedgehog, too, eats many things besides insects. It will eat slugs, small birds and snakes, eggs and even fruit, roots, and mushrooms. It does most of its hunting at night and sleeps during the daytime. When in danger the animal curls up in a tight ball with the sharp spines on its back sticking out in almost every direction. Its close relative, the tenrec, also has prickly spines. The tenrec is the largest animal of the order. It may be a foot and a half long. This creature has no tail at all. Another of its peculiarities is the number of young born at a time. There may be more than 20 in a litter!

The giant pangolin is an anteater, but it is not put in an order with any of the other anteaters. The pangolins, or scaly anteaters, are in an order of their own. They are called 'scaly' because of the horny scales that cover most of their bodies. In the picture of the giant pangolin you see no sign of hair. A pangolin has very little hair on its body, and what it does have is on its unscaled underside.

Giant Pangolin

To rest, pangolins curl themselves into a ball with the tail wrapped around the outside of the coil and hooked in place. They are remarkably strong. A giant pangolin can pull several people along. And once it is curled up, it is almost impossible to uncoil it. In fact, a giant pangolin is not much of a giant. It measures about six feet from the tip of its snout to the end of its long tail.

The hyraxes and the elephants are also in orders by themselves. They are not alike in shape or in size or in habits, but the elephants are about the closest relatives hyraxes have. In Africa, where many hyraxes live, they have been called 'little brothers of elephants'. Both the hyraxes and the elephants are descended from groups once much larger and more important.

Hyraxes are mentioned in the Bible, but they are called conies there. These little animals look much like short-eared rabbits. They are quick to bite any animal that disturbs them. They have long front teeth that are as sharp as daggers. Hyraxes make amazing sounds. They chatter and whistle and scream as if in agony.

Some hyraxes live among rocks, usually in colonies. Pads on their feet that act as vacuum cups help to make them as skilful at climbing steep rocky slopes as mountain goats. Other kinds live in trees. A common name for these hyraxes is dassies.

No other animal of today looks enough like an elephant to be confused with it. An elephant's trunk alone serves to identify it. Almost every zoo has its elephants. They do well in captivity.

Elephants are the biggest land animals alive today. The African elephant is larger than the Indian elephant and its ears are larger. The pictures show other differences between the two.

Indian elephants have long been trained to do different kinds of heavy work. In ancient times they also served as huge warhorses. African elephants, too, used to be used in wars, but they are not such common work animals today as Indian elephants.

Feeding buns to the elephants is part of the fun of going to a zoo. But wild elephants feed on grass and leaves. Their tusks are a big help in digging up roots. An elephant has four huge teeth which are good for chewing tough plants. As the teeth wear down new ones appear.

It is a common idea that elephants live much longer than people, but few elephants live to be more than 70 years old.

Hyrax

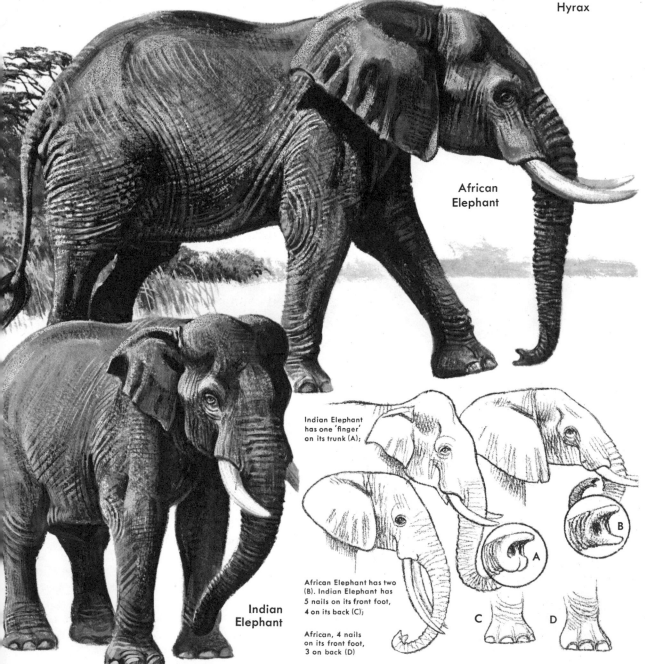

African Elephant

Indian Elephant has one 'finger' on its trunk (A);

African Elephant has two (B). Indian Elephant has 5 nails on its front foot, 4 on its back (C);

African, 4 nails on its front foot, 3 on back (D)

Indian Elephant

Tiger attacking Tapir

Mountain Lion or Puma

Jaguar

Except for the tapir pictured with the tiger, all the animals shown here belong to the order of *carnivores*, or flesh-eating mammals. And they do not eat anything apart from meat.

You have found out that there are food chains in the sea. In the same way, food chains can be traced all over the world. In an area where there are oak trees, acorns are eaten by mice, and mice are eaten by owls. In parts of Africa, grass is eaten by zebras, and zebras are eaten by lions. In the Arctic, plants are eaten by insects, insects by the ptarmigan, and the ptarmigan by the arctic fox. A food chain always begins with green plants. As a rule it ends with a meat-eating animal, in many cases one of the carnivores. The carnivores pictured here are some of the biggest meat-eaters.

There are many families of carnivores. One is the cat family. The tiger, the puma, and the jaguar are all big cats. The lion, the leopard, the bobcat, the ocelot, and the cheetah are other members of the cat family. The tiger is often called the fiercest of the carnivores, but the leopard is just as ferocious.

Coyote

Dhole

The dog family is another well-known group of carnivores. All the animals shown on this page belong in it. You may never have heard of some of them. The dhole and the raccoon dog live in Asia. The dingo is a wild dog only found in Australia. It is the only large native Australian mammal that is not a marsupial or monotreme. Some scientists think that it is descended from the domestic dog taken to Australia by people in prehistoric times and have given it the same scientific name—*Canis familiaris*—with 'dingo' added to distinguish it from all other domestic dogs.

Dingo

Red Fox Colour Variations

Raccoon

Grey Wolf

Ratel

Polecat

Civet

All the animals pictured here are carnivores, too. The ratel, the polecat and the skunk all belong to the weasel family. The others, too, are in this family.

The ratel is often called the honey badger. With its strong, sharp claws it can easily rip open a rotten tree trunk to get honey. The bird pictured with it is a honey guide. Honey guides find stores of honey and then lead ratels to them. The honey guides eat the honeycomb and the honey badgers the honey.

Polecats are like weasels, after which the family is named, and are in the same genus. So are minks. Ferrets are domesticated polecats and are used to hunt rabbits.

Skunks are well known for their way of protecting themselves. They shoot out a liquid with a disagreeable smell. As a rule, however, they go their own way and pay little attention to other animals except for the small ones they capture for food.

Spotted
Hyaena

Striped
Hyaena

Civets are often called civet cats. They do not belong to the cat family, but they are closely related to the cats. Civets are so ferocious that they are hard to handle. A material 'milked' from them is used in making perfumes.

Hyaenas usually only eat the meat which another carnivore has left behind. The striped hyaena will also dig up a corpse for food. But the spotted hyaena will occasionally attack a wounded animal, and a whole pack of hyaenas can attack and kill large animals.

Raccoons are easy to identify from their 'black masks'. These carnivores are very well known in North America. They are often called 'coons' for short. In spite of being much hunted, raccoons have been able to hold their own, partly because they will eat almost any kind of food. As a rule a raccoon dips its food in water before eating it.

Bears are like huge, tail-less dogs. The bear family is closely related to both the dog and the raccoon families. Like raccoons, bears will eat anything they can digest—fish, insects, berries, honey, and much else besides. Bears can move much faster than one would guess from their usually slow and lumbering way of walking.

Raccoon

Striped Skunk

American Black Bear

215

Hippopotamus

The story has already been told of how the horse, over millions of years, became a large animal that ran about on its middle toenails, which had developed into stout hoofs. There are many other hoofed mammals. Scientists call them *ungulates*.

All the hoofed mammals live on the ground. They are all plant-eaters.

Some hoofed mammals have either two or four toes on each foot. Since they have an even number of toes they are called *even-toed ungulates*. All the animals in these two pictures are in this order.

The group is tremendously important, for it has many of the animals that have helped man in it. It includes cattle, sheep and goats, and deer, as well as hippopotami, giraffes, and antelopes.

No animals in the group differ more in appearance than the squat hippopotamus and the long-legged, long-necked giraffe. These two also differ greatly in habits.

'Hippopotamus' means 'river horse'. The hippopotamus is not a close relative of the horse, but it does spend most of its time in rivers. It is one of the least beautiful of all mammals. Like the elephant and the whale, it has almost no hair. The mouth of this big plant-eater is enormous. And the animal has an appetite to match—a bushel of grass is only a taste. Strong tusklike teeth help it to dig up plants to eat.

Klipspringer

Springbok

Hippos, like many of the other hoofed mammals, form herds. A herd spends the daytime in the water, as a rule, and moves out at night to feed in the nearby grasslands.

A hippopotamus often floats in the water with only a small part of its face above the surface. Its beady eyes are raised above the rest of its face. So are its nostrils. Its ears stick up above the water, too. It is easy for the animal to breathe, hear and see what is going on.

A young hippopotamus is always a great attraction in a zoo. It looks tiny indeed beside its bulky mother.

The widespread toes of the hippopotamus are well suited for walking on muddy river bottoms and soft river banks. The hippopotamus can swim well. It is, moreover, one of the best swimmers of all the land mammals.

A giraffe is a most unusual looking animal. Its legs and its neck are so long that they make the giraffe the tallest animal in the world today—18 or 19 feet tall.

This 'animal on stilts' looks very awkward drinking at a water hole. It has to spread its front legs apart to get its head down to the water. But its long legs and neck are a big help to it in eating leaves on trees that other animals cannot reach.

The giraffe has a remarkable ability to go for long periods without water, but it cannot go without drinking as long as a camel can. Of course, it gets some water in the leaves it eats

The draught-board pattern on the giraffe's skin helps the animal to hide. It is like the pattern made by sunlight or moonlight shining down through trees.

If there is no chance to run away, a giraffe defends itself by kicking. With its powerful thigh muscles and big hoofs, it may kick hard enough to even kill a lion.

The klipspringer, springbok, and gnu are antelopes. One can tell antelopes apart by their horns. The klipspringer is one of the pygmy antelopes. The springbok belongs to the group of antelopes called gazelles. A gnu is one of the largest antelopes. It is as big as a cow.

Giraffes

Brindled Gnu

White-bearded Gnu

Red Deer

The red deer, as you would expect from its name, is in the deer family, a very large group of the even-toed ungulates. In most parts of the world, deer are among the commonest of wild animals. As you see, the red deer has antlers. All male deer do, but only female reindeer have antlers. The antlers are different from the horns of the buffalo, the yak and the Barbary sheep in a number of ways. One is that they are branched. Another is that they are shed each year. For the first few years, the new antlers that grow are larger and more branched than those of the year before.

Antlers can be so big that they are a handicap. A giant deer—the Irish elk—once lived in Europe and Asia. The antlers of this deer were the largest known. Except for fighting other males, they must have been a nuisance and a burden to carry about. The big deer died out, but no one really knows why.

Deer chew the cud. Because these animals depend chiefly on their speed to protect themselves from their carnivore enemies, a deer sometimes has to get its food 'on the run'. It swallows the food

Cape Buffalo

Water Buffalo

without chewing it. The food goes down into one division of the animal's stomach. Later, when the animal can rest, a ball of food comes back into its mouth as a cud. Many of the even-toed ungulates chew cud. Giraffes, camels, and all the cattle family do.

Throughout the centuries deer have proved very useful to man. They have provided food and skins for clothing. No deer has been more helpful than the reindeer. It is hard to see how the people of the far north could have lived without reindeer.

Yaks, buffaloes and sheep are in the cattle family. This big family also includes goats, antelopes and all those animals called cattle and oxen. The Cape buffalo from Africa is well known as a fierce attacker. The water buffalo has been used by man in south-eastern Asia for centuries to pull carts and ploughs. The yak is as important to the dwellers in the highlands of Tibet as the reindeer is to the people of the Arctic. The Barbary sheep lives in mountains in north Africa and is a remarkable climber.

The wild boar is in the pig family. It is a dangerous animal when protecting its young.

The alpaca is a member of the camel family. The camels, like so many of the even-toed ungulates, have been very useful to man. The alpaca lives high up in the mountains of South America. Its very long hair is shorn, like the wool of sheep. Then it is woven into blankets and clothes, which are very light and warm.

Yak

Barbary Sheep

Wild Boar

Alpaca

Young Squirrels

The *odd-toed ungulates* are the remnants of a once much larger group. Today they are greatly outnumbered by those with an even number of toes. The horse, as you know, is odd-toed. It runs on the middle hoof, or toenail, of each foot. In the order, too, are the ass, the zebra, the rhinoceros, and the tapir.

The ass and zebra are very close relatives of the horse. They belong to the same genus. They are all descendents of *Pliohippus,* the 'more-like-a-horse' of some 10 million years ago. The ass is found in Asia and Africa. It lives mainly in desert or mountainous areas. The zebra is an animal of the African grasslands.

The rhinoceros has had a long history.

Zebra

There were, you remember, many woolly rhinoceroses in Europe in the days of the mammoths and mastodons. And *Baluchitherium,* the biggest mammal ever to live on land, was a rhinoceros. Now the only rhinoceroses are found in Africa and south east Asia.

A rhinoceros has either one or two horns on its nose. A rhinoceros' horn is not made of real horn as a cow's horns are. It is a closely packed bundle of hair instead. The skin of a rhinoceros is very tough, so much so that 'as tough as rhinoceros hide' is a common expression. A rhinoceros has three hoofs on each foot.

India is the home of the great one-horned rhinoceros. The white rhinoceros, which is really grey in colour, lives in Africa. Among land mammals this big animal is second only to the elephant so far as size and weight are concerned. The hippopotamus weighs more but it is not strictly a land animal.

Zebras can be identified readily by their stripes. These stripes make the zebras hard to see in tall grass or against a background of bushes. But they do not keep them from being the chief food of the lions of Africa.

Tapirs, one of which you saw in a picture on page 212, have three hoofs on each foot. Tapirs are found in south east Asia and in South and Central America from Mexico southward. The broad, silvery-white band around the tapir pictured would seem to make the animal conspicuous, but actually it serves as a protection. This plant-eater feeds at night. On moonlight nights it is harder to see than if it were all dark or all light.

Squirrels belong in the order of *rodents,* the gnawing mammals—by far the largest of all the mammal orders. More than half of the thousands of species of mammals living today are in it. In addition to there being many species of rodents, there are often tremendous numbers of each species. Rodents multiply fast. Mice, for example, may have several litters a year, with five or six young in each. Some rodents grow up fast enough to have a litter of their own when they are only six weeks old.

Grey Squirrel

Rodents are found almost everywhere except in the sea. Some live on the ground, some under the ground, and some in the tops of trees. Some live in the water of swamps and streams. And some are so well adapted for living in desert lands that they never have to have any water to drink. Some hop, some run, some tunnel, and some are excellent swimmers or climbers. The flying squirrels even have flaps of skin which help them to glide through the air.

All rodents are well suited for gnawing and grinding tough food. They can move their jaws sideways and backwards and forwards as well as up and down. Their two pairs of front teeth have such sharp edges that they are like chisels. Their back teeth grind up the food their front teeth have cut off. Even steel chisels wear down. The rodents' sharp front teeth would soon wear down if they were like ours. But they are not. They keep growing at the base.

Great One-horned Rhinoceros

White Rhinoceros

221

Chinchilla

Some of these rodents you are almost sure to recognise. Rats and mice are common, and you may very well have had a hamster as a pet. You probably know the porcupines by their quills.

Chipmunks look rather like squirrels

Hamster

Voles, or Meadow Mice

but they live on the ground, and not in trees. Like hamsters, chipmunks have pouches in their cheeks. They can fill their pouches full of food and then carry it back to their nest or burrow.

The coypu and the marmot live in quite different kinds of places. The coypu builds its nest near water. Marmots dig their burrows on the lower slopes of mountains or on the dry steppe lands of central Europe.

The chinchilla lives in the very high mountains of South America. Many chinchillas are kept in captivity because they have valuable fur which is very soft and warm.

Of the rodents in the pictures the porcupine is the largest. But it is not the largest of all the gnawing mammals. The largest is the capybara. This pig-sized rodent lives in marshes and along streams of Central and South America. It eats plants growing in the water and along the river banks.

Porcupines are not very beautiful or playful. A common belief is that a porcupine shoots its quills when an enemy comes near. This is not true, but the quills become loose easily. An enemy attacking finds itself full of the barbed quills, which are almost impossible to pull out.

Some rodents are valuable furbearers. The fur of squirrels is pretty but not durable. Ranking much higher as furbearers are the chinchilla, muskrat and beaver. Another, the coypu of South America, is the source of the fur called nutria.

The villains among the rodents are the mice and rats. They destroy an enormous amount of food every year. Home owners have to wage a never-ending war against them in their houses. Farmers have to fight them in their storage barns and fields. Rats not only destroy property but also carry disease. The black rat spreads bubonic plague. To keep rats from travelling by ship from one country to another, all big ships are equipped with rat guards to stop these dangerous pests from coming aboard by running up the ropes that moor the ships to the docks.

White-footed Mouse

Coypu

Black Rat

Chipmunks

Prairie Dog

North American Porcupine

European Porcupine

223

The animals shown here all belong to the order of *primates*. The primates make up an enormous group. In it are all the apes and monkeys as well as many mammals less well known. We also are primates.

All the animals pictured on this page are Old World monkeys. There are New World monkeys, too. Many New World monkeys have long tails which serve as extra hands.

The chimpanzee, gibbon, orang-utan, and gorilla are manlike apes. They are man's closest relatives in the animal world. All of them are intelligent. Africa is the home of the chimpanzee and gorilla. The gibbon and orang-utan come from south east Asia and the islands nearby. These big apes are all tree dwellers, but some spend more time on the ground than others.

Of the four, chimpanzees are the best known. They do well in captivity and are able to learn many tricks. A number of specially trained chimps have made flights in space.

The gibbons and orang-utans seldom come down from the trees. Gibbons are much smaller than chimpanzees. Their arms are so long that when a gibbon stands erect its hands touch the ground. An orang-utan has a face like the face of an old man. At times orang-utans act rather like people.

The gorilla is heavier than any of the other manlike apes. It looks fierce and is remarkably strong, but for the most part it is peaceable. This big ape may build a platform of branches in trees to serve as a nest for the night, but it spends much of its time on the ground. It walks on all fours.

Barbary Ape

Mandrill

Proboscis Monkey

Rhesus Monkey

Baboon

Chimpanzee

Gibbon

Orang-utan

Gorilla

Warthog

Babirusa

Armadillo

You may never have heard of some of these strange animals.

Two—the armadillo and the sloth—you may remember are relatives of the giant anteater. They all live in South and Central America. Armadillos are well armoured. They can curl up in their armour if in danger. Armadillos mainly eat insects. Sloths spend most of their lives hanging from branches of trees. They feed on the leaves. Tiny plants growing in their fur make these slow-moving creatures hard to see in the trees.

The warthog and babirusa are members of the pig family. It is not easy to say which one is uglier. The warthog lives in Africa, the babirusa in islands of the East Indies.

The okapi is a close relative of the giraffe. Its home in Africa is in jungle regions so long unexplored that a hundred years ago no scientist knew of this large animal's existence.

'Aardvark' means 'earth pig'. Sometimes aardvarks are called ant bears. But they are neither pigs nor bears. They belong in an order all their own. They are found only in Africa. Aardvarks live in burrows and seldom come out except to find food. Although nearly six feet long, they mainly live on termites or white ants. Their strong claws help them rip termite nests apart.

The flying lemur pictured lives in the forests of south east Asia. Flying lemurs are not lemurs, which are primates, and they cannot fly. They are often put in an order of their own. But some scientists place them with the moles and shrews. Although flying lemurs cannot fly, they

Aardvark

Flying Lemur

can glide more than a hundred feet.

The giant panda and the ringtail are grouped with the carnivores. The panda lives in high bamboo forests in Asia. Most carnivores, as you know, eat other animals, but the panda in its native home only eats bamboo shoots. The ringtail does eat flesh. It is a close relative of the raccoon. So it has been thought, is the giant panda. But some scientists think it may be just what it looks to be—a bear.

The slow loris of Africa and the aye-aye of Madagascar are primates. They are, then, relatives of the monkeys, apes and man.

Two-toed Sloth

Giant Panda

Ringtail

Slow Loris

Aye-aye

Okapi

Man is proud of the great dams he has built. He has a right to be. But he cannot claim to be the first dam builder. Beavers were building dams long before there were any people. By damming small streams they form ponds that provide building places for their homes. Colonies of beavers work together in building dams. With their sharp, strong teeth they fell trees near the water's edge, cut them into pieces, and float them into place. They then plaster the logs together with mud.

Early settlers in North America found the thick fur of beavers very useful for making warm clothing. Trappers killed beavers by the millions and made fortunes from the skins. It seemed that there were enough beavers for this to go on for a very long time. People had the same idea about other animals too. But this idea proved to be wrong. The beaver and many other mammals are now scarce. The bison, which roamed over much of North America in enormous herds before the coming of white settlers, has all but disappeared. So, too, has the pronghorn, another hoofed mammal once almost as numerous as the bison.

Moose do not form big herds as the bison and pronghorn do. They were never seen in such numbers. But they, too, used to be much more common than they are now. Cutting down woods destroyed their homes and they have been hunted too freely in the past. Almost the only places where moose, bison and pronghorn live today are national parks, where hunting is forbidden and the animals are protected.

The mass killing of beavers had some results which people did not connect with beavers for some time. By damming up small streams to form ponds, beavers make the water from heavy rains and melting snow run off much more slowly than it would otherwise. With few beavers left to build dams, the water raced down the streams into the rivers carrying away much of the good soil and causing floods in the lowlands. The value of the land ruined was far greater than the value of the beaverskins. Now beavers are being encouraged in many places as a way of saving the soil and preventing floods.

The story of the American bison is another sad story. When early settlers

Beaver

Pronghorn

American Bison

Moose

Lion

Oryx of Arabia

Numbat, or Banded Anteater

Thamin, or Brow-antlered Deer

Tasmanian Wolf

Javan Rhinoceros

moved westward over the Great Plains the killing of bison—or, as they are commonly called buffaloes—by the thousands began. Buffalo robes kept many people warm in winter. The meat of the buffalo made good food. The tongue was considered a special delicacy. Buffaloes were once so plentiful that sometimes when one was killed only the tongue was eaten.

At the same time that bison were being killed by the thousands for their hides and their meat, their homes and food were being taken away from them by the ploughing of the plains where they roamed. Big herds were reduced to little herds and little herds were reduced to nothing. But just in time, reservations, where buffaloes live undisturbed, were set up for them. Now there are thousands of bison in the herds on reservations.

Other wild mammals have been killed in great numbers for fun or for fur or for food. Fortunately, there are now game laws in most countries and they are helping many wild mammals to hold their own.

The pictures on this page show a few of the other mammals that are in danger of disappearing.

The Tasmanian wolf, found today only in the mountains of Tasmania, is perhaps the rarest mammal in the world. It is a marsupial and therefore not a wolf at all. At times it bounds away like a kangaroo.

Another marsupial in danger of extinction is the numbat of Australia. Unlike most marsupials it has no pouch for its young.

All the Javan rhinoceroses left are on a government preserve. People for centuries killed the rhinoceros and made the horns into powder for medicines.

In a forest in India the only remaining lions in Asia are being protected. The natives used to kill lions because they were a danger to their livestock. Besides, Indian maharajas hunted lions for sport.

The oryx is an antelope. Today the Arabian Oryx only lives in the almost lifeless desert of Rub'al Khali and even there it is being hunted from cars and aeroplanes.

Polar Bear

The thamin of Burma has been killed in great numbers for food. Also the swamps and marshes in which it lives have been drained, to be used as farm land.

The polar bear has been a successful dweller of the Arctic with its perpetual ice and snow. Sportsmen long found the region where it lives difficult to reach. Now, however, they can fly in aeroplanes over the polar bear's forbidding homeland and hunt it down. This big bear is in grave danger of being killed off.

The sperm whale is a living oil tank. Oil it produces from its food is stored in its tanklike head. This whale was once very important for it provided oil for lamps and fat for candles. Hundreds of whaling vessels went out each year to hunt it. Sometimes the whalers found ambergris, a waxy substance produced by sperm whales from indigestible parts of their food. Ambergris is used in perfumes. With the discovery of petroleum the need for whale oil lessened, so a number of nations have banded together to try to save the giant whales. But they could become extinct in future.

Sperm Whale

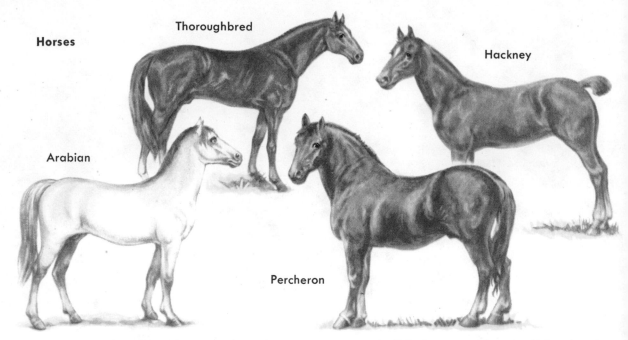

Horses

Thoroughbred

Hackney

Arabian

Percheron

Our early ancestors lived very simply. Their main weapons were crude axes made of stone. They depended on the skins of wild animals for clothing and their only way of getting food was to gather wild plants and hunt wild animals. But their whole way of living was changed when they at last found that they could domesticate some plants and animals and raise them as they needed them. No longer did they have to spend practically all their time in search of food.

Without question, most domesticated animals were first thought of as a source of food—even horses may have been kept first for their meat and milk. But they served many other purposes, too. They provided skins and wool for clothing, they helped with hunting and with tilling the soil, and they carried people and their burdens from place to place. Besides, they guarded property and became

Mule

Pony

Dairy Cattle

Ayrshire

Guernsey

Brown Swiss

Jersey Calf

Friesian

man's close friends and companions.

No one knows the exact order in which animals were domesticated. The order in which our common domesticated mammals were tamed is believed to be this: dog, pig, cow, sheep, goat, donkey, horse, cat.

In the several thousand years since these animals were first domesticated, man has changed them in many ways. He has developed different breeds of animals to serve special purposes or to suit them for living in particular regions.

The many breeds of horses can be classed as draught horses developed for size and strength, light horses developed for speed and beauty, and small horses, or ponies. With the coming of cars, horses, especially work horses and carriage ponies, lost much of their importance. The horse breeders in many countries today are most interested in racehorses, hunters and jumpers.

Arabian horses are the oldest of the breeds of light horses. And almost all our modern breeds have Arabian somewhere in their ancestry. Many people, when they hear that a horse is a Thoroughbred, think that it is simply a horse with good breeding. But Thoroughbred is the name of one distinct breed. Most horses that take part in running races are Thoroughbreds.

The mule is a cross between the horse and the donkey. Such a cross is called a hybrid. It is very hardy and can work very well in hot dry climates.

Cattle have been developed along two lines: better meat production and better milk production. The pictures show five popular breeds of dairy cattle. The oldest breed is Brown Swiss. Its ancestry can be traced back to the cattle raised by the Swiss Lake Dwellers of the New Stone Age. Among the best beef breeds are the Angus, Hereford, Shorthorn, Brahman, Africander, and Charolais. The Red Poll and the Milking Shorthorn are two popular breeds developed to provide both milk and beef.

Sheep

Cheviot Lamb

Hampshire

Merino

Karakul

For tens of centuries shepherds and their flocks have been an important part of the life of many lands. There are still, especially in regions of Asia, shepherds and flocks. But most sheep today are on farms and ranches.

Probably man first tamed sheep for their milk and their skins. Later he found that without killing the sheep he could shear the wool and weave it into cloth. He found, too, that the flesh of sheep is good to eat.

There are now many breeds of sheep. Some are kept for their wool. The world uses more than $2\frac{1}{2}$ million tons of wool a year. Some breeds provide fur, and some are mostly reared for meat. The meat from a sheep less than a year old is called lamb. That from an older sheep is called mutton.

The Hampshire and Cheviot are among the breeds kept in Britain. They are chiefly bred for meat. Their wool is only a few inches long. The Merino is chiefly bred for its wool, which is several inches long. It is also finer than the wool of most other breeds of sheep. Most of the wool from Australia comes from Merino sheep.

The Karakul is a breed common in parts of Asia. The skins of lambs of this breed are made into the furs called caracul, Persian lamb, and broadtail.

Many of the sheep raised in Asia and North Africa have long, heavy tails. They are known as fat-tailed sheep because they store a great deal of fat in their tails. The Karakul, in fact, is a fat-tailed breed. Its tail, however, is not nearly so long as the tails of many sheep in the group.

Fat-tailed sheep can be raised in regions that are dry and barren for long periods. When food is scarce the animals live on the fat stored in their tails. The fat is important to the people who keep these sheep for another reason. The fat from the tails is made into a kind of butter when the sheep are killed.

Goats are much like sheep. Some are kept chiefly for their milk, others for their hair and wool. The Kashmir, a long-haired goat, provides the soft wool

Pigs

Spotted Poland China

Hampshire

Chester White

Tamworth

used for the expensive cashmere sweaters and coats.

The pictures above show four breeds of pigs, popular with farmers in various parts of the world. Until about 25 years ago all pig breeds were divided into two groups, lard pigs and bacon pigs. The lard pigs were those that fattened easily. Their fat was made into lard, much used in cooking. The bacon pigs were those that had less fat and therefore leaner meat. Today cooking fats made from the seeds of such plants as corn, soybeans, and groundnuts have partly taken the place of lard. Now, therefore, most pigs are chiefly raised for their meat. The four pictured are all good meat animals. At agricultural experiment stations, today's breeds are always being crossed to produce better ones. Ways of keeping pigs free from disease and making them grow even faster are being worked out, too.

Bacon is only one of the meats we get from pigs. Ham, pork chops, roast pork and sausages are others. The popular frankfurter, or hot dog, is usually partly pork.

A football is often made from pigskin. Pigskin makes good leather for gloves, luggage, jackets, belts, wallets, saddles, and many other things besides footballs. Pig bristles are used in brushes. In parts of Europe and Asia pigs are trained to dig up truffles, delicious mushrooms that grow underground. But few farmers anywhere would keep pigs if it were not for the meat these animals provide.

Pigs are often thought of as very dirty animals, but they like living in clean conditions. They only get covered in mud and dirt when they cannot keep themselves clean.

Grey Dutch Rabbit

Guinea Pigs

Short-haired

Rough-haired

Long-haired

Blue Persian

Many breeds of rabbits have been developed as food animals. Rabbits are popular pets, too. The white rabbit, often seen as a pet, is an albino. An albino

Cats

Shorthair Tabby

Siamese

Black Manx

Red Persian

is an animal which, for some reason, has its natural pigment, or colouring, missing. As a rule the eyes are pink. Many rabbits are bred for their fur or for the making of felt.

Guinea pigs, which are not related to true pigs, are small tail-less rodents that make good pets. They are among the easiest of pets to take care of. Guinea pigs are also used by scientists in experiments and tests. They have been so much used in this way that 'being a guinea pig' means being used in an experiment.

Cats have been developed almost entirely as pets. They are good mouse catchers, but breeders have done nothing to develop better mousers. They have put all their efforts into getting more interesting-looking and beautiful cats. Cats can be divided into long-haired and short-haired varieties.

The Persians are long-haired cats. Some of them are often called Angoras. They have been developed in more than 20 different colour types. The common tabby and the Manx, both short-haired cats, also come in many colours. Manx cats are tail-less. The aristocratic Siamese, with its beautiful markings, the Abyssinian, the Burmese, the Havana brown and the Russian blue are other short-haired breeds, and some are very valuable animals.

There are well over 115 breeds of dogs —more than of any other domesticated animal. Visitors at dog shows are almost always surprised at the number of breeds on exhibition. The wild ancestors of our dogs today, scientists think, were wolflike. Some of our modern breeds still look more like wolves than they look like certain other modern breeds of dogs. An Alsatian for example, looks more like a wolf than like a chihuahua does.

Probably we have so many breeds because dogs serve so many different purposes. They guard property, help in hunting, pull loads, guide the blind, destroy rats, herd sheep and cattle, help find persons that are lost, and make wonderful companions. Some are bred especially for racing. There are big dogs and little ones, long-haired and short-

Dogs

Springer Spaniel

Smooth-coated Chihuahua

Poodle

Wire-haired Fox Terrier

Basset Hound

Collie

haired dogs, sedate dogs and playful ones, and dogs of different colours. There is a dog to suit the taste of almost everyone.

All the many breeds are classified into six groups: working dogs, toy dogs, sporting dogs, non-sporting dogs, hounds and terriers. Of the dogs pictured here, the springer spaniel is a sporting dog, the chihuahua a toy, and the poodle is a non-sporting dog. The wire fox terrier belongs, as you know, to the terriers and the basset to the hounds. The collie is a working dog on many farms.

Arabian Camel

Animal Adaptations

Every animal has its natural home. It is fitted for living there. The ways it is fitted for living there may make it entirely unfitted for living in another kind of place. A camel is not fitted for living in marshland any more than a crane is fitted for spending its life in a desert. A bat and a mole would certainly be misfits if they changed places with each other.

An animal's natural living place is called its *habitat*. The ways living things are fitted for their particular habitat are called *adaptations to environment*.

The camel is adapted in many ways for life in a desert. It has been used for travelling across deserts, especially those of North Africa and Arabia, for so long that it is often called the 'ship of the desert'. Travel in such deserts is not easy. The places where there is water to drink are far apart. It is hard to walk on loose sand, and sometimes sand is blown about in terrible sandstorms. Desert plants, where there are any at all to serve as food, are small and often bitter and thorny. But such hardships as these are

Sandhill Crane

not too great for a camel's endurance.

Camels do not have to have water as often as most mammals do. They can drink a great deal at one time. Records show that a thirsty camel may drink 20 gallons or more. Some of the water a camel drinks is stored in special cells in its stomach for later use. After a camel has had all the water it wants, it can go for days without drinking. It does not lose water by sweating the way we do in hot weather.

Camels can store up food, too, in their bodies. Their food storehouses are their humps. The food stored is mostly fat. When there is nothing to eat, a camel can live on the fat in its hump.

A camel's lips are covered with tough skin, and its teeth are strong. It can eat thorny desert plants unfit for most mammals.

Its spreading, thickly padded feet keep a camel from sinking into loose sand. The camel's hair is a protection from both heat and cold. Many people think of camels as animals of hot deserts only, but the two-humped, or Bactrian, camel of the desert regions of central Asia often has to endure extreme cold. Long eyelashes keep sun and sand out of a camel's eyes. Hairs in its ears shut out sand. Its nose can be closed during a sandstorm.

The heron lives in marshy areas and like many other birds that live on marshes it has very long legs and large feet, so that it can wade through the soft mud and water. It has a long, strong bill suitable for catching the fish, frogs and water insects on which it feeds.

A bat is adapted for life in the air. Its wings are made of tough skin stretched between its back legs and tail and its

Little Brown Bat

very, very long fingers. Its wings are so big in proportion to its body that it almost floats in the air.

A bat's legs end in sharp claws. With them it can climb rock walls or branches of trees. To sleep, a bat hangs itself upside down by its claws from the wall or ceiling of a cave, an old building, or a cavity in a tree trunk. Some bats can fold up their wings and run about on all fours.

Most bats do their flying about in search of food after dark and avoid bright light by sleeping during the day-time. Bats have beady little eyes. There is no truth to the saying 'blind as a bat', for it is not their eyes that bats depend on for getting about at night. Instead, it is an astonishing adaptation—a sonar system. As it flies, a bat makes sounds too high-pitched for us to hear. But the echoes of these sounds as they bounce off obstacles in the bat's path tell it where to fly. In this way the bat avoids bumping into things, even in pitch darkness.

Moles spend practically all their time underground, a little way beneath the surface. A mole has fur that is like thick velvet. This fur can be brushed forwards or backwards and still be smooth. It allows the mole to move either forwards or backwards through the ground easily.

From its home in the ground a mole digs tunnels in all directions. It can dig a

Mole

Mountain Goat

present. A bat's habitat differs from a mole's chiefly in its relation to the surface of the earth. There are many other important ways in which habitats can differ. Temperature, light, pressure, amount of oxygen, and the nature of the ground surface are among them. Plant and animal populations vary, too. It makes a great deal of difference to an animal what plants and animals share its living place.

The two habitats shown here differ in many ways. The mountain goat lives high up in the Rocky Mountains of North America. The mountainsides are very steep and difficult. The animals shown on the facing page live on the vast plains in the heart of Africa.

The home of the mountain goat is higher above sea level than the home of these African animals. The air is rarer. With each breath it takes, a mountain goat gets less oxygen than it would get if it were breathing the denser air nearer sea level. The average temperature of the mountain goat's habitat is much lower than on the African plains. The air pressure is lower, too.

Mountain goats live above the timber line. No large plants grow there. Not many other animals live there either. The mountain goat does not have to share the little food that can be found. Neither does it have to escape from many enemies.

The African animals would certainly be misfits in the habitat of the mountain goat. The mountain goat has a thick coat of hair. It is very surefooted. The elephant, on the other hand, has almost no hair and its heavy legs and big feet would not be able to climb the steep slopes. Neither the elephant nor the monkeys would be at home in a treeless region. And the lion could not live without such animals as giraffes and zebras for food.

Even in the sea, where conditions are much more uniform than on land, there is a great variety of habitat. But different as different parts of the earth are, there are some animals adapted to all but the very coldest and driest places and those made unfit by poisonous gases.

tunnel without difficulty. Its pointed nose works a little like a snowplough. Its big front feet are excellent shovels. The long, strong claws on its front feet are a great help in digging, too. In a single night a mole, which is only about six inches long, has been known to dig a tunnel of nearly 100 yards. As it digs its tunnels, the mole finds insect larvae and earthworms for food.

Although most moles have eyes to see with, some have eyes covered with skin. Good eyesight is not especially useful to an animal that spends its life in the dark.

A camel's habitat differs from a crane's chiefly in the amount of moisture

At a water-hole in the African Bush

White Pelican

Comman Frog

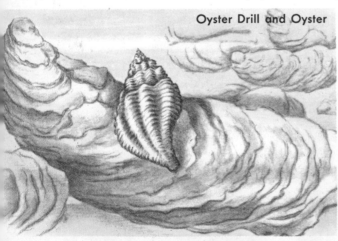

Oyster Drill and Oyster

Sea Anemone

Animals are adapted to live in different kinds of places. They are also built to eat food of different kinds and to get it in different ways.

The white pelican eats fish. It has a built-in fishing net. As it swims through the water, it scoops up small fish with the pouch fastened to its lower bill. It lets the water drain away and then swallows its freshly-caught fish dinner.

The pouch on its bill also serves as a soup bowl for the young pelicans. The adult birds fill their pouches with a sort of fish soup from their stomachs. The young birds stick their bills into the bills of the parent birds to drink the fish soup. A young bird's head may be almost completely hidden inside its parent's bill.

The pelican has webbed feet that enable it to swim fast enough to catch fish. Its strong wings carry it to feeding grounds.

The common frog has a long, sticky tongue. It is excellent for catching insects. The tongue is fastened at the front rather than at the back. When the frog flips its tongue back with an insect sticking to it, the insect is carried far down its throat so that it is easily swallowed.

Oysters are good food for many animals of the sea as well as for us. You may remember how starfish, with their tube-feet, pull open an oyster's shell a little way and then push their stomachs inside to eat the soft body of the oyster. Oyster drills, too, are great enemies of oysters. The oyster drill is a kind of sea snail. The way it eats oysters is quite different from the way a starfish does. The oyster drill does not have to pull on an oyster's shell to open up a crack. It could not possibly do so. Like all snails it has a long, filelike tongue, or radula. By means of its radula, the oyster drill can drill a hole through the oyster's hard shell. After it has drilled the hole, it scrapes out the oyster's body little by little and eats it.

The oyster itself is one of the animals that must wait for food to come to them. It strains food material from the water that flows in and out of its shell.

The sea anemone is another animal that lies and waits. A sea anemone, unlike the oyster, does not completely lose the power of moving about, but it can only move slowly. An animal as slow would have a poor chance of getting enough food if it tried to catch it the way a pelican does. Instead, the sea anemone uses its tentacles. It shoots out poison threads at any animal that comes close enough to touch a tentacle. Then its tentacles bring the paralysed prey to its mouth. The anemone can even catch fish in this way.

Mussels also can creep slowly about, but most of the time they stay anchored in place by fine threads they secrete. They get food the same way that an oyster does.

A lugworm in its burrow gets its food from the sand and mud at the bottom of the water. It swallows a lump of this food material every few seconds for a minute or so. Then it takes a short rest before beginning again. The worm digests the plant and animal material in the mud and sand it has swallowed and expels the rest. It spends most of the time eating.

A barnacle once settled on its rock can

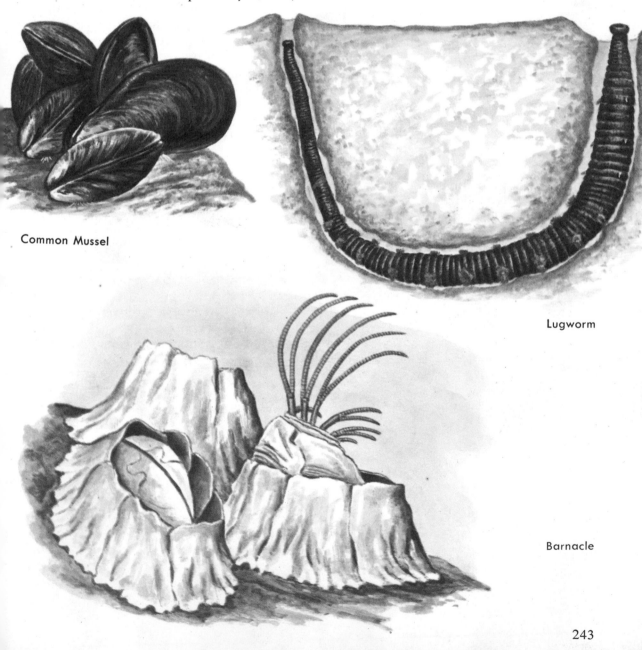

Common Mussel

Lugworm

Barnacle

Bird Bills

Duck

Tern

Eagle

Forest Kingfisher

Chaffinch

Hummingbird

is found at the bottom of the tube. The hummingbird's bill is long enough and slender enough to reach down into such flowers. The tongue has its edges rolled inward so that it becomes a double 'drinking straw'. The bird sucks the nectar up through it. The hummingbird often gets some tiny insects along with the nectar. They are important to its diet.

To drink the nectar the hummingbird must be able to hover in one spot for a time. It is able to do so by beating its wings up and down very fast—so fast that they make the hum that gives the bird its name. This bird is not only able to hover over a flower but can also fly backwards—a feat very rare among birds.

As you know, seeds, insects, toads and frogs, lizards, and small mammals are among the other things birds eat. Every bird has a bill adapted to getting the kind of food it needs. The pictures on the left

never travel anywhere on its own. It uses its featherlike legs to kick tiny animals into its mouth.

A hummingbird's bill is about as different from a pelican's as a bill could be. It is adapted for eating an entirely different kind of food. The hummingbird drinks nectar from flowers. Some of the flowers that produce nectar have their petals joined to form a tube. The nectar

Ruby-throated Hummingbird

244

show how different are the bills of a duck, tern, eagle, kingfisher and chaffinch compared with the bill of a hummingbird.

Flamingo

Both terns and kingfishers are fish-eaters. It may surprise you that their bills are not like the pelican's. The reason is that, instead of scooping up fish as the pelican does, they dive into the water and catch one fish at a time.

The duck pictured finds some of its food in shallow water and some on land. From the mud at the bottom of the water it gets snails and plant roots. It also eats leaves of floating plants. Waste grain and the seeds of grasses provide food for it, too.

The eagle has a bill adapted for tearing apart such animals as rabbits, squirrels, and mice. It is a typical bird-of-prey bill. The chaffinch is a seed-eater. Its short, thick bill is good for cracking seeds.

A flamingo eats a great assortment of food it finds in shallow water—tiny one-celled plants, worms, insect larvae and crustaceans mixed together into a muddy soup. The bird holds its bill upside down as it takes in a mouthful of the soup. Then its lower bill and its tongue push down to squeeze out some of the water before the flamingo swallows the food.

Oxpeckers eat ticks, which are relatives of spiders that bury their heads in the skin of animals and suck blood. It is not easy to pull out a feeding tick. An oxpecker has short legs, sharp claws, and pointed tail feathers that help it stay in place on an animal's back and sides as it pulls out ticks with its broad, thick bill. After it pulls one out and swallows it, it sips up the blood that comes from the wound. The oxpeckers always repay the rhinoceroses and other animals they get their food from, by giving loud warning cries when an enemy is approaching. Of course, it is also a help to an animal to get rid of its ticks.

In the animal kingdom we find countless other adaptations for finding food. The long neck of the giraffe, the big pincers of the lobster, the trunk of the elephant, the giant anteater's long snout and very long, sticky tongue, and the spinnerets with which spiders spin webs that serve as insect traps are only a few of them.

Oxpeckers on Rhinoceroses

Mallard Ducks
Migrating

Many animals have habits which can be thought of as adaptations. Migration is one of them.

Very many birds, as you already know, have summer homes in one region and winter homes in another. They migrate, or make the journey between their two home areas, twice each year. Many birds fly at night and are not seen as they migrate. Others are so small that no one notices them high in the air. But flocks of such big birds as ducks and wild geese, flying northwards or southwards, are common sights in spring and autumn,

and their calls as they pass overhead are familiar sounds. Often migrating birds fly in a V pattern.

In their migrations birds may travel long distances. The arctic tern is the champion bird traveller. It nests as far to the north as there are islands in the Arctic. Healthy young terns have been found in nests partly covered with snow. The bird winters far to the south, chiefly on islands off the Antarctic coast. The terns that nest farthest north and winter farthest south have to make an 11,000-mile journey every spring and autumn.

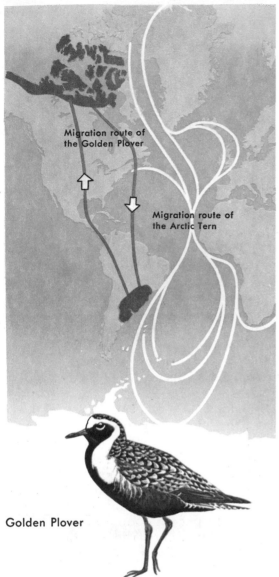

Migration route of
the Golden Plover

Migration route of
the Arctic Tern

Golden Plover

Arctic Tern

The golden plover is another famous bird traveller. It spends its summers in northern Canada and Alaska, as the map shows, and then flies nonstop over the Atlantic to Argentina for the winter.

Some birds that migrates like the little wren only travel short distances. There are other small birds that make long and difficult journeys. The swallows are examples of small birds that make very long journeys when they migrate. Each spring they leave northern Africa and fly to Europe, crossing the Sahara Desert and the Mediterranean Sea.

In many ways bird migration is a puzzle. How did it come about? Did it start in the Ice Age? Why do some birds migrate while others do not? Why do some travel so much farther than others? What tells them where to go? And how do they find their way?

No one knows the answers to these questions. But one thing about migration is certain. It lets the birds that migrate live under better conditions than they could have if they stayed all year round in one place. Swifts, which live almost entirely on insects, spend the whole year in regions where insects are plentiful. Mallards, which feed partly on marshland plants, are able to be where plants are growing all the year round. The arctic tern by its long journeys gets more hours of daylight in a year than any other living creature. By migrating, birds also escape severe cold.

No one should think that birds run no risks in making long journeys. They meet many dangers in their travels—storms, enemies, and the chance of killing themselves by flying into obstacles. But the advantages outweigh the dangers.

Swallow

Monarch Butterfly

Although birds are the most famous animal migrants, many other animals travel periodically from one region to another. The monarch butterfly of North America is one of them.

Towards the end of summer, monarchs form flocks and fly south. Their journey is leisurely, but some of them travel several hundred miles. In the spring they start moving northwards one by one. But most of them fall by the wayside. The monarchs that arrive in the north are mostly young butterflies produced from eggs laid by the females on the northward journey.

Reindeer

Reindeer spend the summer in arctic regions north of the timber line. Their food is chiefly reindeer moss. In July they begin to move southwards in large herds to the edge of the forests. In the spring they move northwards again. The reindeer push on even if they meet danger. Often great numbers of these deer are drowned in trying to cross flooded streams.

Bluefin tuna spend the winters in deep water out in the Atlantic. At egg-laying time, in the spring, they move into the Caribbean. They swim westwards to the warm Gulf Stream and follow it northwards. When they reach Nova Scotia in Canada it is autumn and time to move out into deeper water once more.

The salmon and the eels are great travellers, too. Their round-trip travels, however, are not completed in one year. The salmon begins its life far from the coast in the tributaries of rivers, spending up to three years there. Then it travels downstream and out into the sea. There it lives until it becomes adult and reaches the breeding stage. It now travels back up the stream it travelled down when it was young. It may have to cross dangerous rapids and leap up waterfalls. After it has gone up the river, eggs are laid and fertilised. Then the salmon dies. It thus begins and ends its life in fresh water.

The story of the European and American eel is similar to the story of the salmon but the other way round. Both eels begin life in the Atlantic in the region called the Sargasso Sea. Young eels all

Salmon

look very much alike. As you see from the picture, they are almost transparent. They differ greatly in shape, too, from adult eels.

When they are still too young to look much like fish, they start swimming towards shore. The young European eel swims towards Europe and the young American eel towards America. No one knows what guides them.

Their journey takes months or even years. When they reach land they travel up rivers. They live for several years in fresh water. But sooner or later every eel gets a call to travel down to the sea. Many get the call at the same time. They travel to the Sargasso Sea and lay and fertilise their eggs. But they do not live to return to fresh water.

August—September

ATLANTIC OCEAN

fish dispersed

fish concentrated

May—June

Breeding area— American Eel

Breeding area— European Eel

Bluefin Tuna

Young Eels

Bear in Winter Sleep

they are so quiet that they need little oxygen. Their hearts beat very slowly.

Snakes and salamanders hibernate under rocks or old logs. Toads hibernate in the same kinds of places or in mud at the bottom of a pond. The queen bumblebee hides herself somewhere in the earth, in bark, or inside buildings. Earthworms crawl deeper in the ground.

But hibernation is not limited to cold-blooded animals. Almost no birds hibernate, but many animals do. The squirrel and the dormouse are very well-known hibernators.

The little dormouse gets its name from the French word *dormir*, which means 'to sleep'. It is well named, for it actually

Some animals are able to survive in regions of cold winters because they hibernate. Hibernation can be thought of as a kind of very deep sleep.

Many cold-blooded animals die when winter comes on, and leave only their eggs to endure the cold. Those that do live through very cold weather do so by hibernating. No one sees frogs or snakes or salamanders where ponds are frozen and snow covers the ground. No one sees earthworms, butterflies or bumblebees either.

Frogs bury themselves in mud, often at the bottom of a pond. Before beginning their winter sleep they store food in their bodies by eating a great deal. While they are hibernating they eat nothing at all. They only breathe through their skins—

Red Squirrel

Hedgehog

sleeps for about seven months of every year. A dormouse stuffs itself with nuts and insects during the summer so that it is very fat when it begins its hibernation in a hole in a tree or the ground. During its sleep it is so quiet that it looks as if it were dead. And its body is cold—only a little above freezing. In the spring it takes the dormouse hours to come wide awake. Hedgehogs hibernate too. They build a nest of leaves under a hedgerow and sleep there until the following spring.

Squirrels also eat a great deal before

Queen Bee

Dormouse

they begin hibernation. They sleep curled up in a tight ball, in their warm nests high up in the trunk of a tree. Unlike the dormouse, squirrels may wake up on warmer days during the winter and leave their nests. The squirrels look for something to eat and they try to find some of the stores of nuts and acorns they had buried in the autumn. Often they cannot remember where all their food is hidden but they can usually find enough. When the weather becomes colder the squirrels go back to sleep again.

Many bears sleep through the winter, but their sleep is not like the deathlike sleep of the dormouse and the hedgehog. They may wake up from time to time and move about. Their temperature, their heartbeat, and their rate of breathing are about the same as during the rest of the year. Their winter sleep is a sort of half-hibernation, like the squirrels.

Many warm-blooded animals that do not hibernate have snug burrows or nests where they stay most of the time in winter. They only come out to look for food.

The African lungfish does not need to escape from cold. Its chief problem is to survive the drying up in summer of the ponds where it lives. When the water gets low, the fish crawls into the soft mud. It then builds itself a cocoon by mixing the mud around it with a slimy material it secretes. This fish has both gills and lungs. While in its cocoon it only breathes with its lungs. A tiny tunnel close to the fish's mouth lets in air. The fish waits in its ball of mud till the rains come again. Then it wriggles out into the water.

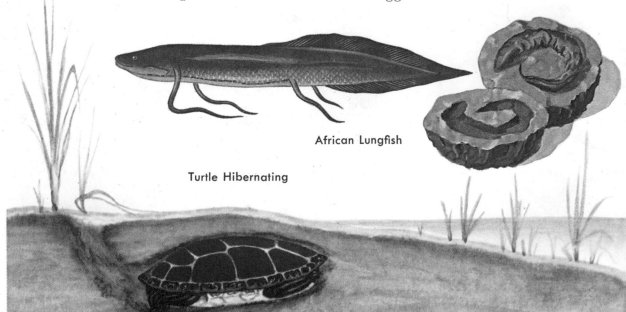

African Lungfish

Turtle Hibernating

Bitterns

The polar bear is an example of an animal that is greatly helped by its colour. The polar bear has no meat-eating enemies. It is the biggest carnivore in the Arctic, where it lives all the year round. But food is not very abundant there. The big white bear lives chiefly on seals and fish. It also eats birds occasionally and birds' eggs. Since it matches its surroundings so well, it can often creep up on the animal it is trying to catch without being seen. It can pounce on a seal, for example, before the seal knows than an enemy is near.

The pictures show a number of other animals that blend into their surroundings. Of those at the bottom of this page, the arctic hare and the kangaroo rat are common prey of carnivores that share their habitat. How clearly these two would stand out if they were to change places!

The kit fox, the stoat, and the jaguar are carnivores. Matching their surroundings helps these animals to get their food. Any of these three in the habitat of one of the others would be so easy to see that it would probably be starving most of the time.

Many animals that live in tall grass, thickets or woods are striped or spotted. As you see, the stripes and spots on their breasts help bitterns to hide. These birds get protection, too, from their way of freezing into position with their long

The main requirement of survival among animals is being able to eat without being eaten. The colour of an animal is a great help for it can make the animal blend into its surroundings so that it cannot be seen easily. Its colour may be a great protection against its enemies. It may also be a help in getting the food it needs.

Ermine

Kit Fox

Arctic Hare

Kangaroo Rat

Jaguar

bills pointing upward when an enemy is nearby.

Fawns, with their spots, are protected from carnivores in much the same way. Their spots match the spots of brightness made by sunlight shining through the trees and keep them from showing clearly as they lie still among the bracken. The spots and stripes of giraffes and zebras, too, as you already know, help to hide them from enemies. The jaguar's spots on the other hand, hide it from its prey.

Trout

Praying Mantis

The general colour plan of fishes is a good one for protection. A fish, as a rule, is darker above than below. Look at the picture of the trout. A fish-eating animal looking down at the water may not see a fish there because the fish's back blends into the depths of the river or lake or sea so well. A fish-eating animal swimming below it may not see the fish because its light underside is no different from the colour of the sky as seen from underwater.

The praying mantis has a great reputation as a destroyer of other insects. It would be much less successful if its colour did not help it to hide while it stalks its prey.

There is one puzzle about protective colouring. Why should an animal that matches the colour of its surroundings almost perfectly have some differences in colour that spoil the perfect matching? Why, for example, should the almost pure white arctic hare have black tips on its ears? And why should the kit fox and the ermine have black tips on their tails? Even the polar bear has a black nose!

Like the polar bear, many of the warm-blooded animals that live the year round in the far north are white. Their colour, in addition to helping them find food or keeping them from being eaten, helps in another important way. Being white helps an animal keep the heat of its body from escaping.

Some animals change the colour of their coats with the seasons. The ptarmigan is one that does. In the spring this bird mostly stays in the last remaining patches of snow until its brown summer

Ptarmigan

253

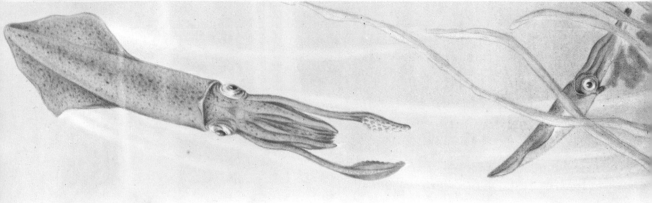

Squid

coat takes the place of its white winter one.

A number of mammals that live far to the north also change colour with the seasons. The ermine, or stoat, is one. During the summer a stoat is brown. It matches the ground and dry leaves and grasses very well. It can creep up on the animals it eats without being seen easily by bigger animals that would welcome a stoat as a meal. This little animal does not hibernate. It must be able to catch food throughout the long northern winter. In the autumn its brown hair drops out and white hair takes its place. The stoat then blends into the snow almost as well as the polar bear.

There are colour changes in animals that have nothing to do with the seasons. Some are caused by moving from one environment to another. By changing colour, an animal can make itself match new surroundings. The plaice or flounder is an example. It can make itself almost any shade of grey or brown. It can also give itself tiny speckles that match sand and big speckles that match gravel.

Chameleons are so famous for changing their colour that this ability is the first thing we think of when we hear their name. But a chameleon's colour changes do not always make it match its surroundings any better. They are caused by changes in light and temperature and by emotions. When a chameleon is cold it is usually brown. With temperature or light changes it may turn green or a pale greenish-yellow. When it is excited it becomes bright green. If it has lost a fight with another chameleon it turns

Ermine or Stoat in Autumn

Hermit Crab

brown. Even though a chameleon's changes in colour do not always make it match its environment better, it often happens that they do.

Unlike squids, which as you know can change colour very quickly, it may take ten minutes for a chameleon to change. A squid's colour changes may be due to emotions. They may also be changes to match new surroundings.

Some animals are made to match their surroundings in the way shown by the pictures of the hermit crabs. Here hedgehog hydroids—tiny colonial animals you will remember as relatives of the jellyfishes—are growing on both the rocks and the shells where the hermit crabs are living. The hydroids help the crabs by making them match their surroundings. In return they get a free ride from the crabs, and have a better chance to get food than if they stayed in one place.

Although hermit crabs do find sea anemones and fasten them onto their shells to prevent them from being eaten, a hermit crab has no intention of cam-

ouflaging itself with hydroids. In contrast, the spider crab—pictured on page 86—does its own camouflaging. It sticks seaweed and small animals on its back and legs that make it match its surroundings. If the crab travels to a new home it may change its camouflage.

The grey tree frog has been much studied by scientists interested in protective colouring. Notice how it matches the bark of the birch tree it is resting on. This little frog can also make itself green

Ermine in
Winter White

255

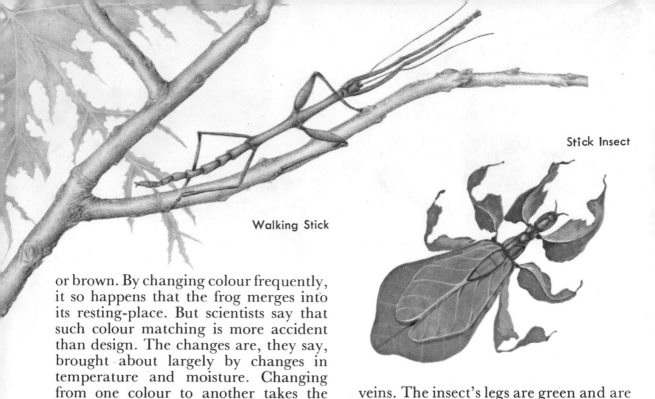

Walking Stick

Stick Insect

or brown. By changing colour frequently, it so happens that the frog merges into its resting-place. But scientists say that such colour matching is more accident than design. The changes are, they say, brought about largely by changes in temperature and moisture. Changing from one colour to another takes the tree frog about an hour.

The stick insect shows a way of matching its surroundings that is called *mimicry*. The stick insect looks like a twig. Insect-eaters are likely to overlook it.

A relative in Asia, the tropical leaf insect, is one of the best examples of mimicry. As you see, the insect's two pairs of wings look exactly like two green leaves, one resting on top of the other. There are even 'veins' that look like leaf

veins. The insect's legs are green and are flattened out so that they look like bits of leaves. In places they have ragged edges as if other insects had been nibbling at them.

An angular-winged katydid, which is related to grasshoppers and crickets, looks very much life a leaf. When it is resting on a green plant it is very hard to see. Treehoppers look like small leaves, thorns or buds.

The viceroy butterfly shows another kind of mimicry. It does not hide by looking like part of a plant. Instead it mimics the monarch butterfly, which is easily seen. The viceroy is good to eat, but the monarch is not. Monarchs are poisonous and make the bird that eats them ill. By looking like the monarchs the viceroy is not eaten by birds that have tried to eat a monarch butterfly.

The bumblebee moth protects itself by copying the bumblebee—an insect with a well-known sting. The moth has no sting, but it looks so much like a bumblebee that enemies pass it by.

Mimicry is not limited to insects. The sargassum fish is a backboned animal that protects itself in this way. It looks like the sargassum weed, common in the part of the Atlantic Ocean where the fish is found.

Sargassum Fish

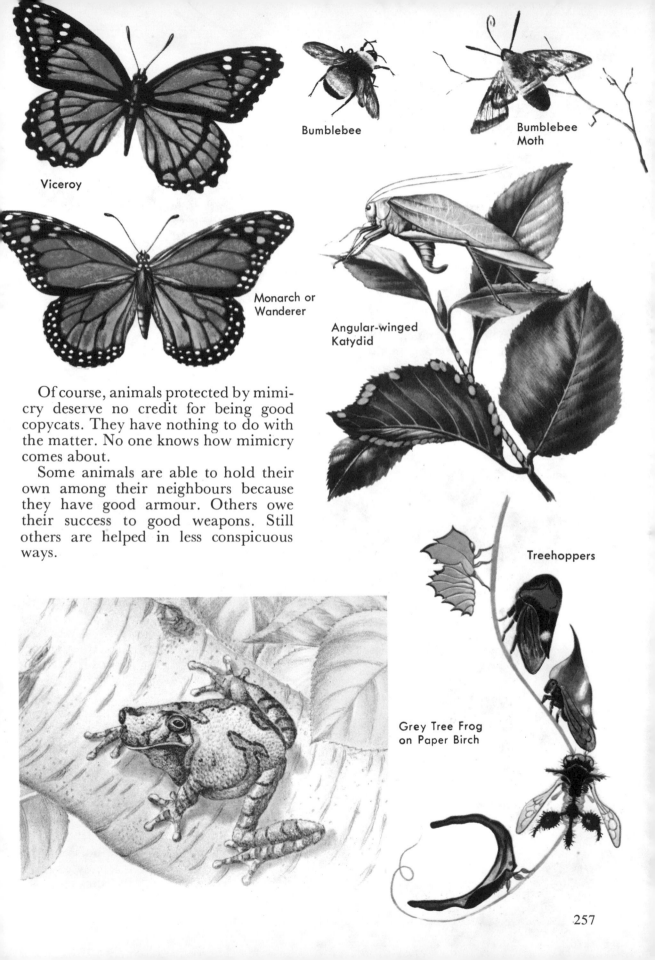

Viceroy

Bumblebee

Bumblebee
Moth

Monarch or
Wanderer

Angular-winged
Katydid

Of course, animals protected by mimi-cry deserve no credit for being good copycats. They have nothing to do with the matter. No one knows how mimicry comes about.

Some animals are able to hold their own among their neighbours because they have good armour. Others owe their success to good weapons. Still others are helped in less conspicuous ways.

Treehoppers

Grey Tree Frog
on Paper Birch

257

Whirligig Beetle

A whirligig beetle's eyes each have two parts. One part is above the surface of the water as the beetle swims about, the other below. The beetle can see an enemy approaching no matter if the enemy is under the surface or above it.

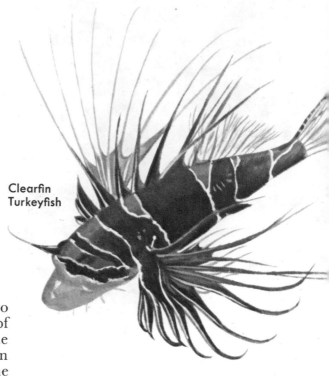

Clearfin Turkeyfish

Striped Skunk

Spotted Skunk

Hog-nosed Skunk

The clearfin turkeyfish is one of the scorpion fishes. All these fishes have poisonous spines on their fins. A jab from one of the spines may cause terrible pain.

You already know about the bad-smelling liquid that skunks spray at their enemies. This liquid is an excellent weapon. But before the animals use it they give warning by lifting their tails or rearing up on their front feet.

The shell of a box turtle forms a very effective suit of armour. The lower part of their shells is hinged, so that when any danger threatens they can shut up their shells. Most other turtles and tortoises cannot shut up their shells in this way, they can only withdraw their legs and head into their shell.

Among the other well-armoured animals you have met are the armadillos, the pangolin, the hedgehog, and a great many molluscs. The sword of the sword-fish, the knives of the surgeon fish, the stings of bees and scorpions, the horns of the yak, the tusks of the wild boar, the quills of the porcupine, the poison fangs of the cobra, the claws of a tiger, and the stinging cells of the jellyfishes and sea

Raccoon and
Box Turtle

anemones are a few of the thousands of weapons animals use to protect themselves from enemies.

Many animals, as you know, protect themselves from the cold by migrating or hibernating. The picture of the arctic fox shows two other means of protection from cold. This fox, as you would guess from its name, lives in the far north. It has a very heavy coat of fur. In addition it has small ears. Since there is not much warmth from the sun in winter, one of the big problems of a warm-blooded animal in that season is to keep the heat of its body from escaping. Both the arctic fox's fur and its colour serve to keep heat in. If its ears were big, much body heat would escape from them.

The fennec, a small fox of the hot, dry lands of Africa, does not need protection from cold. Notice how enormous its ears are. The kit fox lives in the warm southwest of the United States of America. It, too, has big ears, but its ears are not nearly so large in proportion to its size as the ears of the fennec. Hares of one kind or another are found all the way from tropical regions to the far north. The farther north a hare lives, the smaller its ears are.

Arctic
Fox

Fennec

Kit Fox

Cheetah and Gazelle

Of course, their ways of moving about help animals to adapt to their habitat. Hard hoofs for running would be of no use to a whale nor would fins like a fish's be of help to a bullfinch or a rabbit.

There are many big carnivores in the regions where gazelles live. Gazelles are able to run fast enough to have a good chance of escaping from most of their meat-eating enemies. But the speed of some of the meat-eaters is great, too. The cheetah, for example, can run faster than any other land animal. Speed clearly is a help to both the meat-eaters and the animals they prey on.

The gallinule lives near ponds or

Purple Gallinule

Three-toed Sloth, or Ai

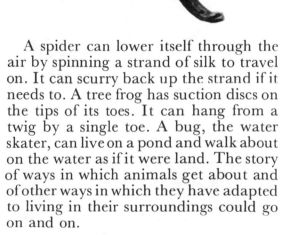

Spider Monkey

Flying Squirrel

lakes. It has very long toes so that it can walk on the leaves of water lilies and other plants that grow on the surface of the water.

The sloth spends its life in trees. Day in and day out it hangs down from a branch. It has to move very little to get the leaves it eats. Its long legs and curved claws fit the sloth for its strange life.

Monkeys are tree dwellers too, but they are very active. A spider monkey's tail helps it swing from branch to branch.

Flying squirrels, like flying dragons and flying lemurs, cannot really fly. But they can glide from branch to branch.

The gecko, a lizard, can walk across a smooth ceiling to catch insects resting there. On its feet a gecko has pads that let it cling to very smooth surfaces, even glass. The pads are not, as many people suppose, sticky. Instead they have tiny hook-like cells on them that catch on any slight roughness. They let geckos hunt for food in places many insect-eaters cannot reach.

A spider can lower itself through the air by spinning a strand of silk to travel on. It can scurry back up the strand if it needs to. A tree frog has suction discs on the tips of its toes. It can hang from a twig by a single toe. A bug, the water skater, can live on a pond and walk about on the water as if it were land. The story of ways in which animals get about and of other ways in which they have adapted to living in their surroundings could go on and on.

Gecko

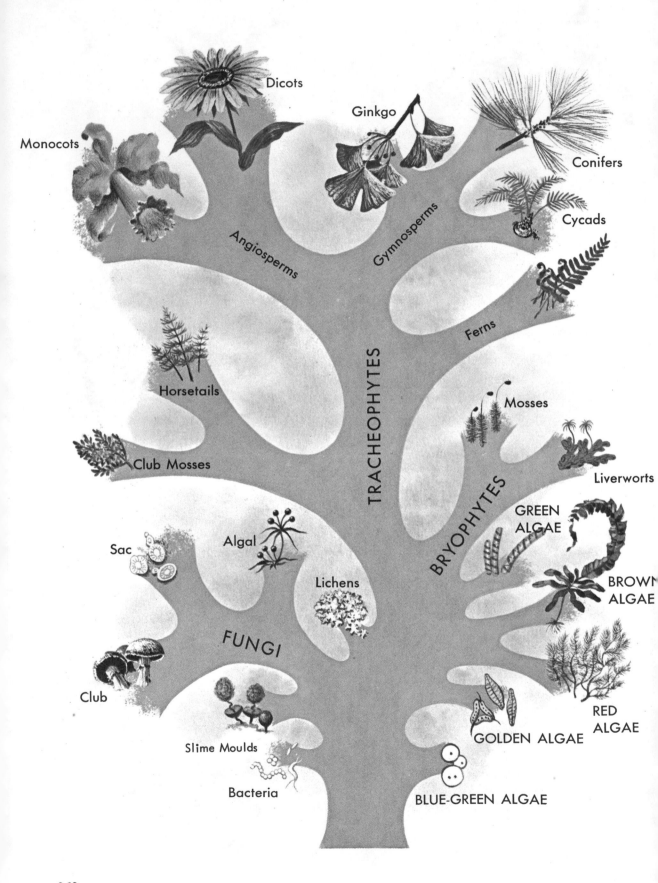

Dicots

Ginkgo

Monocots

Conifers

Angiosperms

Gymnosperms

Cycads

TRACHEOPHYTES

Ferns

Horsetails

Mosses

Club Mosses

Liverworts

BRYOPHYTES

GREEN
ALGAE

Sac

Algal

Lichens

BROWN
ALGAE

FUNGI

Club

RED
ALGAE

GOLDEN ALGAE

Slime Moulds

Bacteria

BLUE-GREEN ALGAE

The Plant Kingdom

There are not nearly as many kinds of plants as there are kinds of animals—at least not nearly so many have been discovered so far. Since some kinds of plants are very small and since there are still some little-known parts of the world, many more kinds of plants are sure to be discovered and named. But many more animals, as you know, are constantly being found, too. So it is not likely that the number of known kinds of plants will ever catch up with the number of known kinds of animals. At present we know of roughly 350,000 kinds of plants as against about 1,000,000 kinds of animals.

Plants are classified very much as animals are. There are phyla, classes, orders, families, genera and species. There are some subphyla, too, and some subclasses.

The common sunflower is a species of plant. It belongs to the sunflower genus. The sunflower belongs to the composite family. The composite family, a very large one, includes such well-known flowers as dandelions, daisies, and goldenrods. The family belongs to the order of bluebells. This order gets its name from the bluebell family, which it also includes. The bluebell order belongs to the subclass of dicots. The dicots are a part of a class called the angiosperms, or flowering plants. The flowering plants belong to the phylum of tracheophytes, or vascular plants—plants with 'little vessels' for carrying water.

Every known plant has been given a scientific name just as every known animal has. The scientific name of the common sunflower is *Helianthus annuus*. The scientific name of the marsh marigold, a member of the buttercup family, is *Caltha palustris*. This small plant has several common names. In the same way, several different plants may have the same common name. From common names, then, it is not always possible to tell what plant is meant. But a plant has only one scientific name and no other plant has that same name.

The 'tree' on the opposite page gives some idea of the whole plant kingdom. All the thousands of plants of today are supposed to have come from very simple one-celled organisms that once lived in the days when the earth was young.

Two branches near the bottom of the tree represent the bacteria and the slime moulds. These groups of living things, you remember, are classed as protists by some scientists.

There are fewer plant phyla than animal phyla. Near the bottom of the tree there are several phyla called *algae*. There is also the phylum of *fungi*. The fungi and all the algae are plants with no true leaves, roots, or stems.

Above the algae and fungi on the tree are the *bryophytes*. Their name means 'mosslike plants'. All the mosses and liverworts are found in this group. Like the algae and the fungi, the bryophytes lack true leaves, roots, or stems.

The whole top of the tree is taken up by the phylum of *tracheophytes*. These plants all have stems in which there are water-carrying tubes. Notice that the tracheophytes branch into the horsetails, club mosses, ferns, gymnosperms or cone bearers, and angiosperms or flowering plants. Both the gymnosperms and the angiosperms, in turn, are branched still further.

The flowering plants were the last of the great groups of plants to appear on the earth. They were so successful that today there are many more kinds of flowering plants than all the others put together.

Caltha palustris

Marsh Marigold
Cowslip
Kingcup
Soldier's Buttons
May Blob
Marybud

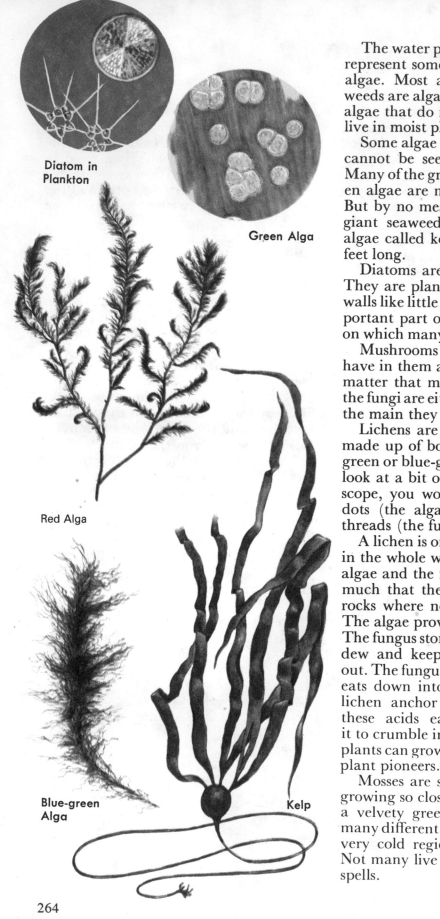

Diatom in Plankton

Green Alga

Red Alga

Blue-green Alga

Kelp

The water plants pictured on this page represent some of the different phyla of algae. Most algae live in water. Seaweeds are algae. So are pond scums. The algae that do not actually live in water, live in moist places.

Some algae are so tiny that single ones cannot be seen without a microscope. Many of the green, blue-green, and golden algae are made of only a single cell. But by no means all algae are small. A giant seaweed, one of the big brown algae called kelps, may grow to be 150 feet long.

Diatoms are one-celled golden algae. They are plants with remarkable glassy walls like little pillboxes. They are an important part of plankton, the 'sea soup' on which many animals of the sea live.

Mushrooms are fungi. Fungi do not have in them any of the green colouring matter that most plants have. Many of the fungi are either colourless or white. In the main they live on land.

Lichens are strange plants. They are made up of both fungus plants and the green or blue-green algae. If you were to look at a bit of lichen through a microscope, you would see many tiny green dots (the algae) surrounded by white threads (the fungus).

A lichen is one of the best partnerships in the whole world of living things. The algae and the fungus help each other so much that the lichen can live on bare rocks where no other plants can grow. The algae provide the fungus with food. The fungus stores up water from rain and dew and keeps the algae from drying out. The fungus also gives off an acid that eats down into the rock and helps the lichen anchor itself in place. In time these acids eat into rock and cause it to crumble into soil, so that soon other plants can grow there. In fact, lichens are plant pioneers.

Mosses are small. We often see them growing so close together that they form a velvety green carpet. They grow in many different parts of the world, even in very cold regions. Some live in water. Not many live where there are long dry spells.

Liverwort

Mosses are not quite so common, how-ever, as plant names might make you think. A number of plants are called mosses that do not really belong to the group. Among them are Irish moss, long moss, and reindeer moss. Irish moss is one of the red algae. Long moss is a flowering plant, a relative of the pineapple. Rein-deer moss is a lichen.

The slender stalks rising from the moss plants pictured have spore cases at the top. Many of the plants that do not pro-duce seeds are spread by spores. Spores are single cells. Some of the mosses are so much alike that it is hard to tell them apart. Often you find that a moss's spore cases give you the best clues for identify-ing it.

The mosses are much better known than their fellow bryophyte, the liver-worts. Some liverworts look rather like mosses. Others are ribbonlike plants that lie close against whatever they are grow-ing on. These liverworts are seen most often on the shaded walls of deep ravines.

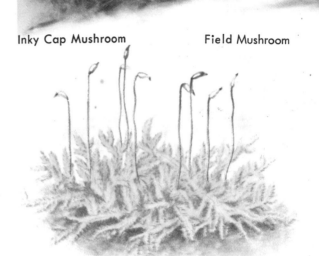

Inky Cap Mushroom   Field Mushroom

Shaggy Moss

Red Cap Lichen

Lichen on Rock

Haircap Moss

265

Wood Fern

Maidenhair Fern

Boston Fern

Tree Fern

Bracken

Horsetail

Nodding Club Moss

All the plants pictured on these two pages are tracheophytes. They all have well-developed tubes for carrying water, which in turn carries food and minerals. In the great forests from which coal was made, there were tree ferns, tree horsetails, and tree club mosses. They were the first really big land plants. Their water-carrying tubes made it possible for them to grow high up from the ground. But these groups of plants no longer play the leading role they once did in the plant world. Now there are no tree club mosses or tree horsetails. All the club mosses and horsetails of today are fairly small plants. There are still some tree ferns in warm, moist regions, but not many of them are more than a few feet high.

Today's horsetails are often called scouring rushes. They get this name because their stems are so gritty that they can be used for scouring pots and pans.

266

Spruce

Pine

For the most part, horsetails grow in barren, sandy areas. But they may not be able to keep their foothold even there.

All the club mosses that are found today are small plants that grow close to the ground. They are only a few inches tall.

Notice in the picture of the bracken that one leaf is rolled up like the head of a violin. This is a young leaf. It is following a common pattern among ferns. When it is young the leaf is rolled into a fiddlehead. It then unrolls from the base upwards. There is a second way in which most fern leaves are alike. When a vein in a leaf divides, it forks into two equal branches.

There are many kinds of ferns. There are ten times as many species of ferns as there are horsetails and club mosses together. But ferns are outnumbered by the plants that bear seeds—the cone bearers or gymnosperms, and the flowering plants or angiosperms—so that they only make up a tiny part of the whole plant world.

The pine and the spruce are conifers. The conifers rank high on the cone-bearing branch of the seed plants. Not all conifers are trees, but most are. They provide most of our timber.

You can see at a glance that the orchid belongs to the flowering plants. It ranks at the top of the monocots, one of the two branches of the angiosperms. No plants have flowers more beautiful or more complicated than those of orchids. Some orchids grow on the ground, but there are many exotic orchids that hang from trees in tropical rain forests.

Shining Club Moss

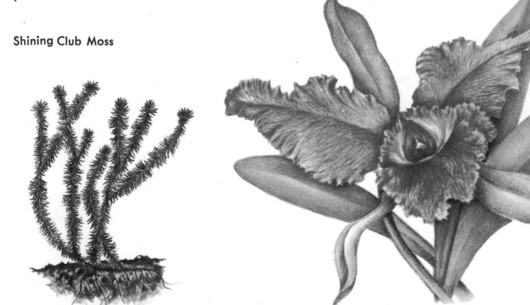

Orchid

Sugar Maple

Plant Factories

Sugarcane is one of the main sources of the world's sugar supply. It is planted in many of the warmer parts of the world, including the West Indies and Mauritius. The sugar is stored in the woody stems of the sugarcane. The cane has to be cut with very sharp knives. It is then taken to a factory where the canes are pressed by powerful mills and a sugary solution is produced.

The impure sugar has to be greatly refined before it can be eaten. Brown sugar has not been refined as much as white sugar, but it is very good to eat.

The story of how the sap in the sugarcane happens to have sugar in it is a very complicated one. A sugarcane plant has only two places from where it can get the material it needs. One is the soil. The other is the air. There is no sugar in either the air or in the soil Since it cannot get the sugar from the air or from the soil the sugarcane must make the sugar itself.

A sugarcane plant is a sugar factory.

Sugar maple trees mainly grow in Canada and North America. The sugar is tapped when the sap begins to rise in early spring. Sugar beet are sugar factories, too.

All green plants make sugar, but most of them do not make very much. Some use it up as fast as they can make it. Some change most of what they make into other substances. Green plants use two common materials in making sugar. One is water. The other is carbon dioxide. The leaves are the chief sugar factories of most green plants—of all green plants, in fact, that have leaves.

A leaf is made up of many cells. In the cells of the leaf of a green plant there are tiny green bodies called *chloroplasts*. 'Chloroplast' means 'green particle'. Chloroplasts are made green by the wonderful green dye, or pigment, *chlorophyll*. This name means 'green leaf'.

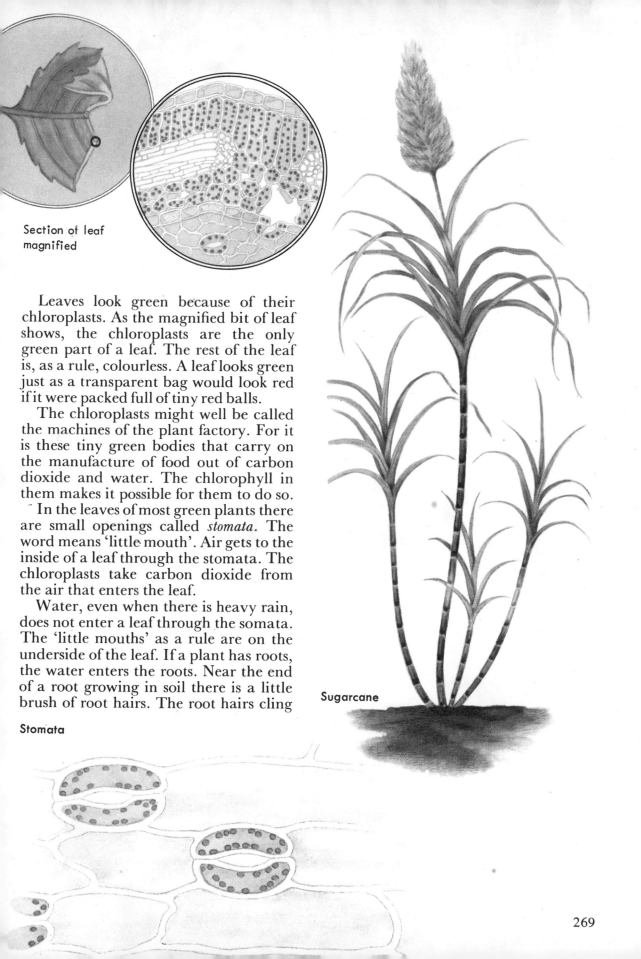

Section of leaf
magnified

Leaves look green because of their chloroplasts. As the magnified bit of leaf shows, the chloroplasts are the only green part of a leaf. The rest of the leaf is, as a rule, colourless. A leaf looks green just as a transparent bag would look red if it were packed full of tiny red balls.

The chloroplasts might well be called the machines of the plant factory. For it is these tiny green bodies that carry on the manufacture of food out of carbon dioxide and water. The chlorophyll in them makes it possible for them to do so.

In the leaves of most green plants there are small openings called *stomata*. The word means 'little mouth'. Air gets to the inside of a leaf through the stomata. The chloroplasts take carbon dioxide from the air that enters the leaf.

Water, even when there is heavy rain, does not enter a leaf through the somata. The 'little mouths' as a rule are on the underside of the leaf. If a plant has roots, the water enters the roots. Near the end of a root growing in soil there is a little brush of root hairs. The root hairs cling

Sugarcane

Stomata

269

Oxygen Rising from Green Plant

Cola

to particles of soil. They soak up water. The water travels from the roots up through the stem and its branches. It goes in special water-carrying tubes. The water at last reaches the veins of the leaf. The veins carry it to the cells where the chloroplasts are.

Chloroplasts cannot work without light. Usually, therefore, the making of sugar only goes on during the daytime. When they are making sugar the chloro-

plasts produce oxygen. If plants are growing underwater, bubbles of oxygen can often be seen rising from them on sunny days.

After sugar is made it may be changed at once into starch and sometimes stored in special stems like potatoes. When grains of starch stained with iodine are examined under a microscope, it is easy to see that the grains have been built up in layers.

Green plants, after they have made sugar, can build it into still other kinds of food by adding minerals from the soil. Green plants cannot live on sugar and starch alone any more than we can.

Animals cannot make food for themselves. They have to get their food from plants or from other animals that eat

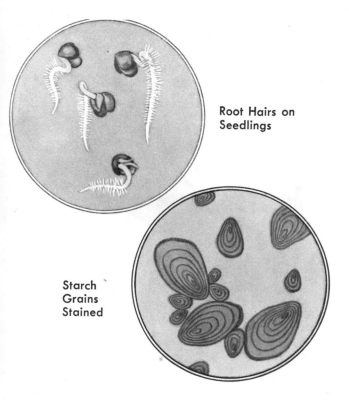

Root Hairs on Seedlings

Starch Grains Stained

Nuts

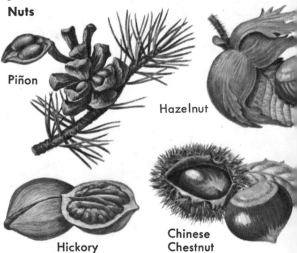

Piñon

Hazelnut

Hickory

Chinese Chestnut

Coffee

Foxglove

plants. Plants that are not green, except for a very few plant protists, must get their food from animals or from green plants. The green plants are the world's food factories.

Much of the food made and stored by plants is for the next generation of plants. Seeds, for example, contain food stored for the young plants that sprout from them. Nuts are seeds. They are only one of many kinds of seeds that animals use as food. The stored food in nuts is mostly fat and protein rather than starch or sugar.

Chocolate comes from the seeds of the cacao tree. The popular drink coffee is made from the seeds of the coffee plant, which may be either a tree or a shrub. Cola drinks have an extract in them from

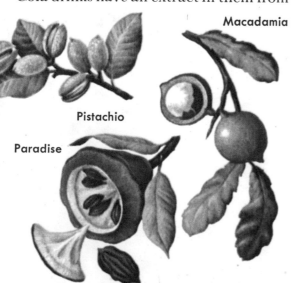

Macadamia

Pistachio

Paradise

the nuts of the cola tree. Tea is another drink we owe to plants. It is made not from the seeds but from the leaves of the tea plant.

Food and drink, however, are not the only products of all these plant factories that are extremely useful to man. Many plants produce drugs. Digitalis, a drug useful in certain heart diseases, comes from foxglove. Belladonna, camphor, and opium are other drugs from plants.

Perfumes, fibres from which cloth can be woven, spices and flavourings, dyes,

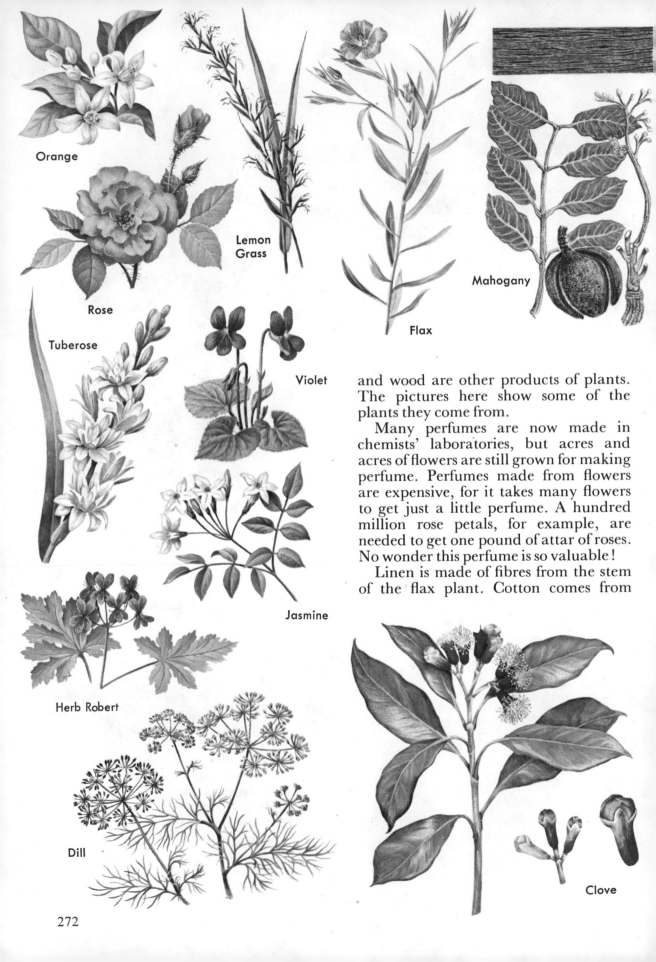

Orange

Lemon
Grass

Rose

Tuberose

Flax

Mahogany

Violet

Jasmine

Herb Robert

Dill

Clove

and wood are other products of plants. The pictures here show some of the plants they come from.

Many perfumes are now made in chemists' laboratories, but acres and acres of flowers are still grown for making perfume. Perfumes made from flowers are expensive, for it takes many flowers to get just a little perfume. A hundred million rose petals, for example, are needed to get one pound of attar of roses. No wonder this perfume is so valuable!

Linen is made of fibres from the stem of the flax plant. Cotton comes from

Ebony

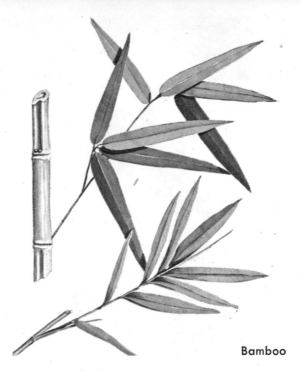

Bamboo

fibres attached to the seeds of the cotton plant. Hemp and jute are other plants with useful fibres.

The plants pictured at the bottom of these two pages all provide us with spices or flavourings. Vanilla, a very popular flavouring for desserts, comes from an orchid. Cloves and nutmeg are spices used in many foods. Saffron, from a crocus, is both a flavouring and a dye. It costs so much, however, that it is seldom used as a dye.

Trees and shrubs give us wood. Ebony and mahogany are two of the most valuable and highly prized kinds. The stems of the giant grass bamboo are often used in place of wood in the Far East. They also serve as water pipes, carrying poles, and fishing poles. Split, they are woven into curtains, baskets, fans and hats.

Rubber, turpentine, oil for soaps and paints, and chicle for chewing gum, are among the other products green plants give us. Even if we did not depend on plants for food, we would go on growing many kinds for the other materials they manufacture.

Vanilla Orchid

Saffron Crocus

Nutmeg

Common Spruce

Trees

Trees are the largest plants that grow on land. You may have the idea that trees are too big to be called plants, but this idea is wrong. A tree is built on much the same plan as a geranium or a rosebush; it is simply larger.

In the warm, wet regions of the world there are some tree ferns. All the trees of cooler regions are seed plants. But they are not all flowering plants. Many of them have cones rather than flowers.

Every tree represented in these pictures is a conifer, or cone bearer. Conifers all have narrow leaves. The leaves of some, like those of the common spruce, are so narrow that they are often called needles. Others, like those of cypresses, are scalelike. They overlap one another on the stems that bear them.

Notice that the pine needles are in clusters while those of the spruce are arranged in spirals along the stem.

The leaves of a conifer, even though they do not have a leaflike look, serve the same purpose that other green leaves serve. They are the plant's food factories.

Most conifers have leaves all the year round. They are evergreens. The fact that they are green all the year round does not mean they never shed any leaves. They do, but they shed them a few at a time throughout the year. The trees are never bare.

Not quite all conifers are evergreens. The tamaracks, or larches, and the bald cypress are among the few conifers that shed their leaves in the autumn and send out new ones in the spring.

The conifers include some of our most valuable timber trees. They are often called softwoods, although that name is not an especially good one. The wood of some conifers is soft, but that of a few is hard and long lasting.

Even people who do not live near any conifer forests are familiar with a number of kinds of conifers. Many evergreens are planted as ornamental trees. And at Christmastime people buy small conifers and their branches for Christmas trees and wreaths.

The names of some conifers are confusing. The Port Orford cedar is not a cedar. Instead, it is, as you might guess from its leaves, in the same genus with the Sitka and Sawara cypresses. The Lebanon cedar really is a cedar. Notice how different its leaves are. However,

Lebanon Cedar

Douglas Fir

Red Pine

Sitka Cypress

Port Orford Cedar

Sawara Cypress

Common Juniper

European Yew

275

Redwood

the Douglas fir is not a fir, and the bald cypress is not a cypress.

Conifers flourished long before any trees with flowers appeared. In the past 60 million years, however, the group has been losing ground. But even now the tallest, the largest, and the oldest trees are found among the conifers.

The tallest trees are redwoods. Many are more than 300 feet tall. The record holder towers 368 feet into the air. It is in a redwood grove in northern California on the west coast of the U.S.A. The closest rivals of the redwoods are found among trees with flowers. They are the eucalyptus trees of Australia.

The largest tree of all is the giant sequoia, a close relative of the redwoods. One giant sequoia, so famous that it has been given a name, has a diameter of 34 feet at the base and is over 272 feet tall— taller, in fact, than a 20-storey building. Inside its trunk there would even be enough room for a church with a tall spire. This giant is called the 'General Sherman'. There are other sequoias almost as big.

The 'General Sherman', scientists say, is probably about 3,500 years old. It began growing at about the same time that the alphabet had its beginnings. The tree was already 3,000 years old when Christopher Columbus and his followers first reached the shores of America.

Scientists cannot tell exactly how old the 'General Sherman' is, but they do know how old some sequoias have lived to be. They have been able to tell the age

Tree Rings

of these trees after they were cut down.

The age of a giant sequoia—and of most other trees, too—can be told from rings in the wood. In the trunks of most kinds of trees, new wood is formed each year in a layer outside the old wood and beneath the bark. When the trunk of a tree is sawn across, each layer shows as a ring. The rings are called annual rings. We find how old the tree is by simply counting the rings.

For many years the oldest giant sequoias were thought to be the oldest of all trees—the oldest, in fact, of all living things. Now some of the bristlecone pines, another conifer, are believed to be older than any sequoia. One bristlecone pine whose rings have been counted began growing nearly 5,000 years ago—before the days when the Egyptians were building great pyramids and over a thousand years before the 'General Sherman' sprouted.

The leaves pictured on this page come from trees whose seeds are produced by flowers, not cones. Such trees are often called broadleaf trees. They are commonly spoken of as hardwoods, too, even though some of them have soft wood.

Many broadleaf trees drop their leaves in the autumn and send out new leaves in the spring just as a few conifers do. During the winter months their branches are bare. Trees that drop their leaves in the autumn are called *deciduous*. The name comes from the Latin word meaning 'to fall off'. As a rule the leaves of deciduous broadleaf trees change colour in autumn.

It is a help to broadleaf trees to drop their leaves in the autumn if they live in a region with cold winters. The living material in the cells of most conifer leaves is much better protected from the cold than the living material in the thin leaves of a broadleaf tree. But in regions where the winters are not cold, broadleaf trees can be evergreen. The holly, which grows over most of western and southern Europe, is a good example.

The ginkgo is unique among the trees of today. It is a seed plant, but neither a flowering plant like the maples and oaks,

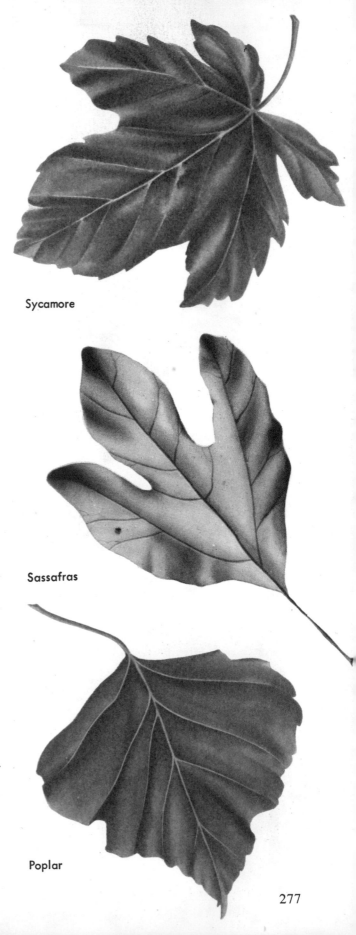

Sycamore

Sassafras

Poplar

Ginkgo

The ginkgo is a living fossil. It has remained almost unchanged for more than 200 million years. Before the days of the flowering plants—in the early days of the dinosaurs—the ginkgo grew in many parts of the world. It flourished in Europe, North America, and Asia. Today it has all but disappeared in the wild. For centuries, however, the ginkgoes have been grown and planted in the gardens surrounding Buddhist temples of the Far East.

But millions of people have seen ginko trees who have never been in the Orient. Ginkgoes are now cultivated in other parts of the world as well and are fairly common along city streets and in parks. They are popular partly because they are resistant to disease and drought and partly because they can stand the smoke of cities. But ginkgoes are not large or especially attractive trees. They are unlikely ever to be as popular as maples and elms and oaks.

nor a conifer like the cypresses and pines. As the tree of the plant kingdom on page 262 shows, the gingko is a gymnosperm. It is, therefore, closely related to the conifers, but it is in a group all its own.

A common name of the ginkgo is maidenhair tree. Ginkgo leaves have much the same shape as the tiny leaflets of the maidenhair fern. The tree bears plumlike seeds. The name 'ginkgo' comes from the Chinese and means 'silver apricot'. The seeds have a silvery sheen. A much older name given to the ginkgo by the Chinese meant 'duck foot'. The shape of its leaves earned the ginkgo this name.

There are hundreds of kinds of trees. Some, like the ginkgo, are seldom mistaken for any other kind, but it is not easy to tell all trees apart. A tree's shape is a help in identifying it. The vase shape of the elm, as you see, is very different from the graceful weeping willow or the rounded head of the common maple. The almost circular crown of the ash can be told at a glance from the slender triangle of a birch. If a tree is deciduous, its shape is one of the best ways of identifying it in the winter.

| Eucalyptus Gum | Birch | Mountain Ash | Weeping Willow | | Douglas Fir | Common Maple |

The shape of a tree is determined by the way it branches. Notice that the Douglas fir branches so close to the ground that the trunk does not show. The elm, on the other hand, branches many feet above the ground. The branches of the fir, moreover, are nearly horizontal, while those of the elm turn up. Some trees, the weeping willow for one, have drooping branches.

Their leaves, of course, are a big help in telling trees apart. Every kind of tree has a leaf of a distinctive shape. Some leaves are narrow; some are broad. Some are very much larger than others. The edges, or margins, of some are smooth; those of others are toothed like a saw. Some leaves have lobes—others are entire—that is, unlobed.

Of the four kinds of leaves pictured on this page the elm and the beech have sawtoothed margins. The holly leaf is lobed, and the lobes end in sharp points. The rhododendron has a smooth margin and no lobes.

Some species of trees have leaves of different shapes, all on the same tree. Sassafras trees are common in North America. They have leaves that are very variable in shape. Some sassafras leaves have lobes on both sides, others have lobes on one side. Still others have no lobes at all. Mulberry trees also have leaves that may vary in shape. It is very hard to identify the tree from which one of these leaves comes, when the leaves are so different in shape.

European Elm

Rhododendron

Holly

Beech

Pine

Common Maple

Hornbeam

White Poplar

Eucalyptus

Tree of Heaven

It is easy to see that the leaves in these pictures all vary in shape and in margins. The pictures show some other ways, too, in which leaves of trees differ.

It may surprise you to find that, with the exception of the clusters of pine needles, each picture shows a single leaf. Three of these leaves, however, are

280

compound. They are made up of separate leaflets. The three are the tree of heaven, the horse-chestnut, and the wattle. The wattle is, moreover, doubly compound. Its leaflets are divided into still smaller leaflets.

Although the tree of heaven and the horse-chestnut both have undivided leaflets, the leaflets are not arranged in the same way. Those of the horse-chestnut spread out like the fingers from the palm of your hand. Those of the tree of heaven are arranged along a leaf stem. They remind one of a feather. We say that the horse-chestnut is *palmately compound* and that the tree of heaven leaf is *pinnately*

compound. 'Pinnate' comes from a Latin word for 'feather'.

The veins, or water-carrying tubes, of different kinds of leaves make different patterns. You cannot see the veins of the pine needles pictured, but the veins of all the leaves from broadleaf trees show clearly. Leaves may be palmately or pinnately veined. The maple leaf is palmately veined. All the other broadleaf leaves shown here have pinnate veining.

The stem of a leaf is called its *petiole.* The petioles of most leaves, if they have them, are round.

Different trees arrange their leaves

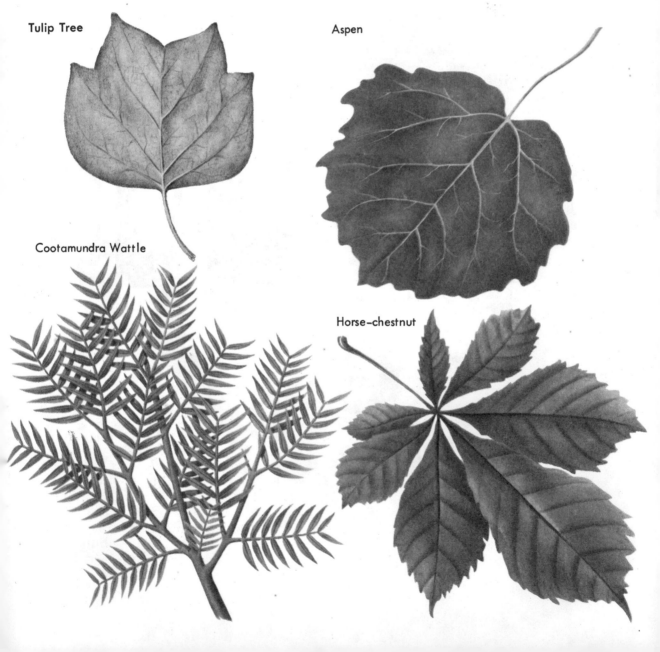

Tulip Tree

Aspen

Cootamundra Wattle

Horse–chestnut

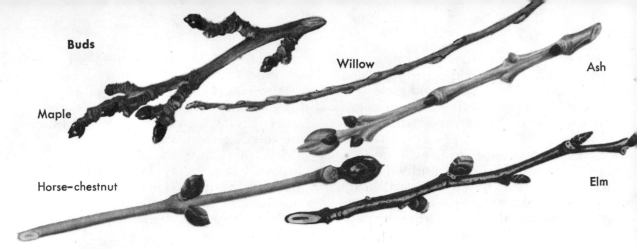

Buds

Maple

Horse-chestnut

Willow

Ash

Elm

differently on their twigs. As you have already found out, pines have their needles arranged in clusters. But different pines have different numbers of needles in a cluster. Some have five, others only two or three. Piñon pine bundles vary from one to five.

The picture below shows three different ways hardwood trees have their leaves arranged. The maple has leaves that are *opposite* each other on the twigs. The leaves of all maples follow this plan of opposite arrangement. So do the ashes.

The leaves of the catalpa grow in rings of three each around the twig. They are said to be *whorled*.

The elm follows by far the most common plan of leaf arrangement. Its leaves come from first one side of a twig

and then the other. They are, in other words, *alternate*.

Some leaves are smooth and glossy. Those of the holm-oak and the magnolia are good examples. Others are rather rough. Some are fuzzy. The white poplar gets its name because the underside of its leaves is covered with soft white down. The white shows clearly when the wind rustles the leaves.

Bark

Shagbark Hickory
Apple
Beech

Some of the leaf shoots of the hawthorn have modified themselves through the ages so that they are now thorns. An easy way to tell a hawthorn tree is by its thorns. The locusts and acacias are also thorny.

When trees are bare, buds help to identify them. In the late summer, before their leaves fall, deciduous trees form buds. Some flower buds. Most are leaf buds. The tiny flowers and leaves inside the buds are well protected from the winter cold. Even though they are all built in much the same way, buds do not all look alike, as the pictures at the top of the page show.

Leaf Arrangements

Elm

Catalpa

Maple

A leaf leaves a scar when it drops off. Some leaf scars are much larger than others. The leaf scars of different trees vary in shape, too. Of the twigs pictured, the leaf scars show most clearly on the horse-chestnut. The leaf scars are horse-shoe shaped.

Many people, especially in winter, can tell trees apart by their bark. Notice how different the three kinds of bark pictured are. Not many trees have bark as smooth as a beech's. Not many have bark as shaggy as that of a shagbark hickory. The bark of most trees is more like that of the apple tree, but the pattern of ridges differs from one species of tree to another.

The colour of the bark varies, too. Grey-brown is the usual bark colour. But some is reddish-brown and some, as you see, is pale grey. The bark of the silver birch is white.

All conifers have cones of one sort or another that help to identify them. Even the cones of the different species in one group such as the pines are distinctive. Those of sugar pine, for instance, are long—often almost two feet long—while those of Scots pine are oval. Two of the cones shown have already opened and lost their seeds. The cones of firs and larches are erect. Those of spruces hang

Sugar Pine

Mountain Pine

Scots Pine

White Pine

down. Long pinecones, hang down, too, but most short, wide cones stand up.

In the spring the flowers of the hardwoods are a help in telling one tree from another. Later in the year the fruits and seeds are like labels to those who know trees well enough to read them. Acorns, for instance, grow only on oak trees, and every kind of oak has its own special shape and size of acorn. Notice how the

Common Oak with leaf

Sessile Oak

Turkey Oak

Flowering Cherry

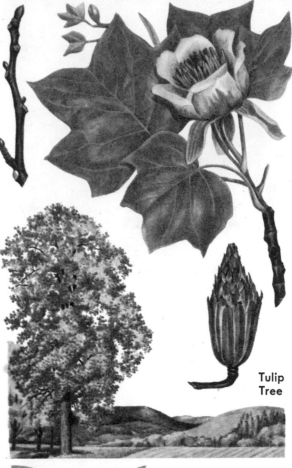

Tulip Tree

Spike Wattle

Laburnum

Bottlebrush

Hawthorn

cups as well as the shells of these acorns vary.

Our broadleaf trees belong to the great group of flowering plants, the angiosperms, but the flowers of many of them go unnoticed. No one would gather walnut or oak or maple flowers for a bouquet. Some trees, however, have large and showy flowers. The six hardwoods shown on these two pages are among them. They are often planted as ornamental trees.

Most of our cultivated fruit trees, too, have showy flowers. No flower garden is ever more beautiful than an apple orchard in full bloom.

For some reason which no one understands, one branch of the flowering plants—the dicots—produced many more kinds of trees than the other branch—the monocots. But there is one huge family of trees on the monocot branch—the palms. There are more than a thousand—there may even be several thousand species of palms. To the people of tropical lands the palms are enormously important. They provide shelter, food, drink, fibres, oil and vegetable ivory.

The coconut palm is a common sight on the shores of warm seas. It often grows right down to the edge of the sea on small islands. Although its flowers are small, its seeds—the coconuts—are among the largest of all seeds.

Some small palms can be grown successfully as house plants. So it is possible to see palms growing even if the climate is too cold for them to grow outside in the garden.

Coconut Palm

flowers

Banyan

Palm trees do not have the solid woody trunks that dicot trees and conifers have. Their trunks are more like giant cornstalks. Bundles of woody water-carrying tubes are scattered through them with soft pith between. No one can tell the age of a palm by counting rings. There are no rings.

The banyan, a 'strangling' fig, is famous for its many trunks. The extra trunks develop from roots dropped down from branches. A famous banyan tree in India covers nearly two acres. It has some 230 trunks more than two feet thick and over 3,000 smaller ones.

The silk tree of southern Asia has, you can see, doubly compound leaves and pink flowers. It is used as an ornamental tree. As you might guess from its leaves, it is related to the sensitive plant.

The monkey puzzle tree of South America is an araucaria, or Chile pine—a conifer but not a true pine. The way its branches bend at the ends reminds people of monkey tails.

The sausage tree of Africa is a relative of the catalpa. It is called after its sausage-shaped fruits.

The bottle tree gets its name from the shape of its trunk. This tree grows in the grasslands of Australia. Its trunk serves as a storage tank for water. The stored water tides the tree over dry periods.

Unfortunately, trees of all kinds have enemies. There are countless kinds of insects that live on the trees of our forests and orchards and the shady trees of our towns and cities. There are many tree diseases, too.

Smoke is also an enemy of trees. Many

kinds cannot stand the soot of cities.

Fire is one of the worst enemies of our forest trees. Forest fires, many started by carelessness, have destroyed hundreds of acres of good timber. Replacing a forest takes many, many years, even centuries. A forest fire may so damage the soil that trees cannot grow in it.

Trees are a great help to a city or town. But choosing shady trees for planting around our homes and on our streets is not easy. A tree that is likely to be killed by a disease or that is so infested by many kinds of insects that a war against them will have to be carried on constantly is not a good choice. Neither is a short lived tree nor one with wood so brittle that it breaks easily in storms.

Some trees are unsuitable for city streets because they produce so many roots that they clog up sewers. Some are unpopular because their flowers have an unpleasant smell. Some litter up the ground under them with their flowers or fruit or seeds. But, although there are many questions to be asked about any tree that is being considered for city planting, there are many trees to choose from. Except in the very arid parts of the world, there are almost sure to be several kinds of trees that do well.

Silk Tree

Monkey Puzzle

Bottle Tree

Sausage Tree

Bacteria and Slime Moulds

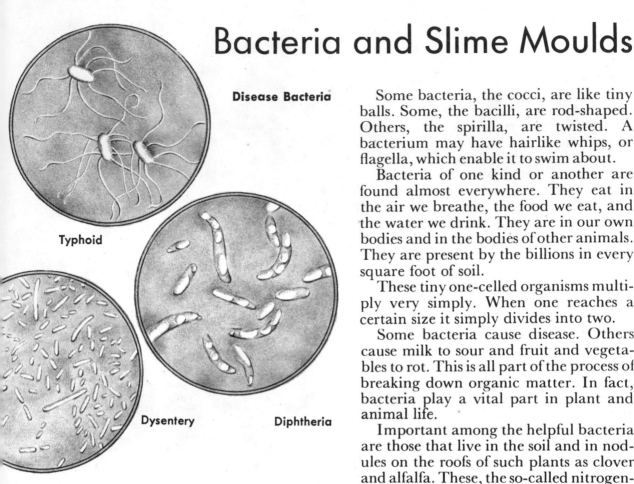

Disease Bacteria

Typhoid

Dysentery

Diphtheria

Some bacteria, the cocci, are like tiny balls. Some, the bacilli, are rod-shaped. Others, the spirilla, are twisted. A bacterium may have hairlike whips, or flagella, which enable it to swim about.

Bacteria of one kind or another are found almost everywhere. They eat in the air we breathe, the food we eat, and the water we drink. They are in our own bodies and in the bodies of other animals. They are present by the billions in every square foot of soil.

These tiny one-celled organisms multiply very simply. When one reaches a certain size it simply divides into two.

Some bacteria cause disease. Others cause milk to sour and fruit and vegetables to rot. This is all part of the process of breaking down organic matter. In fact, bacteria play a vital part in plant and animal life.

Important among the helpful bacteria are those that live in the soil and in nodules on the roofs of such plants as clover and alfalfa. These, the so-called nitrogen-fixing bacteria, help keep soil fertile by taking nitrogen from the air and building it into compounds green plants can use.

Early in its life history a slime mould is a creeping animal-life blob of protoplasm. Later it develops spores just as many plants do. The tiny spores scatter in the wind. Each may then start a new slime mould.

Bacteria and slime moulds, as you know, are called plants by some scientists and protists by others. They are certainly not much like the plants we are used to seeing. Bacteria are all far too small to be visible without a powerful microscope. It would take 50,000 of some kinds to make a row an inch long. Each bacterium is a single cell, but in many cases several may stay together and form a chain. Slime moulds are much larger, but they are still tiny.

The spore cases of slime moulds vary greatly in both colour and shape. Those of the slime mould pictured here, you will notice, do not look much like those of

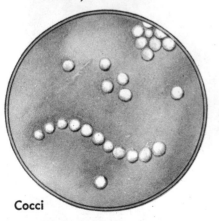

Cocci

Bacilli

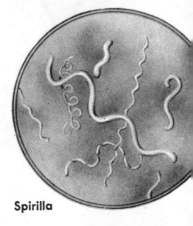

Spirilla

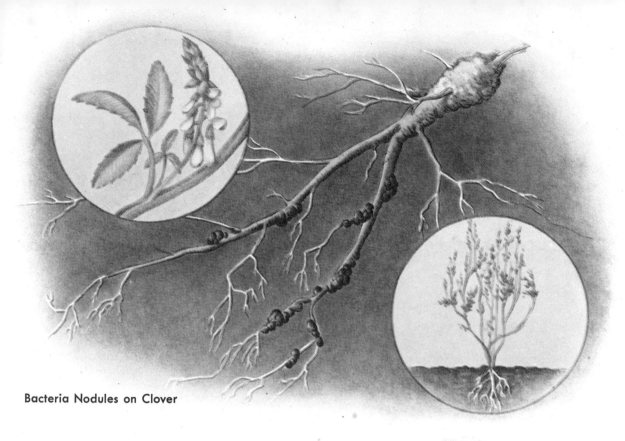

Bacteria Nodules on Clover

the one pictured on page 63. Some slime moulds have spore cases without stalks, and so they lie flat instead of standing upright like the one pictured here.

Slime moulds are puzzling and fun to study. Scientists have found their animal-like stage useful in learning about protoplasm. These strange plant-animals, however, are far, far less important than bacteria.

Slime Mould

Plants that are not Green

More than three-quarters of all the thousands of species of plants are green. With the help of their chlorophyll they can make the food they need. The other plants that make up the plant kingdom lack chlorophyll and cannot make food for themselves. Like animals, they must get their food ready-made.

Some plants that are not green obtain their food from other live plants or from live animals. Others get food from dead plants or animals or from such plant and animal products as flour, sugar, and leather.

Plants that must get their food ready-made are often called 'dependent plants' or 'saprophytes'. More than ninety-nine out of every hundred saprophytes are fungi.

Yeasts are one-celled fungi. They are larger than bacteria but they are far too small to be seen without a microscope.

Yeast plants depend chiefly on sugar for food. The sugar must be dissolved. As yeast plants use up sugar, they produce carbon dioxide and alcohol. When

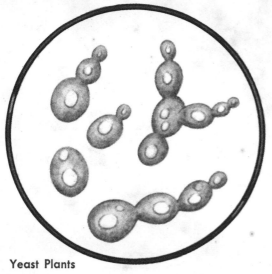

Yeast Plants

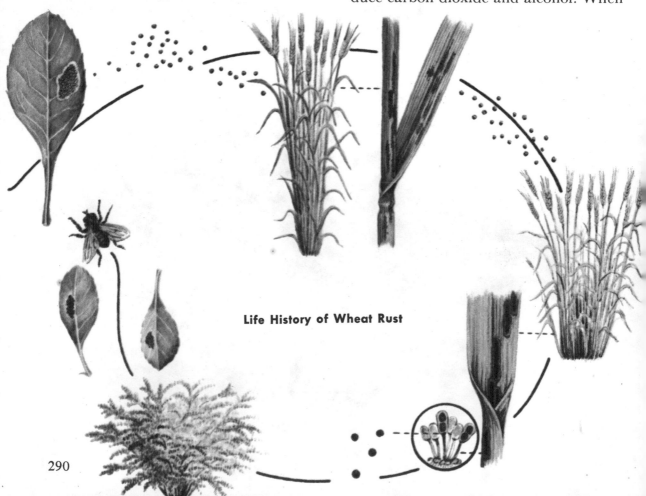

Life History of Wheat Rust

290

yeast is at work in a solution, we say that the solution is souring, or fermenting. These tiny plants float about in the air like bacteria. They may well drop into any fruit juice or other sugar solution left uncovered and begin growing there.

The yeast plants floating about in the air are wild yeasts. Yeasts are cultivated for use in making bread and in making alcohol and alcoholic drinks. The cakes and packages of yeast used in making bread are made up of millions of yeast plants pressed together. In bread-making, it is the carbon dioxide produced by the yeast that is important. The bubbles of this gas make the dough rise.

As a rule yeast plants multiply by budding. A small bud grows out of a cell. A wall soon divides it from the parent plant. In turn a bud may grow from it and another bud from that one. A whole chain may be formed. But at any time a chain may break apart into separate plants.

Moulds are fungi, too. They are considerably larger than yeasts. The main part of a mould plant is a mass of colourless threads called a *mycelium*. From the mycelium tiny stalks arise which bear a capsule containing spores. Spores serve mould plants as seeds: new plants grow from them. Their spores capsules give moulds their colour. Common colours among the moulds are black, blue green, brown, and pink.

Moulds will grow on almost anything which comes from a plant or an animal. Moulds growing on foods are usually a nuisance. But many kinds of cheese like Stilton and Danish Blue owe their flavour to moulds growing in them. Moulds

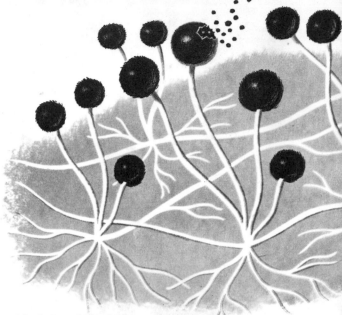

Black Bread Mould

growing on leather, cloth, or wood ruin it in time. But some moulds are a great help to us in fighting disease. The drug penicillin, for example, is produced from a green mould.

Mildews are fungi, too. They are much like moulds. The white powder one often sees on lilac or rose leaves is made of spores of a powdery mildew. Late potato blight is caused by a downy mildew. The 'mildewing' of books and paper and of belts, shoes, and rolled-up clothes in hot, humid weather is caused by moulds rather than by mildews.

None of the fungi cause the farmer more trouble than rusts. They may ruin whole fields of grain. Rusts have complicated life histories. Many spend part of their lives on one plant and part on another. Wheat rust spends part of its life on barberry.

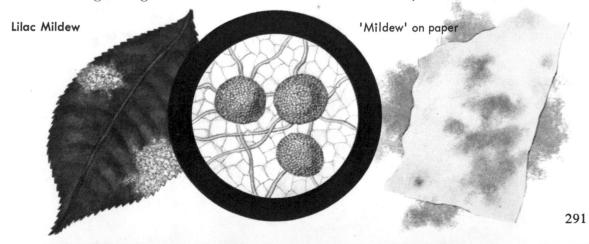

Lilac Mildew

'Mildew' on paper

291

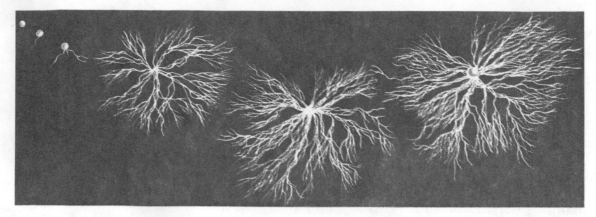

Mycelium Developing

Spore Print

Mushrooms are the largest of the fungi. The general plan of a mushroom is like that of a mould. The main body of the plant is a mass of colourless threads, or mycelium. Early stages of a young mycelium are pictured above. Stalks bearing the spores grow up from the mycelium. As a rule the mycelium is well hidden by whatever the fungus is growing on. The spore-bearing stalks of mushrooms are far larger than those of moulds. What we usually call a mushroom is only the spore-bearing part.

Life History of a Field Mushroom

Suppose the spore of a field mushroom reaches a good place for growing. A cobweb-fine white thread, the beginning of a mycelium, grows from it. It begins getting food from decaying plant materials in the soil. The young mushroom plant grows and branches. It spreads out in the soil. It may grow for many weeks underground.

At last tiny bumps the size of a pinhead appear on the mycelium. They are the beginnings of the mushrooms—the spore-bearing stalks. The little mushrooms get bigger. Soon they are large enough to push their way above the ground.

When a field mushroom first appears, it looks like a round white button. As the button grows, the top opens up into an 'umbrella'. The umbrella is called the cap. The handle of the umbrella is the stem. As the cap opens up, it leaves a collar around the stem. The cap may grow to be large. Field mushrooms with caps five inches across have been found. Usually the caps are smaller.

The underside of the cap is made up of many thin folds. These folds are called gills. They spread out from the centre of the cap like the spokes of a wheel. The gills are pink when the cap first opens up. Later they turn brown and then nearly black. The top of the cap becomes darker, too.

The spores of the field mushroom are brown. When they are ripe the gills are covered with them. There are so many millions on a single mushroom that it would take twenty years to count them one by one.

Some of the spores fall to the ground. The wind blows some away. Any animal that brushes against the mushroom sends spores travelling. The spore print pictured was made simply by resting the cap of a field mushroom on a sheet of white paper for several hours and letting the ripe spores drop down on the paper. The cap must be lifted off the paper very carefully.

The ink cap and the fairy-ring mushroom have gills just as the field mushroom has. The ink cap's gills are white at first. But when the spores are ripe the

Shaggy Inky Cap

gills and cap turn to a black, inky liquid.

Long ago people thought that the rings formed by the fairy-ring mushroom were actually made by fairies. We know now that the plant's mycelium spreads underground to form the circle. The mycelium in the centre dies. Each year the ring is bigger than it was the year before. This little mushroom's spores are white.

Sometimes mushrooms push their way up through hard-packed soil. It is difficult to see how they can do so, for they are not woody plants. They break through by taking in a great deal of water and swelling fast.

Fairy-ring Mushroom

Orange Peel Fungus

All mushrooms have histories much like that of the field mushroom. But they do not all bear their spores on gills. None of the mushrooms ·pictured here have gills. They have other ways of spreading out their spore-bearing surfaces. These mushrooms, too, produce spores in huge numbers.

The bright-orange lining of the orange peel fungus is the spore-bearing layer. Each pit in the cap of the morel is like one of the cups of an orange peel fungus. The lining of each pit bears spores.

The bolete and the bracket fungus are in a group called pore fungi. On the underside of the cap of a bolete and the shelf, or bracket, of a shelf fungus there are pores that open into slender tubes. The spores are borne on the lining of these tubes. When they are ripe, they fall out through the pores and are blown about.

Shelf fungi grow on trees of many kinds. This one, the common shelf fun-gus, may be as much as two feet wide. The undersurface is white and fairly soft. Pictures can be drawn on it easily with a stick. Each mark is brown because the pores darken when they are damaged. Another common name for this shelf fungus is artist's fungus.

The horn of plenty has an outer layer of spore-bearing cells. This layer is not nearly so smooth as that of an orange peel fungus. The many branches of the coral fungus serve to spread out the spore-bearing layer of this mushroom. The delicate little hedgehog hydnum bears its spores on soft, hanging teeth, or spines. This mushroom when young and pure white is considered one of the most beautiful of all plants. It is easy to imagine it as a winter scene in a dwarf forest. Later it turns brown.

The stinkhorn forms its spores underground in an egg-shaped case. When the spores are ripe, the case breaks open and a stalk grows up with amazing speed bearing a slimy cap of spores with a very bad smell. The odour attracts flies and other insects which scatter the spores. Not all stinkhorns have the lacy veil that this one has.

The spores of puffballs are borne on a network of threads inside the balls. These fungi get their name because, when they ripen and open, clouds of spores puff out at the lightest touch. The number of spores puffballs produce is amazing even for mushrooms. A giant puffball may produce more than a thousand million.

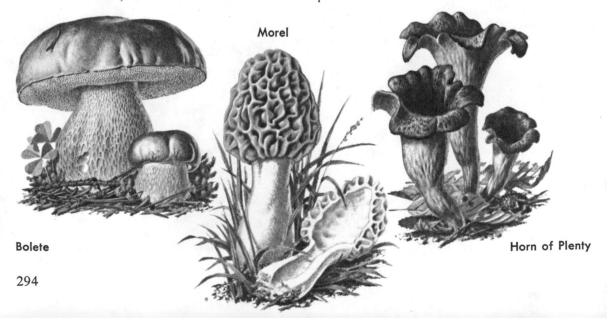

Bolete

Morel

Horn of Plenty

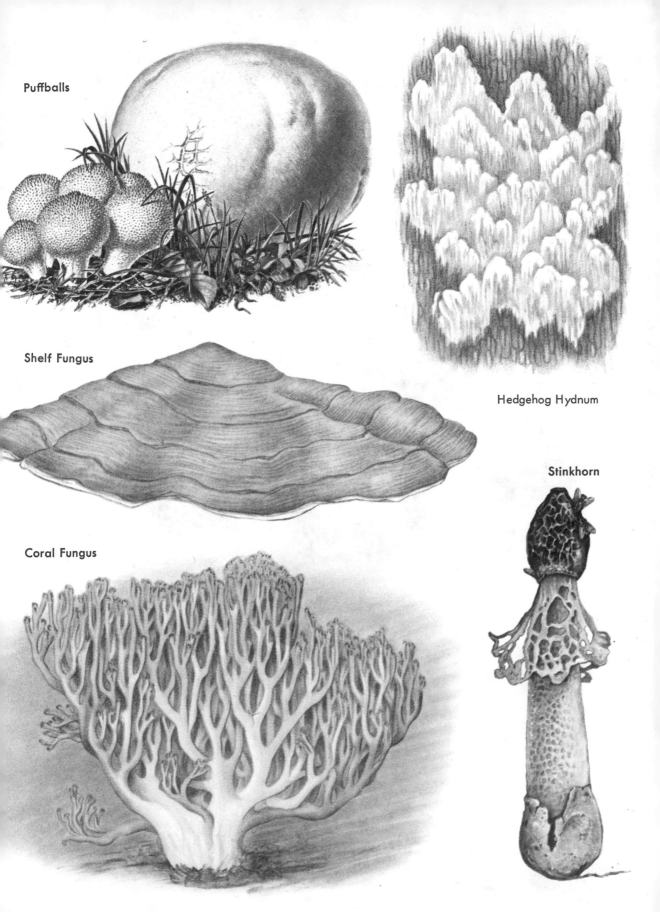

Puffballs

Shelf Fungus

Coral Fungus

Hedgehog Hydnum

Stinkhorn

Blewits

Honey Fungus

Shaggy Cap

Rooting
Collybia

Orange-Brown Lactarius

Beefsteak Fungus

Parasol
Mushroom

Grape Coral

Oyster Fungus

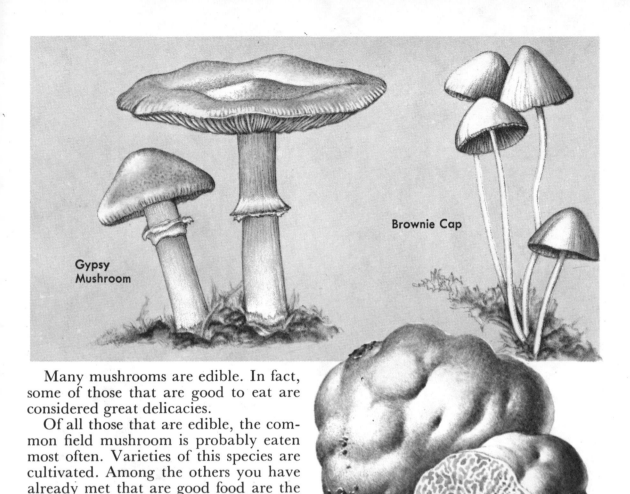

Gypsy Mushroom

Brownie Cap

Many mushrooms are edible. In fact, some of those that are good to eat are considered great delicacies.

Of all those that are edible, the common field mushroom is probably eaten most often. Varieties of this species are cultivated. Among the others you have already met that are good food are the puffballs, ink cap, fairy-ring mushroom, bolete, morel, hydnum, and horn of plenty.

All those pictured here can be eaten. The brownie cap, however, is so small that unless there are a great many close together it is scarcely worth picking. Its cap may be only half an inch across.

In contrast with the little brownie cap, a truffle may weigh as much as two pounds. This fungus grows wholly underground. As you already know, pigs are sometimes trained to sniff out truffles and dig them up. Poodles also make good truffle hunters. Many people consider truffles the most delicious of all fungi.

There are many other edible mushrooms. Of those that are not good to eat, some are too woody or have a bad taste or smell. But some are not safe to eat. More than a few, in fact, contain deadly poisons. All these mushrooms are deadly poisonous. None of them can safely be eaten.

Truffle

Chanterelle

Death Cap

Fool's
Mushroom

Green Stropharia

Emetic Russula

Lurid
Bolete

Mexican
Sacred
Mushroom

Fly Agaric

Olive Clitocybe

Morgan's
Lepiota

False Morel

The death cap, fool's mushroom, and fly agaric are closely related. They are all amanitas. As you might guess from its name, the death cap is so poisonous that it is likely to kill anyone who eats it. The fool's mushroom is just as deadly. The poison in these mushrooms acts slowly. A person may not know until several hours after eating them that he has been poisoned. By that time it may be too late to do anything to fight the poison.

The poison of the fly agaric is not quite so deadly and it acts rapidly. In most cases the life of a person who has eaten it can be saved. This mushroom got its name because a growing one is likely to be surrounded by a circle of dead flies, killed by sipping juice secreted by its cap. Its poison has been used to get rid of flies.

Amanitas always have a cup at the base of the stalk and a collar around the stem. Not all the amanitas are poisonous, and some are edible. But, since about nine-tenths of all people killed by eating mushrooms are killed by amanitas, any mushroom with a cup at the base and a conspicuous collar should be avoided.

Morgan's lepiota is a close relative of the edible parasol mushroom and looks much like it except that its spores are green. The poison of this mushroom causes indigestion but is not likely to cause death.

The lurid bolete also causes indigestion and is not deadly. Except for colour this mushroom looks much like the edible bolete pictured on page 294. It deserves the 'lurid' in its name. As you see, the stem is red shading into orange. The underside of the umbrella is vermilion at first and orange later. The flesh is yellow, but it becomes blue when bruised. The spores are greenish-grey.

Their beautiful colours help identify the stropharia and emetic russula. Their poisons usually cause indigestion.

The poison of the olive clitocybe acts like that of the fly agaric. This mushroom owes its name to the fact that it glows in the dark.

Eating the Mexican sacred mushroom has a strange effect. Its poison causes the eater to see visions and to stagger about drunkenly, as if in a trance.

The false morel, easily confused with morels we eat, is likely to have in it a poison that attacks red blood cells and may cause death. Strangely, this same mushroom may have no poison and be edible. But no one should take a chance with it.

Unfortunately, as you know from looking at Morgan's lepiota, the lurid bolete, and the false morel, some poisonous mushrooms look very much like some that are edible. We should trust no one but·an expert to tell us exactly whether mushrooms found growing wild are really safe to eat.

Many people think that mushrooms should not be called mushrooms unless they can be eaten. If they are not good to eat, these people say, they should be called toadstools. But 'mushroom' to a scientist does not mean just a mushroom that can be eaten. Instead, it may mean any fungus large enough to be called fleshy. To many it means any mushroom that has gills. Still other scientists prefer the name only for those in the genus *Agaricus*—the genus containing the field mushroom. 'Toadstool' is simply a nickname for mushroom. Probably the 'toad' comes from the unpleasantness of some of the mushrooms—some people call anything distasteful a toad. The stool-like shape so common among mushrooms explains the rest of this slightly unusual nickname.

Olive Clitocybe at night

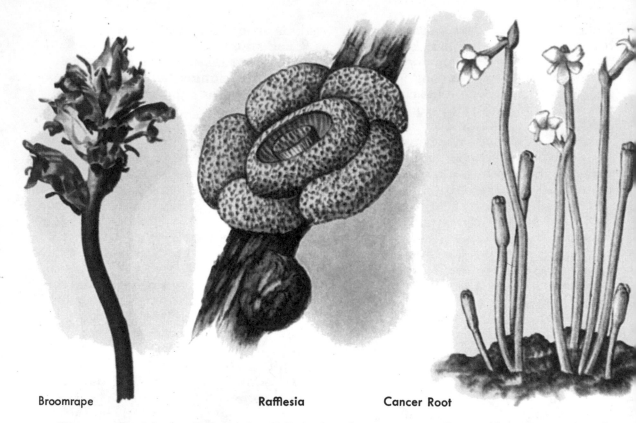

Broomrape   Rafflesia   Cancer Root

Compared with the thousands of kinds of fungi, the other plants that are not green make up a very small part of the plant kingdom. All those pictured here belong much higher in the plant kingdom than the fungi. They are all flowering plants. But they have no green leaves to serve as food factories. The only green leaves in these pictures are those of the clover on which dodder is growing.

Some saprophytic plants, it has been pointed out, take food from living plants or animals by growing on them or inside them. Such plants are called parasites. The rusts and mildews and a few moulds are parasites. Shelf fungi that grow on living trees, many of the cup fungi, and a number of other mushrooms are parasites, too. There are also parasites among the flowering plants that have no chlorophyll.

Cancer root is one of the flowering-plant parasites. As you would guess from its name, it grows on the roots of other plants.

Suppose a seed of cancer root falls on the ground and begins to grow. The seed has enough food in it to enable the little plant to grow for a time. But unless it finds a plant it can grow on before it uses up all its food, the little plant dies.

The biggest flowers in the whole plant kingdom are produced by plants that cannot make their own food. The plants are rafflesias, members of a family of parasites that only grow in tropical regions. One blossom may be a yard across. But it is fleshy and not at all pretty. It has, moreover, an unpleasant smell. Rafflesias have no stems or leaves. The only part of them besides their flowers is inside the host plant.

Dodder twines around other plants. It, too, is a parasite. It sends suckers into the stem of the plant it is growing on. The vine does not have either roots or leaves. It must get water as well as food from the plant it twines around. Another name for dodder is love vine. Still others are devil's sewing thread and strangleweed.

There are more than a hundred different species of dodder, but they are all much alike. Some species must have one special kind of green plant as a host. One species, for example, will only grow on clover. But many species will grow on almost any kind of green plant within reach. Dodder is a close relative of morning glory.

Once in a while an Indian pipe plant grows on the roots of another plant. But as a rule it is found growing in piles of dead leaves and branches in thick woods. There it has a mass of fungus threads around its roots. The fungus gets food from the dead wood and leaves, and the Indian pipe in turn gets food from the fungus.

Indian pipe is sometimes called a ghost flower because it is so white. Some Indian pipe plants, however, are not so ghostly as others. Some of them are pale pink.

Orchids are among our most beautiful flowering plants. But orchids may be almost colourless. Coral root and brunetta, both orchids, get their food in the same way as the Indian pipe.

Dodder on Clover

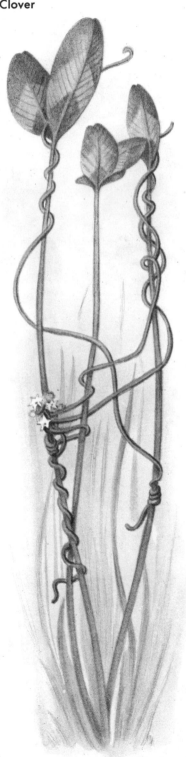

Coral Root   Indian Pipe   Brunetta

Vegetables

All vegetables are parts of green plants. They are storehouses in which plants store up the food they make. Different plants make different parts of themselves into storehouses. A vegetable may be several parts of a plant.

Roots are common storehouses. Carrots, turnips, beets and sweet potatoes are all root vegetables. So are radishes, parsnips, and yams. Many of the root vegetables keep well. Before the days of swift transportation from one part of the world to another, these vegetables, stored away in vegetable cellars or other cool storerooms, were almost the only fresh foods that people of northern lands had in winter.

The white, or Irish, potato is not a root, although it looks much like a sweet potato. It is, instead, an underground stem. Such an underground stem is called a tuber. The story is told that when potatoes were first grown in Europe the people did not know what part of the plant to eat. They first ate the green seedballs, which they found unpleasant. They were about to give up growing the potato when they learned that they were supposed to eat the tubers instead.

We eat the stems of asparagus and celery, too, but their stems are not tubers. They grow above ground. Stalks of asparagus are the main stems of young plants. At the top are the beginnings, or buds, of leaves and branches. Stalks of celery are the stems of leaves. They have leaflets at the top. A bunch of celery is

Carrot

Beetroot

Turnip

Sweet Potato

Potato

Asparagus

Celery

302

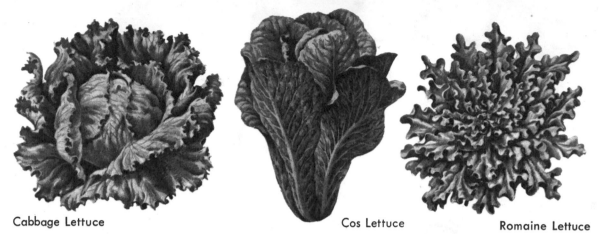

Cabbage Lettuce

Cos Lettuce

Romaine Lettuce

really a bundle of leaves. The fibres that make some celery and asparagus stringy are the water-carrying tubes.

When we eat lettuce or parsley we are eating the leaves of a plant. As you can see from the pictures, the leaves of lettuce

Onion

Leek

Parsley

underground, away from the sunlight. A leek is a bulb, too. It is like a young onion.

A head of cauliflower is a bunch of flowers which have not yet opened out. We eat both the stems and the flowers of broccoli. The artichoke, which many people think ranks above all other vegetables for flavour, is a flower bud.

may be curly or smooth. They may be quite free from one another or crowded into a head. Spinach and cabbage are other leafy vegetables. The cabbage leaves form a head like that of a cabbage lettuce. Brussels sprouts are tiny bundles of leaves. They are like cabbages except that they are much smaller. Some root vegetables have leaves as well as roots that are good to eat. Many people prefer the leaves of beet and turnips to the roots.

The part of the onion plant we eat is a bulb. A bulb is chiefly made of thick leaves that overlap one another. These leaves are colourless because they are

Globe Artichoke

Garden Pea

Sweet Corn

Beans

parts of the world. Parched corn was important to the diets of American Indians and pioneers. Dried peas are chiefly used for soup. Lentils, much like peas, are eaten both as a vegetable and in stews and soups.

In some cases we eat not the seeds themselves but the packages that hold the seeds. Green peppers, marrows and some of the many squashes are good examples. We scoop out the seeds before eating these vegetables.

Scientists call any part of a plant that contains seeds a fruit. To them a fruit does not have to be sweet. Peppers and marrows are, therefore, fruits to a scientist's way of thinking. A number of vegetables are fruits which we eat seeds and all. Among them are aubergines,

Okra

Many plants, as you already know, store a great deal of food in their seeds. Sweet corn, peas, and beans are seeds we eat as vegetables. They are good tinned or frozen as well as fresh from the garden. Seed vegetables have a big advantage over most other kinds—they can be dried and stored and still be good to eat long after they are picked. When dried they do not have to be kept cold. Dried beans of various kinds are staple foods in many

sometimes called eggplants, okra, cucumbers, french beans, and tomatoes. Tomatoes were raised in flower gardens long before anyone thought of eating them. They were called 'love apples' and were believed to be poisonous. Now tomatoes have become one of the most popular vegetables.

One of the foods stored in many vegetables is starch. Another is sugar. This is not surprising, since sugar and starch are the food which green plants make from water and carbon dioxide. The potato is a storehouse mostly filled with starch. Some vegetables have enough sugar in them to taste sweet. Sweet corn is one. Sweet potatoes are another. Beet, peas, yams, carrots, and parsnips are still others even though 'sweet' is not in their names.

Some vegetables have quite large amounts of protein. They can be used as substitutes for meat. Peas and beans are among the vegetables high in protein.

Perhaps more important than the starch, sugar, and protein stored in vegetables are the vitamins and minerals stored in them. Leafy green vegetables are now one of our very best sources of iron and calcium, two minerals our bodies must have. Green vegetables and tomatoes are excellent sources of vitamin

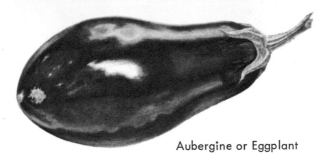

Aubergine or Eggplant

C. Yellow vegetables such as carrots, sweet corn, potatoes, yams, and tomatoes provide us with vitamin A. It is almost impossible to have a balanced diet without vegetables. A rule many meal planners follow is: serve at least two different vegetables besides potato every day. One should be raw and one green or yellow.

Squashes

Labels on map: Carrot, Cabbage, Horseradish, Cos Lettuce, Jerusalem Artichoke, Turnip, Parsnip, Endive, Tepary Bean, Pepper, Artichoke, Onion, Eggplant, Yam, Cress, Lima Bean, Squash, Pea, Cucumber, Sweet Corn, Okra, Lettuce, Green String Bean, Sweet Potato, Tomato, Radish, Spinach, New Zealand Spinach, Potato, Pumpkin, Beetroot, Celery, Asparagus

Origin of Common Vegetables

As the map shows, the vegetables grown in the gardens of Britain came, in the beginning, from many different parts of the world. Very few of them are natives of Europe. Our vegetable markets would look very empty and poverty stricken if they only sold vegetables which were of European origin.

You may wonder whether there are other wild plants which could have been developed into vegetables in our gardens. Out in the country in the spring many people gather the leaves of such plants as dandelion and nettles for greens. We could doubtless grow other such leafy plants instead of lettuce and endive and spinach. But the list of wild plants that we might have cultivated as vegetables is, so far as we know, very short. It is lucky indeed that vegetables that are not natives do well in our gardens.

A vegetable's name may give the wrong idea of its history. The so-called Irish potato is not a native of Ireland but

came from South America. The Jerusalem artichoke has no connection with Jerusalem; it is a native of North America. But, as an exception, New Zealand spinach really is a native of New Zealand.

As the map shows, South America has provided some of our most popular vegetables. But more than half of the kinds of vegetables we plant in our gardens were originally cultivated in the lands near the eastern end of the Mediterranean. These lands are sometimes spoken of as the cradle of civilisation. Probably plants have been grown as food there longer than in any other part of the world.

The map does not show the origin of broccoli, cauliflower, Brussels sprouts, kale, collards, or kohlrabi. The reason is that these vegetables are all descendants of the wild cabbage of Europe. They do not look much like their wild cabbage ancestor now. But the big heads of cabbage so common today do not look much like their wild ancestor, either. Would you guess from the picture of wild cabbage that any of the vegetables pictured with it were even relatives? Gardeners down the centuries have been very interested in getting better vegetables from those they had. An illustration of such an improvement is seen in the potato.

Many years ago a plant breeder called Luther Burbank saw a seedpod growing on one of the potato plants in his garden. Usually potatoes are not grown from seed. Instead a potato is cut into pieces, with at least one eye or bud on each piece, and the pieces are planted separately. Some varieties of potatoes do not form seeds at all. But Burbank decided to plant the seeds from the seedpod, when

they were ripe. He was very interested in finding ways of producing better strains of plants. Perhaps by experimenting with potato seeds he could grow some potatoes that were better than any available at that time.

When he opened the seedpod he found 23 seeds. In the spring he planted them in his garden. They all grew. When the time came to harvest the crop, he carefully looked at the potatoes from each plant to see what they were like. He found that the potatoes from each plant were different. The potatoes from some of the plants were very small and misshapen. Those from others had deep-set eyes. Those from yet others had rough skins. These were no improvement over the ones that he had been growing

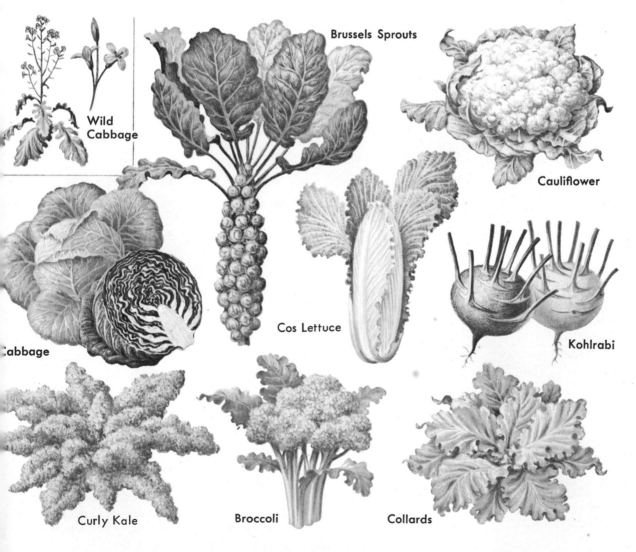

Wild Cabbage

Brussels Sprouts

Cauliflower

Cabbage

Cos Lettuce

Kohlrabi

Curly Kale

Broccoli

Collards

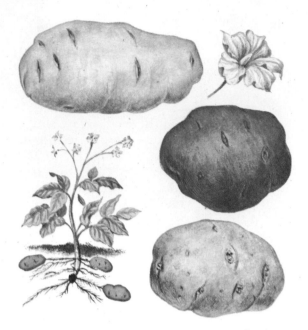

Potatoes

smooth potatoes. Soon he had enough of this new kind of potato to sell. Thus the Burbank potato was developed.

Burbank called this experiment with the potato his most important experiment because it was his first one. If this one had failed, he might have turned in discouragement to some other kind of work.

Careful selection of the plants from which new plants are to be raised is one way in which our vegetables have been improved and good varieties developed.

Many new strains of rice have been developed by treating the seeds and plants with various chemicals. These new strains of rice are being grown in countries where rice is the principal food. Some of the new rice plants give a much

before. But some of the other potatoes were good. Two of the plants had produced large smooth potatoes that were different from any that were on the market at that time.

Burbank examined these potatoes carefully. The potatoes from one of the two plants, he decided, were slightly better than those from the other. He saved these potatoes and planted them in the spring. They all produced big smooth potatoes. He selected the very best of these for raising new plants the next year. They, too, produced big

Peppers

Radishes

higher yield of seeds for each plant. A much larger amount of food can now be grown using the same area of land and involving the same amount of work by the farmer.

Rice is not the only plant which is being developed in this way. Wheat is another. Some of the new strains of wheat can grow in places that were too hot and dry for the old ones. When a new kind of plant or animal suddenly appears that has changed and can pass on the characteristics to its descendants, it is called a *mutant*. 'Mutant' comes from a

Latin word that means 'to change'. It is a good name for a plant or animal that differs noticeably from its ancestors.

Many mutants appear that are far worse than the parent plants they came from. But watching for desirable mutants and taking care of them when they do occur is another way in which our vegetables have been improved. All the many vegetables that have been developed from cabbage are thought to be mutants. The changes that gave us cauliflower were especially big ones.

Still another way of improving our vegetables has been to cross different varieties. A plant produced by crossing two different kinds of plants is called a hybrid. You have already read about hybrid animals. We shall read exactly how plant hybrids are produced when we come to the chapter on flowers.

Just a glance at a garden catalogue gives some idea of the great number of varieties there are of our common garden vegetables. The pictures on the opposite page show a few of the many different varieties of potatoes, radishes and peppers that we raise.

The picture of potatoes brings out the fact that varieties differ in colour of skin. The picture cannot also show that different varieties are suited for growing in different kinds of soil and climate, and for being cooked in different ways.

Not all the peppers shown are eaten as vegetables. Some are used chiefly to season other foods. They are too peppery to be eaten in large amounts.

As you see, radishes may be long or round, red, white, red and white, or almost black. Of course, you cannot see from the picture that some are much more spicy than others. Although radishes are usually eaten raw in this country, they are often cooked in other countries. In the Far East radishes weighing several pounds are grown. These are cooked before they are eaten.

A way in which we have produced better vegetables, but not new varieties, is by fertilising the soil in which they grow. For example, scientists have found that tomatoes grown in one field may be richer in vitamins than those grown in another.

Some of the recent improvements in vegetables have been brought about through the use of growth hormones. Growth hormones are chemicals. Seedless tomatoes are produced by the use of a growth hormone. A seedless tomato is not altogether seedless, but it has fewer seeds than other tomatoes. Experimentation with growth hormones is being carried on with many different kinds of vegetable.

Seedless Tomato

Concord Grape

Fruits

In a modern green-grocery there is sure to be fruit of many kinds. They come to the markets of Great Britain from all over the world. The demand for fruit is so great that it is brought to us by the boat-load from other lands. Special machines have been invented for unloading bananas and other easily damagable fruits from fruit boats. Out of our own orchards and fruit farms, fruit is carried to our towns and cities by train and lorry.

A good diet calls for some fruit every day. But we should eat great quantities of fruit even if it were not an important part of a good diet. No other kind of food looks more attractive or, people think, tastes better or does you so much good.

The chief food stored in most fruit is sugar. Sugar is excellent energy-giving food. And it is much better for us to get it in fruit than in the form of granulated sugar, for in fruit we get vitamins along with the sugar, and some minerals, too. The citrus fruits, for example, are one of the best sources of vitamin C and mineral calcium, while prunes are a good source of vitamin A and of iron and copper.

One vegetable, as you know, may be one part of a plant, another vegetable a different part. Fruit, on the other hand, is always the same part of the plant. They are the packages in which the plants provide food and bear their seeds.

Although all fruits are packages of seeds unless they are seedless varieties developed by growers, fruits are built on a number of different plans. Some fruits have only a single seed. Some have several seeds. Some have a great many.

Each type of fruit has a name. The grape is an example of one type. In it several seeds are surrounded by a soft pulp. This pulp, in turn, is surrounded by a skin. The gooseberry and currant are built on this same plan. No one commonly calls a grape a berry, but 'berry' is the name scientists give to this kind of fruit. Oranges, oddly enough, are berries,

Apple

too. So are all the other citrus fruits. These fruits are different from other berries in that the pulpy part is divided up into sections.

The apple is a pome. The seeds are in a core in the centre of the fruit. There are thousands of varieties of apples.

Citrus Fruits

Grapefruit

Orange

Lime

Lemon

Tangerine

311

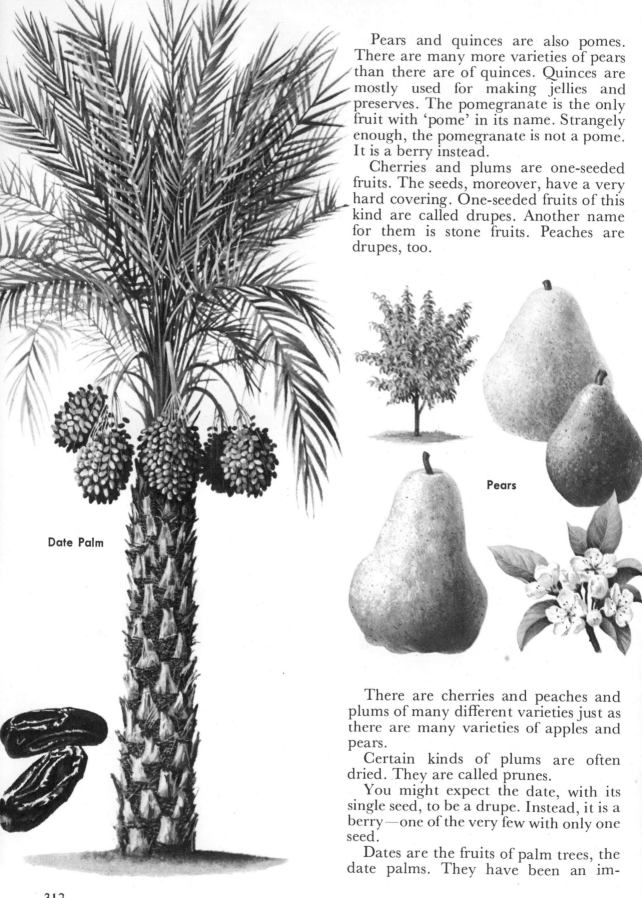

Pears and quinces are also pomes. There are many more varieties of pears than there are of quinces. Quinces are mostly used for making jellies and preserves. The pomegranate is the only fruit with 'pome' in its name. Strangely enough, the pomegranate is not a pome. It is a berry instead.

Cherries and plums are one-seeded fruits. The seeds, moreover, have a very hard covering. One-seeded fruits of this kind are called drupes. Another name for them is stone fruits. Peaches are drupes, too.

Pears

Date Palm

There are cherries and peaches and plums of many different varieties just as there are many varieties of apples and pears.

Certain kinds of plums are often dried. They are called prunes.

You might expect the date, with its single seed, to be a drupe. Instead, it is a berry—one of the very few with only one seed.

Dates are the fruits of palm trees, the date palms. They have been an im-

312

Quince

Cherry

portant food for the people to the south and east of the Mediterranean since before the dawn of history. Dates can be dried and kept for a long time.

An old saying is that date palms must have their feet in water and their heads in the sun. Many, for example, are grown on irrigated lands along the Tigris and Euphrates and beside the Nile. Date palms are also common in oases of the Arabian and the Saharan deserts. As you see, dates grow in big clusters.

Some other fruits are called pepos. A pepo is a large fruit with a thick rind. Inside it there are many seeds, often hundreds. Pumpkins, cucumbers and melons are pepos. Pumpkins and cucumbers are not sweet enough to be called fruit as the word 'fruit' is commonly used, but melons are. The picture shows several kinds of melons that are good fruit for breakfast or for dessert. Another name for these melons is muskmelons. The 'musk' in the name comes from the fruit's strong, pleasant

Plums

smell. Of course, the banana melon owes its name to its shape and colour. The watermelon is another popular fruit in the pepo group.

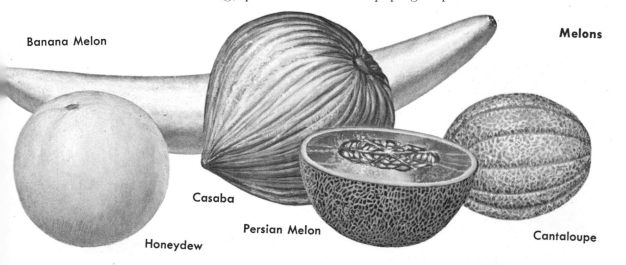
Banana Melon

Melons

Casaba

Honeydew

Persian Melon

Cantaloupe

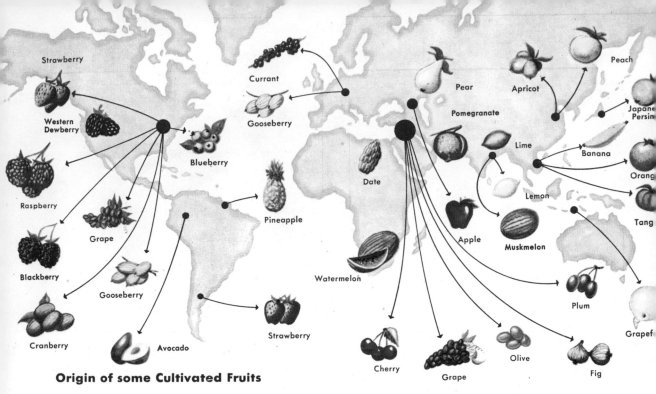

Origin of some Cultivated Fruits

A pineapple is made up of many fruits crowded so closely together that they seem to be one. It is a so-called multiple fruit. No seeds develop ordinarily in a pineapple. This seedless fruit can be grown only in warm, moist lands. It is one of the most important crops of Hawaii and many are also grown in Malaya and South Africa.

The fig, although it looks like a simple fruit with many seeds, is a multiple fruit, too. Many little fruits grow together to form a single fig. Figs, like dates, have been an important food in Mediterranean lands for thousands of years. Like dates, figs can be dried and kept for a long time.

Of the 'berries' pictured below, the

Pineapple

currant, gooseberry and cranberry are true berries. The raspberry and the blackberry are made of many tiny drupes joined together. Each little round section has a single seed in it, just as does a cherry or a plum.

The strawberry is not a true berry, either. Its seeds are on the outside. The pulpy part of a strawberry is a cushion on which the seeds rest.

If we had to limit ourselves to the fruit that grows wild in Britain we would only have the small wild strawberry and the blackberry. Most of the fruits that are grown in orchards and gardens are natives of other parts of the world. As the map shows, the peach and apricot, for example, came from China. Apples were originally grown in the Middle East, as were cherries and plums. The grapefruit is a native of the East Indies, the banana and orange of south east Asia, and the pineapple and avocado pear from northern South America. Australia is the only continent which has not sent any fruits to our orchards and gardens.

A few fruits are shown by the map to be natives of two different regions. The grape is one. Wild grapes grow in both

Fig

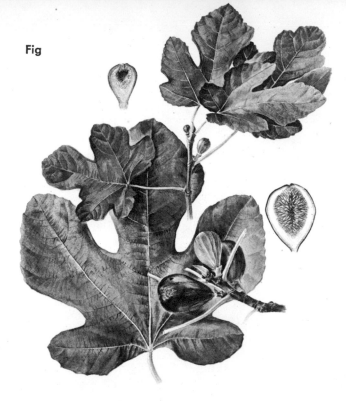

the Old World and the New. The Concord grape came from one of the wild American grapes. Many of the other grapes that are grown to make wine came from the wild grapes of Europe and the Near East.

Gooseberry

Redcurrant

Raspberry

Cranberry

Strawberry

Blackberry

Akee

Cherimoya

Barbados
Cherry

Soursop

Sugar Apple,
or Sweetsop

Mangosteen

Sapodilla

Surinam Cherry

316

Mango

Sapote

The banana is a tropical fruit known around the world. Great quantities are shipped to other lands from the regions where they grow. In contrast, few of the tropical fruits pictured here reach our markets. You are not likely to know many of them.

The mango, an ancient fruit of India now grown in many tropical regions, is often called the most delicious fruit of all. The mangosteen of the East Indies —not like a mango in spite of its name— is also highly praised. It seems to melt in your mouth.

People of Hawaii and visitors to the islands know the papaw well. This fruit of tropical America thrives there as well as in warm regions of Asia, Africa and Australia.

The cherimoya, sugar apple, and sour-sop are closely related New World fruits. They are large, with custard-like flesh. The akee of Africa has white pulp around shiny black seeds. Both the pulp and the seeds are said to be poisonous until the fruit is ripe enough to split open.

Barbados and Surinam cherries are natives of tropical South America. So are the sapodilla and the sapote, or marmalade plum. The sapodilla comes from the tree that provides the chicle used in chewing gum.

Fruit gathered from wild plants made up much of the food of our early ancestors. But the fruit they ate was very different from the fruit for sale in our markets today.

We have improved our fruit, just as we have improved our vegetables, partly by growing them under better conditions than they had in the wild. We have raised new plants from only the best parent plants. And we have done other things, too.

Papaw

Loganberry

Occasionally mutants—or sports, as they are often called—appear among fruits just as they do among vegetables. Fruitgrowers have improved our fruits greatly by watching for sports and propagating them when they turn out to be desirable. They have produced many new varieties in this way.

The loganberry is thought to be a mutant. In 1881 Judge Logan of California found growing among his blackberries a new kind of berry that was later named after him. The loganberry is shaped like a blackberry but it is red like a raspberry. It grew, scientists believe, from a blackberry seed. The nectarine, a smooth-skinned fruit, is a mutant of the fuzzy-skinned peach.

Sometimes only one branch of a plant will bear fruit of a new and different kind. The navel orange, a freak or sport because it is seedless, began in this way.

Dozens of strains of the common varieties of apples have come about as branch sports.

Fruitgrowers have improved our fruit, too, by crossing different varieties. The boysenberry is a cross between the loganberry and the raspberry. Many of today's varieties of fruits are hybrids.

The Golden Delicious apple is thought to be a chance hybrid—a hybrid that no one helped bring about. It may instead be a mutant. The first tree found bearing this fruit was growing in an orchard. The grower carefully protected it. Thousands of Golden Delicious apple trees have been grown from this tree.

Some hybrid fruits are crosses between two different kinds of fruit. The plumcot is a cross between the plum and the apricot. The ugli is a cross between the tangerine and the grapefruit. There have been many other crosses of citrus fruits.

Apples

Delicious

Greening

McIntosh

Crab Apple

Jonathan

Golden Delicious

Rome Beauty

Nectarine

Attempts to cross different kinds of fruit are unsuccessful unless the fruits are fairly close relatives. The apple and the orange, for example, cannot be crossed.

A new hybrid fruit is really as much of an invention as a new kind of machine. Our government, therefore, grants patents on distinctive hybrid fruits. It also grants patents on new varieties developed from sports. Nursery catalogues often call attention to patented plants they sell.

On the whole, fruit spoils rather easily. Refrigerated railway trucks and lorries and cold-storage houses help fruitgrowers get their fruit to market in good condition. Fruitgrowers have helped solve the problem of spoilage with some fruits by shipping them while they are still green. The bananas that reach our country are almost always green. They travel to us in refrigerated banana ships. From ports they are carried by train and lorry to centres of distribution all over the country. There they are ripened in special rooms, then delivered to fruit and grocery stores. Lemons and pineapples are other fruits that are harvested and shipped before they are ripe.

Another way of keeping fruit from spoiling before it reaches us is to coat it with an invisible protective chemical. Scientists keep searching for ways to provide us with better fruit in better condition.

Banana

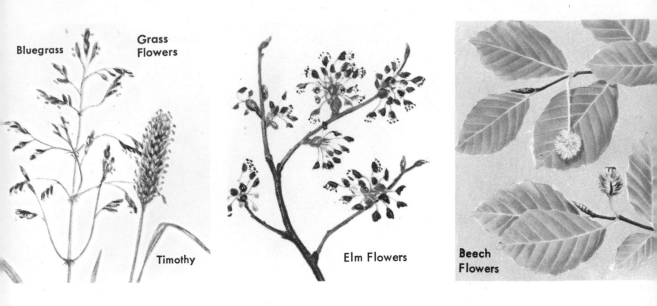

Bluegrass · Grass Flowers · Timothy · Elm Flowers · Beech Flowers

Flowers

Learning to call by name all the kinds of flowers in the world would mean learning to know some 250,000 kinds, for there are that many different species of plants that bloom. Not all flowers, of course, are colourful. It takes careful looking to find the flowers on some plants that are in bloom. Probably most people see certain flowers without recognizing them as such. They may not know, for example, when they find the paths on a spring morning littered with yellowish catkins from hazel trees, that these catkins are clusters of tiny flowers.

A number of trees besides the hazel have flowers so simple that they are not easily recognized as flowers. The maple and elm are among them. Grass flowers, as you see, are simple, too. In contrast, the orchid pictured is very showy.

The thousands of flowering plants are

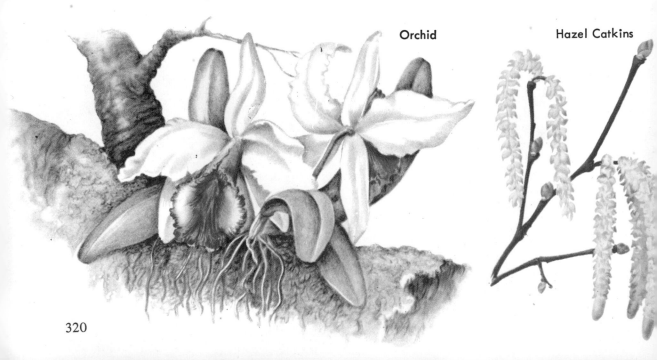

Orchid · Hazel Catkins

divided up into about 300 families. Flowers are the identification tags that tell what family a flowering plant belongs to.

Five different families are represented by the flowers on page 320. The hazel tree is the willow family. The beech, grasses, elm, and orchid belong to the beech, grass, elm, and orchid families named after them.

All the plants pictured on this page are members of the grass family. This family is a very large one. About 10,000 different plants belong to it. It is, moreover, the most important to man of all the families of flowering plants, for it includes our most important cereal grains. Some of these grains have been cultivated since prehistoric times. Egyptian paintings 5,000 years old show farmers harvesting wheat.

The giants of the grass family are found among the bamboos. A stalk of

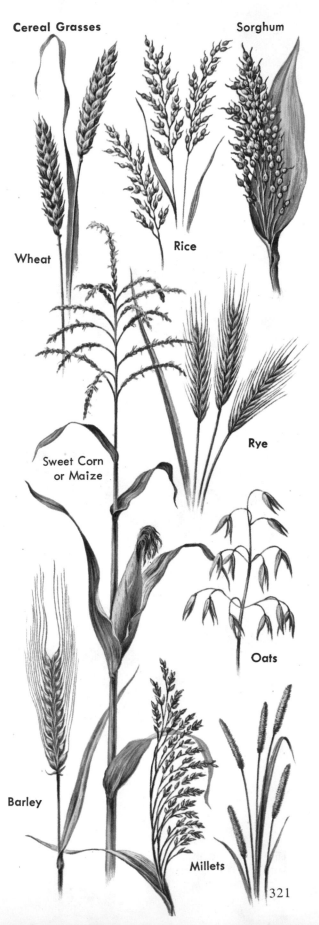

Cereal Grasses

Sorghum

Wheat

Rice

Sweet Corn or Maize

Rye

Oats

Barley

Millets

Bamboo

Trillium

Narcissus

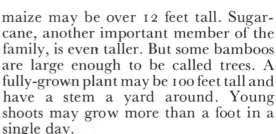

Tulip

Lily

Hyacinth

Lily of the Valley

maize may be over 12 feet tall. Sugarcane, another important member of the family, is even taller. But some bamboos are large enough to be called trees. A fully-grown plant may be 100 feet tall and have a stem a yard around. Young shoots may grow more than a foot in a single day.

In the grass family, too, are the lawn and pasture grasses as well as all those growing wild in the meadows and grasslands of the world. Many food chains begin with grass. Grasses play much the same role on land that diatoms do in the sea.

The flowering plants are divided into two groups—the *monocots* and the *dicots*. Monocot is short for *monocotyledon* and dicot for *dicotyledon*. These names come from the number of seed leaves, or *cotyledons*, a young plant has immediately it has germinated from seed. A monocot has only one seed leaf. A dicot has two.

The grass family is a monocot family. The orchid family is another. Grass flowers are among the simplest monocot flowers, orchids among the most complicated.

All the flowers pictured on this page are monocots. Except for the narcissus, they all belong to the lily family. Strangely enough, onion, leek, and garlic also belong to this family. So does asparagus. But not many people grow any of these four 'lilies' for their flowers. The narcissus belongs to a family closely related to the lilies—the amaryllis family.

Chamomile

Dandelion

Zinnia

Dahlia

The flowers on this page are dicots. They all belong to the largest of plant families—the composites. The family is well named, for every so-called flower is composed of many tiny flowers, or flowerets.

The flowers of composites, however, are not all built on the same plan. The daisy is made of two different kinds of tiny flowers. Those around the edge are quite different from those in the centre. The dandelion, on the other hand, is made up of flowerets all of the same kind. The zinnia and the dahlia follow the daisy pattern. Most of them have so many flowerets like those around the edge of the flower that it is not easy to see those in the centre. But one of the dahlias shows clearly that it is built like a daisy.

The willow, maple, and elm families also belong to the dicot group. Among other well-known dicot families are the pea family and the rose family. The pea family includes peas, peanuts, sweet peas, beans, and clover. The rose family includes not only our roses but also most of our fruit. Apples, plums, apricots, peaches, pears, strawberries, and raspberries are all relatives of the rose.

The chart on pages 372-75 lists 22 families of flowering plants and names several plants in each. Some of these relationships may surprise you.

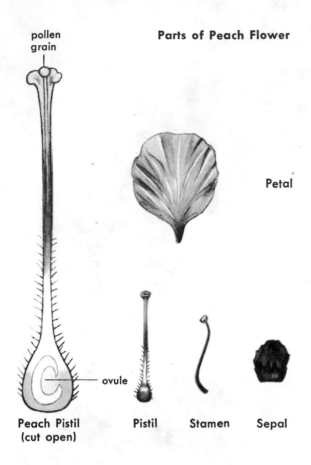

pollen grain

Parts of Peach Flower

Petal

ovule

Peach Pistil
(cut open)

Pistil   Stamen   Sepal

Ovules contain female cells, or eggs. Pollen grains contain male cells, or sperm. Male cells from pollen grains must reach the female cells in the ovules before the ovules can grow into seeds. The male cells and the female cells must join—the eggs must be fertilised.

Fertilisation in the case of a peach blossom comes about in this way: as soon as a peach blossom opens, bees come to it to get nectar. As a bee gets nectar, it brushes against the stamens. Some of the pollen from the pollen sac sticks to its fuzzy body. When the bee rubs against the stamens it rubs against the pistil, too.

At the same time that the bee is getting pollen on its body, it is rubbing pollen from the last peach blossom it visited off on the top of the pistil. The top of the pistil—the *stigma*—is sticky. It holds any pollen grains that reach it.

The picture on the left tells the next step in the story. It shows a section down through the pistil of a peach blossom as it would look if it were greatly magnified. One of the ovules in the base of the pistil can be seen. A grain of pollen is resting

Life History of Peach

The role of all flowers, whether they are simple or showy, is to produce seeds. The story of how a peach seed is formed will serve as an example of how seeds are produced by flowers.

A peach blossom has four sets of parts. In the centre of the blossom there is a *pistil*. It looks like a tiny green vase with a long narrow neck.

Surrounding the pistil are many pinkish stems with sacs full of yellow 'dust' at the top. They are *stamens*. The yellow dust in the sacs is *pollen*.

Outside the stamens are five bright-pink *petals*. The petals, of course, are the conspicuous part of a peach blossom. It is the petals that make a blossoming peach tree into a cloud of pink.

A ring of five reddish-green *sepals* surrounds the petals. They form a tiny cup for the rest of the flower.

Down inside the base of the vase-shaped pistil there are two small greenish-white bodies shaped like eggs. They are *ovules*. Ovules are the beginnings of seeds.

on top of the pistil. A tube is growing down from it. The tube grows till it reaches an ovule. Then all the living material from the tiny pollen grain enters the ovule. A male cell reaches and joins the female cell. The ovule is now ready to grow into a seed.

As soon as the egg in one ovule is fetilised, the other ovule in the pistil dries up. It does not develop into a seed. A single peach blossom only produces one seed.

After fertilisation has taken place, the petals, stamens, and sepals wither and fall off. So do the neck and top of the pistil. Only the base of the pistil is left, with the tiny young seed inside.

The seed grows. While it is becoming a large peach seed, the wall of the part of the pistil that holds it is developing into the rest of the peach, the sweet, juicy part of the fruit that we eat.

When the peach seed is ripe, it is ready to be planted to grow into a new peach tree. The new tree will bloom, the blossoms will produce seeds, and the seeds will produce new peach trees. The cycle of tree—blossom—seed is repeated over and over again.

All complete flowers have the same four kinds of parts peach blossoms have: pistils, stamens, petals, and sepals. But many flowers lack one or more of these parts. However, a flower must have either stamens or pistils. It cannot play any part in producing seeds if it has neither.

Of the flowers that have already been pictured, the trillium best shows the four parts of a complete flower. In the centre there is one pistil. You can just see its top in the picture. Surrounding the pistil are six stamens. Around them there are three white petals, and on the outside of the petals three green sepals.

Many of the monocots have three petals and three sepals. The petals and sepals of the dicots more often come in fives or in fours. A peach blossom has five sepals and five petals. The peach, you remember, belongs to the rose family, which is one of the families of dicots.

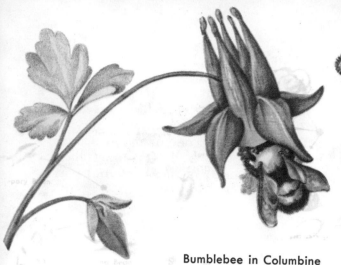

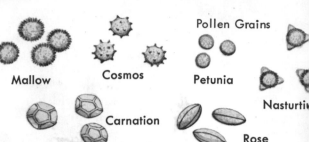

Mallow Cosmos **Pollen Grains** Petunia

Carnation Rose Nasturti

In some cases it is not easy to tell whether a flower has both petals and sepals. Petals and sepals may look very much alike. They do, for example, in a tulip. The only way of telling them apart is that the three sepals are outside the three petals.

Columbine is another flower with sepals and petals both brightly coloured. But the petals can be recognized by their long spurs. The picture shows the spurs clearly.

In orchids the petals themselves differ in shape. And when the sepals as well as the petals are beautifully coloured it is hard to tell which are petals and which sepals.

A flower does not have to be large to be complete. Even the tiny flowerets that make up a dandelion have sepals, petals, stamens, and a pistil. Five petals are joined together to make a yellow 'strap'. The sepals are white bristles. A pistil rises from the centre of the flower. Joined in a cuff around it are five stamens.

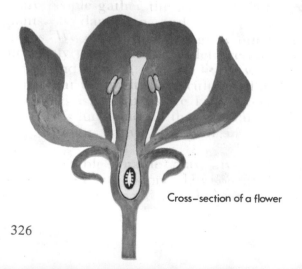

Cross-section of a flower

Bumblebee in Columbine

The diagram below shows a section through a complete flower. You can see easily the pistil in the centre surrounded by stamens. The stamens are surrounded by petals, which in turn have sepals outside them. This flower, however, differs somewhat from a peach blossom. Notice that the sepals, petals, and stamens are attached above the enlarged part of the pistil. In a peach blossom the sepals, petals, and stamens grow out from around the lower part of the pistil. Noticing where the petals and sepals are attached helps to tell flowers apart.

The words 'calyx' and 'corolla' are often used in descriptions of flowers. All the sepals together form the *calyx*. The petals form the *corolla*. 'Calyx' means 'cup'. 'Corolla' means 'crown'.

The hazel catkins on page 320, you remember, are bunches of tiny flowers. Each flower is about as simple as a flower can be. It consists of many stamens fastened to a tiny cup-shaped disc. There are no sepals, no petals, and no pistils.

Stamens alone, however, cannot produce seeds. Hazel bushes would never have seeds if they only bore flowers with stamens—*staminate flowers* they are called. As a matter of fact, the hazels that bear these staminate flowers never do produce seeds. Hazel seeds are produced on other hazel bushes that bear catkins made up of only flowers with pistils—*pistillate flowers*. Each pistillate flower consists of a single pistil.

Of course, the staminate flowers are just as important as the pistillate flowers. Pollen from them must reach the ovules of the pistillate flowers if seeds are to form.

Scientists call the hazel a *dioecious* plant. 'Dioecious' means 'two households'. The hazel gets this name because

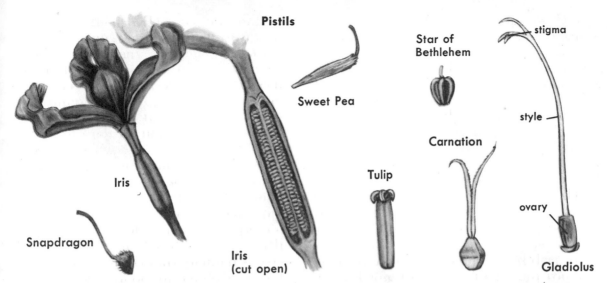

Pistils

Sweet Pea

Star of Bethlehem

stigma

style

ovary

Carnation

Tulip

Iris

Iris (cut open)

Snapdragon

Gladiolus

its pistillate flowers are on one tree and its staminate flowers on another. The willow, a close relative of the hazel, is another two-household plant.

Some plants have two kinds of flowers —one with pistils and one with stamens —but bear both on the same plant. Maize is a good example. These plants are *monoecious*. The word means 'one household'.

Maple and elm flowers, which, you have seen, are not at all showy, are not as simple as willow and hazel flowers. But they are not complete flowers either. Both of them lack petals.

Even though flowers of all kinds have either stamens or pistils or both, the stamens of different flowers do not all look alike and neither do the pistils. The pictures on this page show some ways in which stamens and pistils vary. An iris pistil, for example, has stigmas that spread out to look like petals. The stamens of anemones are squat, those of snapdragon long and curving. Even the pollen grains flowers produce are different. The pictures of pollen grains show them greatly magnified.

You might expect that there would be no problem of fertilisation for flowers that contain both stamens and pistils. But in many cases there is no fertilisation unless pollen is brought from another flower, often from a flower on another plant of the same kind. Many flowers must, in other words, be *cross-pollinated*.

Wind blows pollen about easily. Many flowers are pollinated by the wind. But many flowers depend on insects, just as the peach tree does, to carry their pollen from blossom to blossom. Most plants without showy petals are wind-pollinated. Those with showy petals need the help, as a rule, of insects or other small animals. Red clover, for example, depends on bumblebees. In the story of life on the earth, insects and flowering plants go hand in hand. Neither could have developed as they did without the help of the other.

Gay petals are like signal flags—calls to insects for help in carrying pollen from flower to flower. It is when the pollen sacs open up that the petals are freshest and brightest. The perfume of a flower helps attract insects, too.

The bees, moths, and other insects that carry pollen do not know, of course, that they are helping the plants. To them the petals and perfume are simply dinner bells.

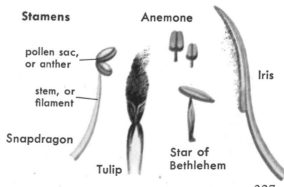

Stamens

Anemone

pollen sac, or anther

stem, or filament

Snapdragon

Tulip

Star of Bethlehem

Iris

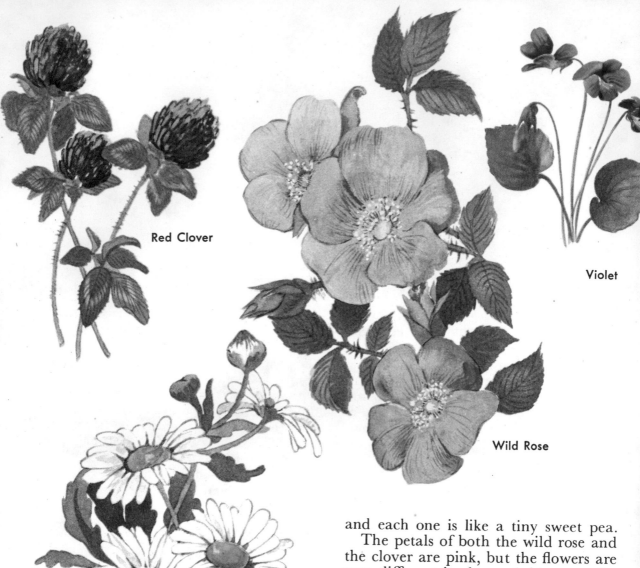

Red Clover

Violet

Wild Rose

Moon Daisy

The flowers shown here are common spring and summer flowers. They are all quite different in appearance.

The daisy, as you know, is a composite. It is the only composite pictured here, although many wild flowers, especially those of late summer and autumn are composites. A clover blossom is made of many tiny flowerets, too, but it is not a composite. The flowerets are arranged in a different way. All of them are alike,

and each one is like a tiny sweet pea.

The petals of both the wild rose and the clover are pink, but the flowers are very different in shape. A blossom of a rose consists of one large flower only.

Both the wood anemone and the tea-tree have white petals but they have different coloured stamens. Bluebells are monocots. All the other flowers shown here are dicots.

You probably know these flowers by sight. But you are almost sure to meet some wild flowers that you do not know. There are flower guides to use in identifying wild flowers. Most of them help by illustrating many of the flowers. But it would take a very large book to illustrate all our wild flowers. You may very well have to identify a flower just by its description. If so, the answers to these questions will help you to find out what it is.

How many petals, sepals, stamens,

Wood Anemone

Tea-tree

Bush Iris

European Bluebell

and pistils does it have in each flower?

Are the petals, if any, joined?

How large and what colour are the flowers?

Are the sepals and petals attached above the base of the pistil or below it?

How tall is the plant the flower is on, and where is it growing?

What time of year is it in bloom?

Many of our spring wild flowers are found in woodlands. They come into bloom before the trees are fully in leaf. Before there are leaves on the trees, sunshine can reach the floor of the woods. The spring woodland flowers take advantage of this sunshine. Some wild flowers are *perennials*. They live, that is, for several or many years. They store up food in bulbs or roots or underground stems which they use to come into bloom quickly. In the spring sunshine their leaves make food which is stored for the next year's blooming.

Although many spring flowers are hardy perennials, as a rule nothing remains above ground during the winter to show that the plant is still living. Instead of merely losing its leaves for the winter as elm trees and rosebushes do, the whole part of the plant withers and dies.

329

Wild Sunflower

Goldenrod

Yellow Toadflax

Cardinal Flower

Michaelmas
Daisy

Black-eyed
Susan

Heather

The flowers on these two pages are flowers of late summer and autumn. They are for the most part not woodland but roadside or garden flowers or they grow on moorlands and other open spaces. Most of them are perennials. The sunflower is an *annual* instead—that is, it grows from seed, blooms, and dies all in one season. The ragwort is usually a *biennial*. It often lives for only two years, but it may live longer.

Some wild flowers have the word 'weed' in their names. They are weeds in the sense that they can take care of themselves; they do not have to be planted and cultivated as our garden flowers do. But a better definition of the word 'weed' is 'a plant that grows where it is not wanted'. Any plant can be a weed. Grass, for example, can be a real nuisance in a vegetable or flower garden. And violets and buttercups, although beautiful in the spring, do not help the appearance of a lawn later in the season.

The dandelion, everyone agrees, is a weed. But if it did not bother us by getting into our lawns we would surely think of it as a lovely wild flower.

To the men who work to keep roadsides clear, some of the flowers pictured here are weeds. To most of the people who see them they are wild flowers.

Some of our wild flowers are in danger of disappearing. People have been too careless about picking them. If all the flowers are picked from a plant, it cannot make seeds to start new plants. To get its flowers, people often pull up a whole plant. Sometimes, too, they dig up plants to take home to their gardens. Many wild flowers die if they are transplanted.

We are killing off our wild flowers, moreover, by taking away their homes.

We have cleared woodlands, ploughed up meadows, and covered thousands of square miles with roads and motorways. We are mowing or burning over our roadsides and our railway embankments. We are keeping our fields clear of weeds. Our growing cities take over open country. Sooner or later many of our wild flowers are bound to disappear unless everyone does his fair share in protecting them.

Even now some of our best-loved wild flowers are very hard to find. The showy lady's-slipper is one of them. Anyone who finds a showy lady's-slipper should be careful not to pick it and should try to keep others from doing so.

Many orchids grow under strange conditions. The hyacinth orchid is very difficult to grow in gardens as it needs a certain species of fungus in the soil around its roots. In the wild state this fungus is always found in the soil where the hyacinth orchid is growing.

Some wild flowers, and some cultivated flowers as well, have to be several years old before they bloom. The century plant, a native of Mexico, got its name because the time it lives before it blooms seemed to people like a hundred years. Actually a century plant may have flowers in 10 to 15 years. After the plant has bloomed it dies. In contrast, most of the perennials that grow in this country come into bloom year after year once they begin.

Day Lily

Hyacinth Orchid

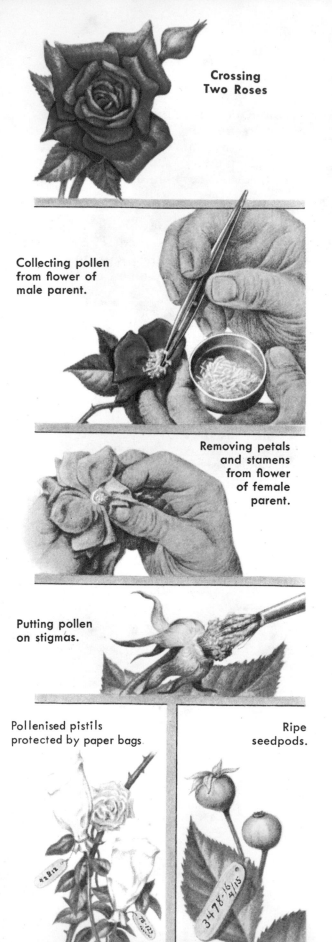

Crossing Two Roses

Collecting pollen from flower of male parent.

Removing petals and stamens from flower of female parent.

Putting pollen on stigmas.

Pollenised pistils protected by paper bags.

Ripe seedpods.

Many plants—hundreds of kinds—are grown just for the beauty of their flowers. Flower catalogues list many varieties of them.

Plant breeders have gone about improving our flowers just as they have improved our fruit and vegetables. The chief ways are carefully selecting the best plants for propagation, watching for sports and taking care of desirable ones, and producing hybrids.

The three roses pictured at the top of the next page are hybrids. Knowing about the parts of flowers helps us to understand exactly how hybrids are produced.

Crossing two flowering plants means taking the pollen from the flower of one plant and putting it on the pistil or pistils of a flower of a different variety. Often a plant breeder has in mind some new characteristic he would like the new flower to have. He may have in mind some special colour, or some special shape, or a certain number of petals. He may be thinking more of the plant itself and want an especially hardy one, or one that climbs well, or one that will thrive in poor soil, or one that can stand the attacks of certain insect pests or plant diseases.

The plant breeder may, perhaps, be trying to get a very hardy climbing rose that has big bright-red flowers. He has a red rose of the colour he wishes, but it is a small bush. He has a very vigorous climbing rose that stands cold weather well, but its flowers are pale pink. The two roses are in bloom at the same time. He decides to cross the two.

First he cuts away the petals and sepals and stamens of several of the roses of one plant. Let us suppose it is the plant with pink flowers. He takes some of the pollen from the red flowers of the other plant and, using a soft brush, puts it on the pistils of the pink flowers. Then he ties paper bags carefully over these pistils so that no other pollen can reach them.

Perhaps no seeds will develop. The pollen of the red rose may not be of any use in fertilising the eggs in the ovules of the pink rose. If seeds do develop, some

Hybrid Roses

of the plants that grow from them may have the worst traits of their two parents. But perhaps one will have the characteristics the breeder is looking for.

Obviously the plant breeder might cross the two plants the other way round. He might put the pollen of the pink rose on the pistils of the red one. The results might be either better or worse.

Every year new hybrid roses are listed in garden catalogues. Some of them are different enough from other roses to be given a patent. The popular Peace rose is a patented hybrid rose.

Garden catalogues list hybrids of many flowers besides roses. Tulips, irises, peonies, marigolds, petunias, chrysanthemums, and zinnias are only a few of them.

Not all new varieties, however, are hybrids. Some of them are sports. Recently, for example, a rosegrower found in a field of tea roses with big red flowers one rose that was growing twice as fast as any of the others. It kept on growing and turned out to be a climbing rose with flowers like those of the tea roses around it. Many plants were then raised from this one sport.

The catalogues which list and describe the kinds and varieties of flowers that a certain nurseryman sells, may appear very confusing to a gardener. They seem to be full of so many different varieties. It is very difficult for the gardener to know which varieties will grow best in his garden. He must con-

sider the type of soil that forms his garden; he must also think where he is going to put the plant. Some plants need a sheltered position away from the wind, some need to be shaded from the sun, others will grow almost anywhere. He must also consider how this new variety will fit in with the other plants in his garden.

Walter Faxon Peony

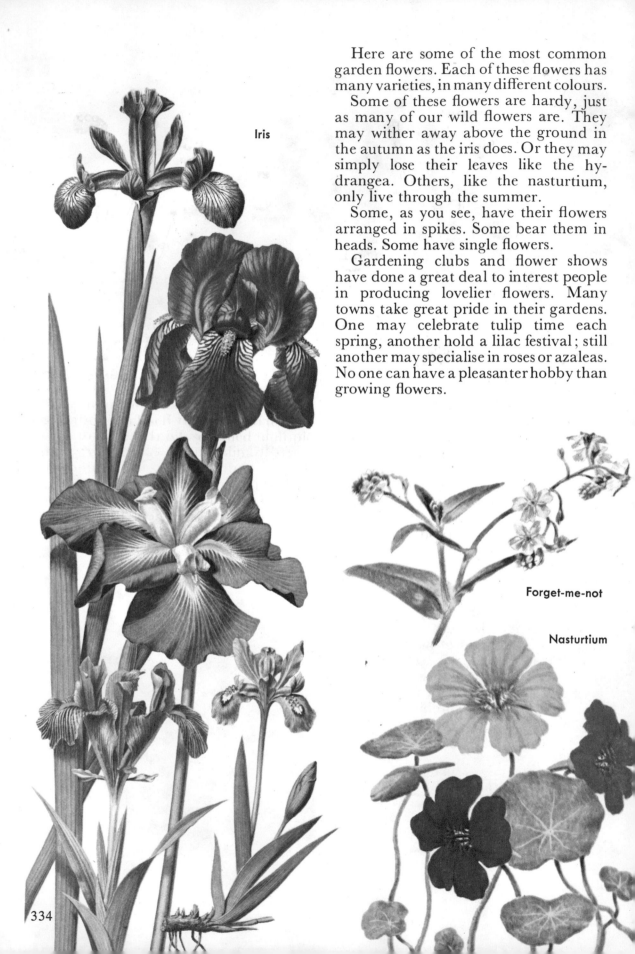

Iris

Forget-me-not

Nasturtium

Here are some of the most common garden flowers. Each of these flowers has many varieties, in many different colours.

Some of these flowers are hardy, just as many of our wild flowers are. They may wither away above the ground in the autumn as the iris does. Or they may simply lose their leaves like the hydrangea. Others, like the nasturtium, only live through the summer.

Some, as you see, have their flowers arranged in spikes. Some bear them in heads. Some have single flowers.

Gardening clubs and flower shows have done a great deal to interest people in producing lovelier flowers. Many towns take great pride in their gardens. One may celebrate tulip time each spring, another hold a lilac festival; still another may specialise in roses or azaleas. No one can have a pleasanter hobby than growing flowers.

Stock

Snapdragon

Hydrangea

Candytuft

Phlox

Crocus

Sweet Pea

Canna

Larkspur

It goes without saying that the ancestors of all our cultivated flowers once grew wild. But even if we could see these wild ancestors the chances are we would not recognise them. Wild tulips like the one pictured below can still be found in western Asia. They do not look much like the tulips we are used to seeing.

No garden flower has had a more exciting history than the tulip. Many of

Tulip

Geranium

Wild Geranium

the tulips in our gardens today can trace their ancestry back to tulips brought from Turkey to Europe in the 16th century.

When tulips reached Holland they became very popular there. In fact, in the 1700's there was a tulip craze that came to be called 'tulipomania'. Enormous prices were paid for new varieties of tulips. A single bulb of a variety of tulip named Semper Augustus sold for what would be hundreds of pounds in our money.

The craze ended, but tulip breeding is still important in Holland. New varieties are being developed in other countries, too. There are now hundreds of varieties.

The wild geranium pictured is one of our wild flowers. But the geranium we see most often came to us from South Africa.

In our flower gardens there are many other immigrants. Flowers were first imported into Britain in the 17th century. The flowers that came from our own wild flowers rub shoulders not only with tulips and geraniums, but also with such foreigners as strawflowers from Australia, hollyhocks from Asia, snapdragons from Europe, nasturtiums from South America, and marigolds from Mexico.

Wild Tulip

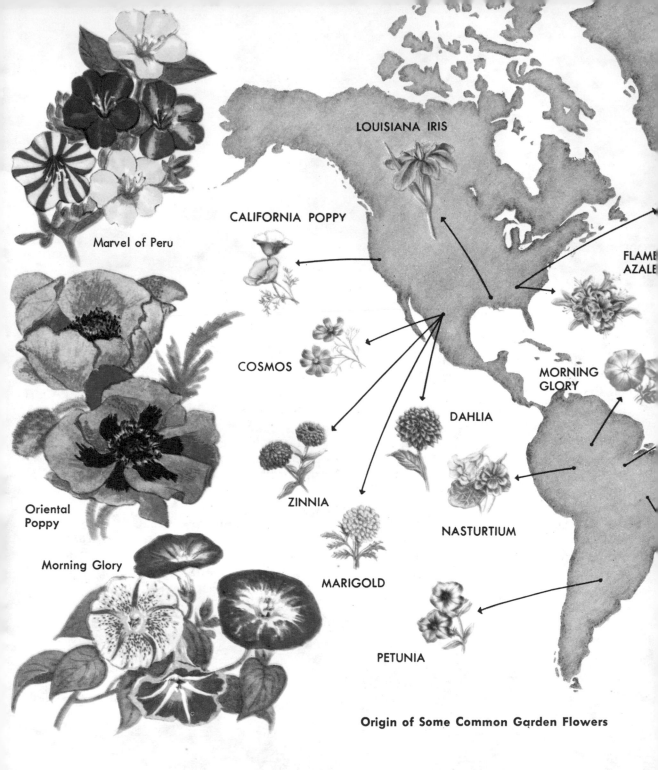

Marvel of Peru

CALIFORNIA POPPY

LOUISIANA IRIS

FLAME
AZALE

Oriental
Poppy

COSMOS

ZINNIA

DAHLIA

MORNING
GLORY

Morning Glory

MARIGOLD

NASTURTIUM

PETUNIA

Origin of Some Common Garden Flowers

This map tells us from what lands 30 of our common garden flowers came. Comparing it with the map on page 306 shows that the petunia and the potato reached us from the same region of South America. It is not surprising that they did, for they are cousins. Both of them belong to a family especially common there—the nightshade family.

The morning glory and the sweet potato are both natives of another region of South America. They, too, are cousins; they belong to the morning-glory family. Asparagus, onions, and tulips were

SNAPDRAGON

CANDYTUFT

PANSY

ANEMONE

HOLLYHOCK

DODENDRON

CHRYSANTHEMUM

DAISY

CARNATION

TULIP

JAPANESE IRIS

CANNA

REGAL LILY

ORIENTAL POPPY

CALLA LILY

STRAWFLOWER

GLADIOLUS

SALVIA

GERANIUM

BLUE LACE

brought from south-western Asia; they, as you know, are all members of the lily family. Candytuft and cabbage belong to the mustard family. They both came to us from southern Europe.

Some flowers had been cultivated for centuries in other parts of the world before they appeared in our gardens. A trip through a flower garden of today may well take us back in imagination to the gardens of the ancient emperors of China, the monastery gardens of the Middle Ages or the flower-bordered highways leading to Aztec temples.

Seeds

A seed is made up of a tiny plant, food for the plant, and a seed coat for protection. The tiny plant inside is sometimes spoken of as the *embryo*. No other part of the seed can grow. A seed may look perfect from the outside, but if the embryo plant has died the seed will never sprout.

How long an embryo plant will live inside a seed depends partly on what kind of plant the seed came from. Gardeners usually want seeds which were produced the previous season. And the seeds of many plants seldom sprout if they are more than three years old. Quite a number of seeds, however, are likely to be good even if they have been stored for 15 years. And more than a few kinds have been known to grow after over 100 years.

The record for long life is held by some water lily seeds that were found buried deep underground in a layer of peat in China. They were about 1,000 years old when they sprouted.

A few plants, the cocklebur for one, produce two kinds of seeds. Those of one kind sprout quickly, if they are going to sprout at all. The others stay dormant— alive but unsprouted—for a long time.

Of the three kinds of seeds pictured on this page, two come from monocots. The other one—the bean—is a dicot. A monocot embryo, you remember, has one seed leaf, while a dicot embryo has two.

A grain of maize shows the general plan of a monocot seed. The embryo

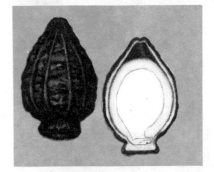

Maize

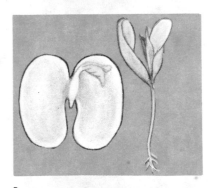

Marvel of Peru

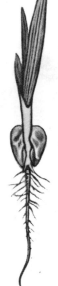

Maize Sprouting

Bean

Bean Sprouting

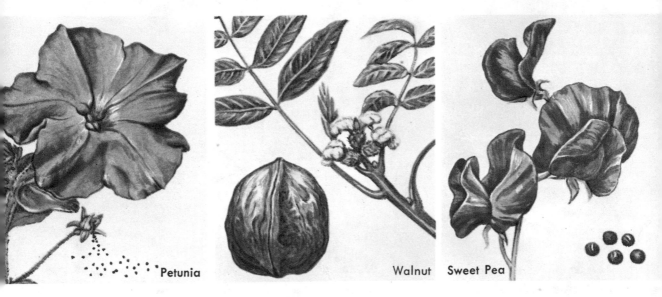

Petunia   Walnut   Sweet Pea

plant only takes up a small part of the seed. It rests on the food that has been stored up for it. The tiny plant's one seed leaf never leaves the seed. When maize sprouts, the growing plant forces its way out of the seed coat. Through the seed leaf it takes in the stored food.

Although the coconut and the bean are both dicots, their seeds are built on rather different plans. In the coconut the two seed leaves are thin. They are wrapped around a ball of food.

The embryo bean plant fills the whole seed. No food is stored beside it. Instead, the food is stored in its two thick seed leaves. When the bean sprouts, the stem of the young plant pulls the two seed leaves out of the seed coat and up out of the ground. Soon, after the food stored in them has been used up, they drop off the plant.

Some seeds are far larger than others. They range all the way from orchid seeds, which are so tiny and light that it would take millions and millions to weigh a pound, to palm seeds that may weigh more than forty pounds. These enormous seeds—sometimes called twin coconuts—are produced by palms of the Seychelles Islands in the Indian Ocean.

The flowering plants form by far the biggest group of seed plants. Most seeds, therefore, are produced by flowers. Some kinds of flowers are very much bigger than others. But big flowers and big seeds by no means always go together.

Petunia flowers are larger than sweet peas, but sweet pea seeds are far larger than petunia seeds. Walnut flowers are not nearly so large as sweet peas, but their seeds are much larger. The seeds of even the biggest most beautiful orchids are like dust.

Seeds come in so many different sizes and shapes and colours that collecting seeds is an interesting hobby. It is easy to learn to tell many kinds of plants by the size and shape and colour of their seeds. Can you pick out in the assortment of seeds pictured below the three maize, four bean, one pea, and two sunflower seeds?

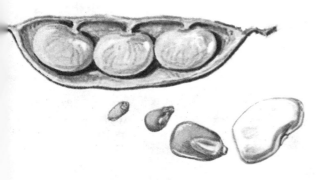

White Willow

Clematis

Willow herb

Some plants form millions of seeds in a season. The poplar and white willow are two that produce enormous numbers.

If all the seeds of a willow were to fall under the tree that bore them, they would not have a proper chance to grow. Many of them might start growing, but one tiny tree after another would die because it was so crowded that it could not get all the water, minerals, and sunshine it needed. It is important for every seed plant, if it is to hold its own, to have some way of getting its seeds scattered.

Many kinds of seeds travel by air. The smaller the seed, as a rule, the better it can ride the wind currents. The tiny seeds of orchids are so light that during much of their journey they are actually floating like tiny balloons in the air. The slighest breeze carries them a long way.

The pictures on these pages show a number of other seeds that are airborne. These seeds are all helped in their travels through the air by having parachutes of down. As you would expect, they, too, are small, light seeds. Only light seeds are equipped with parachutes. The parachutes may be tufts of silky hairs like those of the willow herb or feathery plumes like those of clematis.

In some cases the parachutes are fastened to the seeds themselves. In others they are fastened to a close-fitting covering around the seeds. Many so-called seeds are really one-seeded fruits even though the part of the fruit that surrounds the seed is not at all thick and juicy like that of a peach. The wall of the pistil the seed was formed in has become just a sort of extra seed coat.

A willow herb seed is a seed. A dandelion 'seed' is actually a fruit. It does not make any difference so far as the scattering of the seeds is concerned.

Dandelion

Spear Thistle

Seeds that travel by parachute are sometimes called flyaways. A seed with a parachute may fall to the ground and then be picked up again and again to continue its travels. A single seed with a parachute may be carried more than a hundred miles.

Some kinds of plants whose seeds travel by parachute have spread for many thousands of miles. Each cattail of a bullrush plant is made up of thousands of tiny one-seeded fruits with parachutes. Bullrushes now grow on the edges of swamps and ponds all over the world. The constant fight we have to carry on to keep our lawns free from dandelions is another sign that parachutes are a great help in getting seeds scattered.

There are many different species of thistles found in different parts of the world. But every species has seeds that have parachutes to help their dispersal. Each thistle flower head consists of many tiny flowers called florets. Thistles belong to the large family of composites, just as the dandelion does. Each floret forms a small fruit with a plumed parachute. Cotton seeds also have long downy parachutes. Cotton is spun from the fibres of the parachute. Cotton is grown as a very important crop in many of the warmer countries. Some of the seeds blow away and cling to an animal, as the down is very sticky. Cotton seeds could also be grouped among the seeds that are dispersed by animals.

Cotton

Bullrushes

Plane

Russian Thistle, a tumbleweed

There are many kinds of tumbleweeds. They have the help of the air in scattering their seeds but the seeds are not borne aloft. Instead, when the seeds of a tumbleweed are ripe, the plant dries up and its stem breaks. Then it goes rolling along the ground in the wind, dropping its seeds as it goes. Tumbleweeds are found on prairies and deserts all over the world.

Some seeds and fruits fly through the air on wings rather than parachutes. The picture below shows a few. Winged seeds and fruits mostly come from trees. The wind close to the ground is not likely to be strong enough to lift them.

Winged seeds and fruits turn and twist as they fall through the air. They are something like tiny helicopters. As the wind drives them they are more like aero-planes. One kind of seed is even called the aeroplane seed. It comes from an East Indian vine. Its wings measure six inches from tip to tip.

Some seeds make long air journeys without the help of either wings or parachutes. They travel 'by bird'. Wading birds carry many seeds in mud on their feet. Birds may carry sticky seeds for a long way on their bills. When they clean their bills they scrape the seeds off. Mistletoe is one of the plants that have been scattered in this way. Birds may also carry small seeds in their feathers.

Riding on the feet or in the feathers or on the bill of a bird is like riding on the outside of an aeroplane. There is always a danger of falling off. Sometimes seeds ride on the inside of their bird aeroplanes.

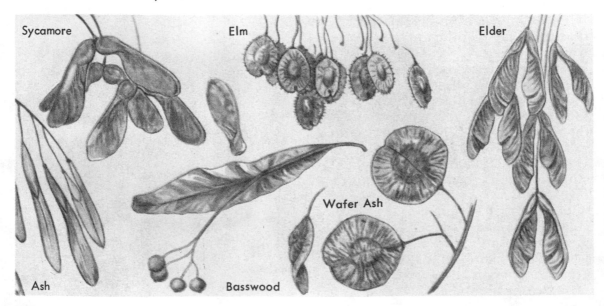

Sycamore   Elm   Elder

Wafer Ash

Ash   Basswood

Birds eat fruit. If the seeds are small, as they are in such a fruit as a blackberry, they swallow the fruit, seeds and all. The bird digests the soft part of the fruit, but it may not digest the seeds. They may go through the bird's body and still be able to grow.

Birds are not the only animals that scatter seeds by carrying them inside their bodies. Box turtles scatter the seeds of wild strawberries in this way. Lizards, snails, freshwater fishes, and land crabs are seed carriers too. The famous scientist Charles Darwin once found water lily seeds in the stomach of a fish that was in the stomach of a heron.

Animals usually carry seeds quite by accident. But sometimes they carry seeds to store them away as food. They may even plant them. Jays, for example, often dig holes in the ground and put acorns in them. They may never come back to get the acorns they have buried. Then the acorns have a chance to grow. Squirrels plant nuts of different kinds in the same way.

Burdock

Goosegrass

Devil's-claw

Starling

Squirrel and nuts

Witch Hazel

Touch-me-not

Pansy

Violet

Sandbox Tree

The seeds that catch a ride on the feet, bills, and feathers of birds are often called hitch-hikers. The seeds pictured on the right are hitch-hikers, too. They are carried in the fur of mammals and in people's clothing. The sharp prickles on the hard cases that hold the seeds can catch in fur or clothing easily. They often cling so tightly that the seeds are hard to pull off. Anyone who has walked through a patch of goose grass knows how easy it is for goose grass seeds to get a free ride.

The seedpods of some plants shoot out their seeds. Witch hazel pods pop open when the seeds are ready to be scattered. The ripe pod of a touch-me-not plant shoots out its seeds if touched. Violet and pansy seedpods explode, too.

Another plant that shoots out its seeds is the sandbox tree that grows in the hot, wet lands of tropical America. Travellers have given this tree another name—the

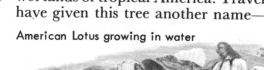

American Lotus growing in water

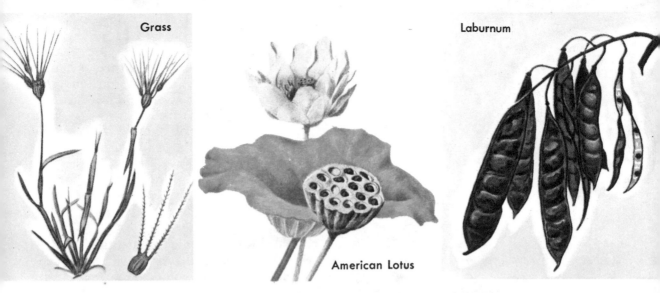

Grass

Laburnum

American Lotus

monkeys' dinner bell. Its ripe seedpods explode with so much force that the noise is like a pistol shot. There are monkeys in the forests where the tree grows. The explosions of the pods gave people the idea that the tree calls the monkeys to dinner.

Wings not only help seeds to travel by air; they also help them to travel by water. Seeds cannot stand being in water long, but with wings to help them, they may float on the surface of a pond or stream until they reach a bank. They may float for several miles. The coconut's fibrous shell keeps it afloat. Snug in its outside husk, this seed can safely island-hop if the trip by sea is not too long.

The American lotus has an unusual way of sending its seeds on journeys by water. The seed holder it produces serves as a boat. It can float for a long way. The seeds are held firmly inside it until the 'boat' breaks or rots away.

Such seeds as walnuts may roll quite a distance. The water that runs off after a heavy rain often washes seeds along the ground. Seeds in pods may go coasting over ice and crusty snow. A few seeds can actually crawl a little way. Some grass seeds, for example, do so by means of stiff hairs that move when they get wet.

Some seeds have gluey seed coats. They may stick to dead leaves and be carried as the leaves are whirled along.

Seeds can endure long periods of bad weather. They make it possible for seed plants to hold their own in many places where other plants cannot. And, as you have seen, seed plants have any number of ways of getting their seeds scattered. Is it any wonder that, after seed plants once appeared, they spread over most of the earth?

Coconut Palm

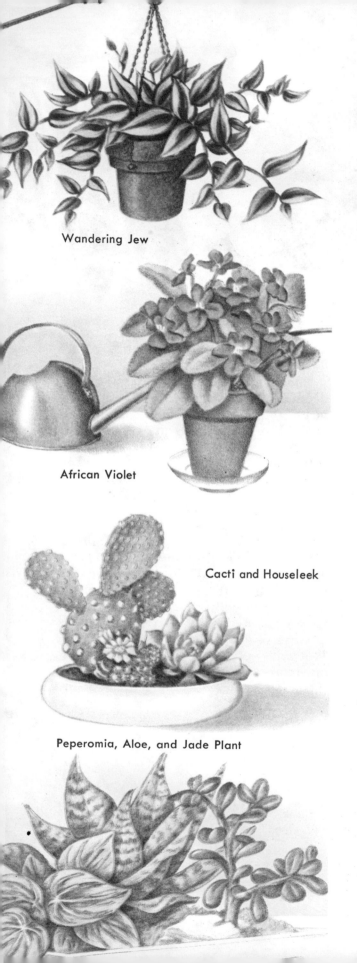

Wandering Jew

African Violet

Cacti and Houseleek

Peperomia, Aloe, and Jade Plant

House Plants

Even in cold winter weather, when the trees are bare and our gardens show nothing but dead stalks, we can have growing plants around us. For many different kinds of plants can be grown indoors. Florist shops are full of plants for indoor gardens. Some of these plants are liked for their flowers, others for their leaves. These pictures show a few of the plants that can be grown indoors successfully.

Wandering Jew is a trailing plant. It was a favourite with our great-grandmothers because of its pretty leaves. Now other trailing plants have become just as popular. Ivy and philodendron are two of them. Philodendron is often seen growing without soil. It will do well if it is simply planted in water.

African violets are very popular, partly because they bloom so well when properly taken care of. Many varieties will bloom almost the year round.

Cactus plants make an interesting indoor garden. Different kinds have different shapes, some of them rather grotesque. Cactus plants have no leaves. But they have beautiful flowers when they bloom.

Some cactus plants are tiny. Several can be grown in a bowl only a few inches across. In the picture of the bowl with the two cacti there is also a houseleek plant. A houseleek does not need to be grown indoors as it can often be seen growing on some thatched roofs of old houses. Another name for this plant is cobweb, because of the very fine hairs on each of the small leaves. It is mainly grown for its leaves, but as you can see from the picture it has small flowers too.

Houseleeks and cactus plants are *succulents*, plants with special ways of storing water. The word 'succulent' means 'full of juice'. Cacti store water in their stems, a houseleek in its thick leaves.

The three plants in the bottom picture are also succulents with thick leaves for storing water. The jade plant, with the small leaves, grows into interesting

Geranium

shapes and throws pretty little shadows when the sun shines on it. It is a relative of the houseleek. Aloe belongs to the lily family. Peperomia, the plant with the heart-shaped leaves, is in the pepper family—the family that includes not the green pepper but the plant black pepper comes from.

In early summer, geraniums are planted by the millions in gardens, parks, and window boxes. They make good indoor plants for the winter, too. There are more than 650 varieties to choose from. The varieties differ chiefly in the colour of their blossoms. There are pink, deep red, and white blossoms as well as scarlet ones.

Poinsettia

The secret of being a successful indoor gardener is knowing that not all plants that will grow indoors should be treated the same way. They do not all thrive with the same amount of light. Some do best in a sunny south window, others in a north window. They do not all need the same amount of water. Some must be protected from draughts. Some can stand higher or lower temperatures than others. Some need well-drained soil, while others will grow in pots that have no drainage.

A good rule is to try to give plants, as nearly as possible, the conditions they would thrive in outdoors. Cacti, for example, are desert plants. They live in regions where there are occasional heavy showers. A cactus plant, therefore, should be watered thoroughly. Then it should not be given any more water until the soil is quite dry. If the soil around it is kept wet all the time, a cactus is likely to rot. As another example, begonias grow outdoors in cool regions. If a begonia is to last long indoors, it should not be kept in a warm room.

At Christmas time and other special times potted plants by the thousands are sent as gifts. Some of them do not last any longer than a bouquet of cut flowers. A poinsettia that has lost all its leaves is, for example, a common sight a day or two after Christmas. Many florists now send a card with every potted plant telling how the plant should be cared for. The directions should be followed.

Aquarium

Terrarium

An aquarium is too often thought of only as a home for fish. But if it is planted carefully, it can be made into an attractive underwater garden.

A little glassed-in garden, or terrarium, is fun to plan and plant. The one in the picture above has four kinds of plants in it: twinberry—the plant with the red berries—moss, a small fern, and a lichen of the kind called red cap, because of its red tips.

To have an attractive indoor garden it is not necessary to buy plants from a florist. If you cut off the leafy top of a pineapple and plant it in a small pot, roots will form and it will soon grow. If you want fruit, you must keep it in a warm place and put it in a larger pot as the roots grow bigger. Grapefruit seeds grow into plants with shiny dark-green leaves. If the top third of a carrot is stood in a shallow bowl of water and held in place with pebbles, it will send up dainty feathery leaves. Slips taken from such plants as begonias and geraniums may be started in moist sand, then planted in pots with every hope of their growing well. Interesting plants for a terrarium can be gathered anywhere.

Begonia

The paper-white narcissus is among the most successful blooming plants that can be grown indoors. Paper-white narcissus bulbs can be planted in water and pebbles, and need little care. On a cold, dark morning in winter a bowl of blooming narcissus does a great deal to make one forget the weather.

Paper-white Narcissus

351

New Plants from Old

Almost all the plants we grow in our fields and orchards and gardens are seed plants. The commonest way of growing them is to plant their seeds. The story of a great many of our crop plants is much like the pumpkin life history pictured here.

Planting a seed means putting it in a situation that will allow the small plant inside the seed to break its way out through the seed coat and keep on growing. Warmth, moisture and air must be provided. Many people who plant seeds do not understand that seeds need air. It is possible to drown the tiny plants in seeds by pouring on so much water that it shuts air out.

The depth at which a seed is planted is important. In every seed some food is stored for the embryo plant. If the seedling is to keep on growing, this food must last until the plant is above the surface of the ground and can make food for itself.

A marrow seed has enough food stored in it to let the young plant grow a few inches. It can be planted some two inches deep without any danger that the seedling will run out of food. There is an advantage in planting a large seed rather deep. If it is planted close to the surface, a heavy rain is likely to wash away the soil from around it. If, on the other hand, a tiny petunia seed is planted deep in the ground, the seedling will run out of food and never reach the sunshine.

Life History of a Marrow

In some cases there are other ways of growing new seed plants that are better than planting seeds. Many kinds of flowers are commonly raised from *bulbs*. Almost no one, for example, plants tulip seeds except flower-growers who are trying to produce new varieties of tulips.

Bulbs provide an easy way of growing sturdy plants. A bulb is mostly made up of thick leaves that overlap one another. A great deal of food is stored in them. There is very much more food in a tulip bulb than there is in a tulip seed. A strong, vigorous plant can grow from a bulb and come into bloom much more quickly than from a seed.

A *corm* is very much like a bulb. Crocuses and gladioli are commonly grown from corms rather than from seeds. Corms are swollen stems, filled with food.

Some plants can be grown from *roots*. The dahlia has fleshy roots in which a large amount of food is stored.

As you know, a potato is a thick underground stem of the kind called a *tuber*. A gardener, to plant potatoes, cuts potatoes into pieces, each piece with an eye, or bud. There is enough food in the pieces to let their buds grow.

A *rhizome* is another kind of thick underground stem. Iris plants are usually grown from rhizomes. Tubers, rhizomes, corms, and fleshy roots have the same advantage over seeds that bulbs have.

The branches of some plants send out roots wherever they touch the ground. New plants can be started by bending a branch down to the ground, fastening it in place until it sends roots down and a shoot up, and then cutting the branch so that it is no longer joined to the parent plant. This plan of starting new plants is called *layering*. Many new blackberry and raspberry canes are started by layering.

Geraniums are usually grown from *cuttings* often called slips. A cutting is a piece—in many cases a branch—cut from a plant. Geranium slips, as you know, will send out roots when put in moist sand. A cutting may include both a young branch and a part of the stem it grew from.

Such woody plants as apple trees are often raised from cuttings fastened in certain ways, or *grafted*, to other similar woody plants so that the different plants grow together. A cutting of Apple A, for example, could be grafted on to a hardy crab apple tree. The whole top of the crab apple tree would be cut off with only the cutting of Apple A grafted in its place left to grow. Soon the tree would look like the parent Apple A tree. No one would know by looking at it that it had crab apple roots. It would bear apples like those on Apple A.

It has been said that there is really only one Golden Delicious tree in the world. This saying is true in the sense that every Golden Delicious tree except the first one

Rhizome

Cuttings

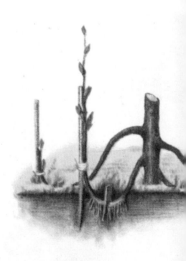

Layering

354

Golden Delicious Apple

Geranium Slip

came from a cutting that was grafted on to the roots of some other kind of tree. The same thing could be said of countless other varieties of woody plants. For many of the fruit trees, rosebushes, grapevines, and ornamental shrubs and trees that nurseries sell are grafted. Grafting is an important help in multiplying plants of new varieties that are developed.

In some cases it is not possible to grow a seed plant from its seeds. Suppose a new kind of apple—let us call it Apple X—has been produced by crossing two kinds of apples. Suppose, too, that Apple X proves to be one of the many kinds of apples that do not produce seeds unless pollen has been brought to their flowers from apple trees of a different variety. The trees that grow from Apple X seeds are not, then, Apple X trees. The reason that they are not is that they have two parents—the Apple X tree and the tree that provided the pollen. They are crosses between Apple X and the variety the pollen came from.

Of course, seed plants that rarely or never produce seeds, such as the pineapple, must be grown in some other way then by seeds. It is lucky that such plants have other ways of multiplying.

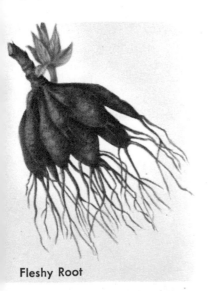

Fleshy Root

Bulb

Corm

Houseleeks

Thimble Cactus

Plant Adaptations

Many plants, like many animals, are specially adapted for living where they do. They may be so well fitted for living in certain kinds of places that they cannot live anywhere else. A seaweed and a willow tree could not change habitats any more successfully than could a swallow and a cod.

A desert is one of the places that present special problems to plants. The deserts are likely to be very hot in the daytime and cold at night. The air as well as the soil is usually dry. When rain does fall, it frequently comes down in torrents. Much of the water runs off instead of sinking in.

The plants called succulents have solved the problems of living in such deserts. Most cacti have no leaves at all except when they are very young. Their stems do similar work that leaves do for such plants as elms and daffodils. Cactus stems are thick and pulpy. As you already know, they make good water storage tanks.

It would do a cactus plant no good to have a storage tank if it had no way of filling the tank. Its roots spread out near the surface of the ground. They are ready to soak up fast any water that reaches them.

Having no leaves helps a cactus to save the water it has stored. Many gallons of water may evaporate from a maple tree on a hot summer day, because there is an enormous amount of surface from which evaporation can take place. In the case of a cactus there is little surface exposed to the air.

Juicy cactus plants would not have much of a chance to escape being eaten by thirsty desert animals if it were not for their spines. Spines, then, are another desert adaptation.

The thick leaves of houseleeks—their water reservoirs—form a rosette close to the ground. Not much surface is exposed.

Welwitschia grows in the deserts of south-western Africa. In its whole life of perhaps more than a hundred years it has only two leaves. They grow from the

Welwitschia

Cacti

Torch

Saguaro

Hedgehog

Englemann's Pear

Purple Tinge Pear

Barrel

Pincushion

Beavertail

Joshua Tree

broad top of the plant's thick root-trunk. The wind tears the leaves into narrow ribbons, and pieces break off the ends, but the leaves keep growing at the base. The root-trunk stores water as well as food. Welwitschia is a living fossil. It has no close relatives.

The Joshua tree is very common in the hot deserts of the southern U.S.A. It may grow 30 to 40 feet tall. Very little water can evaporate through the thick tough leaves.

Venus's-flytrap

Sundew

Pitcher Plant

A swamp is a very different habitat from a desert. Here there is always a great deal of water. But there may be a shortage of another important material—nitrogen. Plants as a rule get all their nitrogen from the soil or water in which they grow. But a swamp plant may get some nitrogen just as many animals do—by 'eating' meat.

The pictures on this page show four plants well adapted to living in swamps because they are meat-eaters. They eat insects.

The hairy leaves of the tiny sundew are insect traps. At the end of each hair there is a drop of liquid. The plant gets its name from these drops of liquid, which look like dew. But this dew does not disappear when the sun shines.

The dew is sticky. A little insect that alights or crawls up on a leaf gets stuck in the dew. The hairs it touches bend over to the centre of the leaf. The other hairs bend down, too, and trap the insect. The dew helps to turn the soft part of the insect into a liquid, which is absorbed by the leaf. When the sundew has finished digesting the insect, the hairs open out again. The hard parts of the insect blow away and the leaf is ready for another meal.

The ends of the leaves of a Venus's-flytrap are its traps. They catch insects by folding together. On each half of the trap at the end of a leaf there are some stiff hairs that stand up. These are the triggers that make the trap work. When an insect touches one of them the trap closes. Stiff hairs around the edges keep the insect from escaping. The trap stays closed until the insect is digested. Then

Bladderwort

insect trapped in bladder

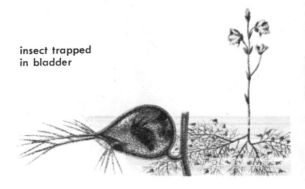

it opens again, ready for another meal.

Pitcher plants trap insects in pitcher-shaped leaves that are usually partly full of water. Inside are downward pointing hairs. Insects can crawl down into a pitcher but not back up again. They drown in the water and are then digested.

Small hollow balls with one-way doors grow on the stems of bladderwort, a water plant. Insects that swim in cannot escape.

The water hyacinth, duckweed and water lily are also water plants. Bullrushes grow in marshes and other very wet areas. None of these plants, however, depend on insects for food. They live where they can get all the materials they need for making food.

The water hyacinth floats about in many of the streams and ponds in warm countries. Often it is a serious nuisance as it can almost stop boats using a river. No plant is better adapted to floating. The stalk of each leaf is an air-filled balloon.

The common duckweed floats, too. This tiny plant without stems or leaves is very light.

The roots of a water lily are in the mud at the bottom of the water, but its leaves usually float on the surface. These leaves differ from most aerial leaves in an important way—the stomata, or air openings, are on the upper side of the leaf. Otherwise they could not take in from the

Water Hyacinth

Duckweed (greatly enlarged)

Water Lily

Bullrush

Air Pine

Strangler Fig

air the carbon dioxide needed for food-making.

In warm, rainy forests plants have to struggle to get the light they need. Some put themselves in the sunshine by perching on the branches of trees. Such plants are called *epiphytes*. Perching high on a tree makes it hard for a plant to get water. Different epiphytes solve the problem in different ways. Some, like the air pine, have stiff leaves cupped at the base that form a rain barrel. Many small animals, from tree frogs to mosquitoes, use the rain barrels of these epiphytes as nurseries.

Long moss is a close relative of air pine. It too is an epiphyte on trees, but it has a different method of getting water. This plant has many fine stems and leaves covered with hair scales. The hair scales catch the water when it rains, then close up trapping the water.

Many orchids are epiphytes. These epiphytes have aerial roots that quickly soak up water from rain.

The primrose shows how a small plant can be adapted to getting enough light. Its leaves spread out in an open rosette.

The strangler fig has a strange way of establishing itself in a crowded forest. A seed alights in a crevice or fork somewhere on another kind of tree—often a

Bristlecone Pine

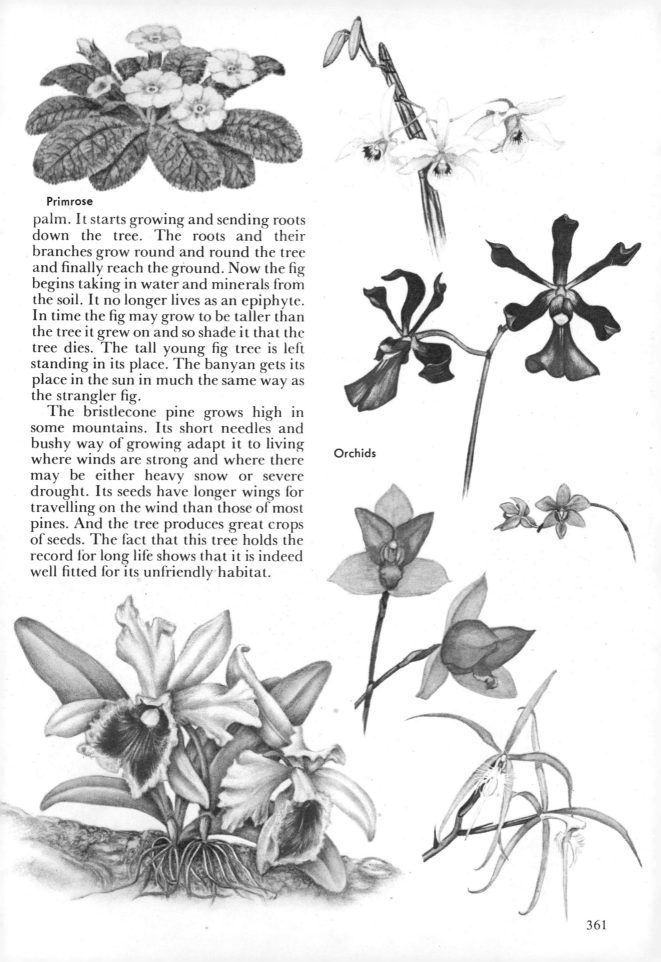

Primrose

palm. It starts growing and sending roots down the tree. The roots and their branches grow round and round the tree and finally reach the ground. Now the fig begins taking in water and minerals from the soil. It no longer lives as an epiphyte. In time the fig may grow to be taller than the tree it grew on and so shade it that the tree dies. The tall young fig tree is left standing in its place. The banyan gets its place in the sun in much the same way as the strangler fig.

The bristlecone pine grows high in some mountains. Its short needles and bushy way of growing adapt it to living where winds are strong and where there may be either heavy snow or severe drought. Its seeds have longer wings for travelling on the wind than those of most pines. And the tree produces great crops of seeds. The fact that this tree holds the record for long life shows that it is indeed well fitted for its unfriendly habitat.

Orchids

These pictures show a few of the many other ways in which various plants fit into their surroundings. The sweet pea and morning glory have tendrils which help them climb. Climbing devices are especially important in tropical forests where there is a constant fight for sunlight.

The kelp has a holdfast which anchors it securely to rock along the shore. It can stand the buffeting of the waves partly because of this good anchor.

The trunk of the kapok tree of tropical America flares out at the base into giant folds that are like the flying buttresses of Gothic cathedrals. They help to keep this tall, heavily branched tree from being uprooted in windstorms.

The dense covering of hairs on mullein leaves, the arrangement of prickly-lettuce leaves so that they always face the sun, and the stilt roots of the mangrove tree are still other plant adaptations. The list is almost endless. Any species of plant that is alive and thriving today, you may be sure, has adapted itself in many ways for living where it does. Survival depends on adaptation.

Sweet
Pea

Morning
Glory

Alaria, a
Kelp

Kapok Tree

Charts

The charts that begin on this page will summarize for you some of the things you have discovered about the history of the earth and about the world of living things. They will also add a great deal of new information. These are the charts:

EARTH'S DIARY

ERAS		EVENTS	LIFE
	PRE-CRUSTAL TIME 200 million years or more	Earth 'born'. Mantle and core of earth separated. Earliest rocks formed.	No life.
EARLY PRECAMBRIAN	100 million years	Great volcanic activity. Mountains pushed up and worn away. First sedimentary rocks formed.	Very simple one-celled plants and animals probably present. At least blue-green algae by end of era.
LATE PRECAMBRIAN	100 million years	Many sedimentary rocks formed. Earliest known glaciers. Great mountains formed in Scotland, now much worn away.	Sponges and many other invertebrates probably common. Many seaweeds.

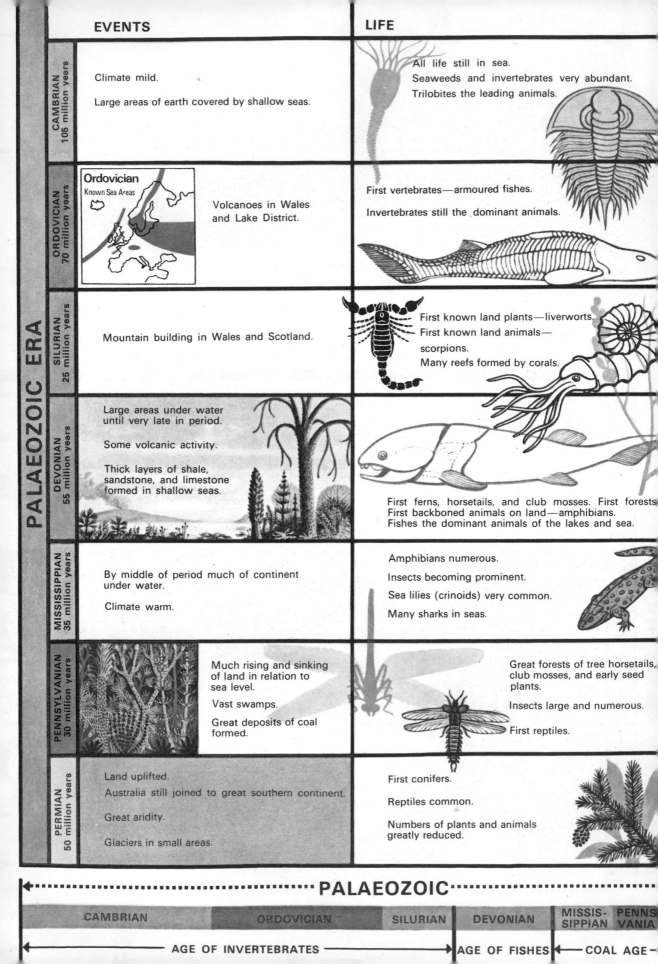

PALAEOZOIC ERA	EVENTS	LIFE
CAMBRIAN 105 million years	Climate mild. Large areas of earth covered by shallow seas.	All life still in sea. Seaweeds and invertebrates very abundant. Trilobites the leading animals.
ORDOVICIAN 70 million years	 Volcanoes in Wales and Lake District.	First vertebrates—armoured fishes. Invertebrates still the dominant animals.
SILURIAN 25 million years	Mountain building in Wales and Scotland.	 First known land plants—liverworts. First known land animals—scorpions. Many reefs formed by corals.
DEVONIAN 55 million years	Large areas under water until very late in period. Some volcanic activity. Thick layers of shale, sandstone, and limestone formed in shallow seas. 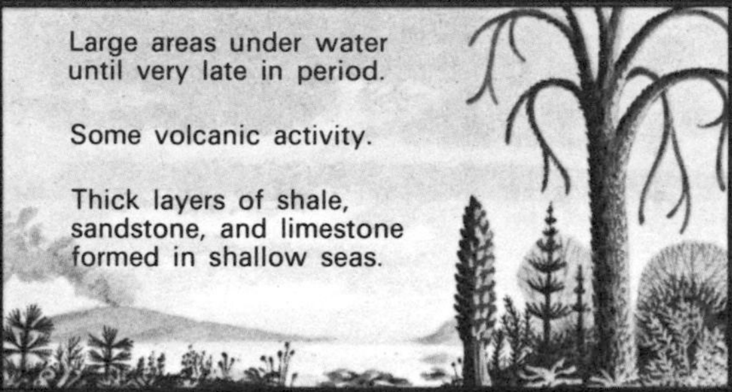	First ferns, horsetails, and club mosses. First forests First backboned animals on land—amphibians. Fishes the dominant animals of the lakes and sea.
MISSISSIPPIAN 35 million years	By middle of period much of continent under water. Climate warm.	Amphibians numerous. Insects becoming prominent. Sea lilies (crinoids) very common. Many sharks in seas. 
PENNSYLVANIAN 30 million years	 Much rising and sinking of land in relation to sea level. Vast swamps. Great deposits of coal formed.	Great forests of tree horsetails, club mosses, and early seed plants. Insects large and numerous. First reptiles.
PERMIAN 50 million years	Land uplifted. Australia still joined to great southern continent. Great aridity. Glaciers in small areas.	First conifers. Reptiles common. Numbers of plants and animals greatly reduced. 

PALAEOZOIC

CAMBRIAN	ORDOVICIAN	SILURIAN	DEVONIAN	MISSIS-SIPPIAN	PENNS-VANIA

AGE OF INVERTEBRATES — AGE OF FISHES — COAL AGE

EVENTS		LIFE	

MESOZOIC ERA

TRIASSIC — 50 million years

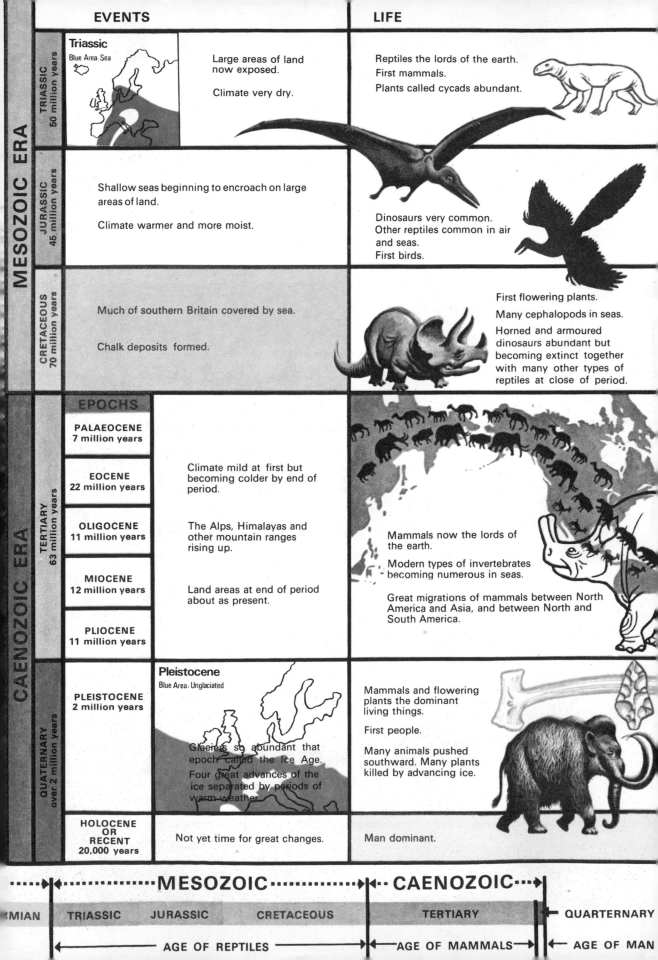

Triassic
Blue Area: Sea

Large areas of land now exposed.

Climate very dry.

Reptiles the lords of the earth.
First mammals.
Plants called cycads abundant.

JURASSIC — 45 million years

Shallow seas beginning to encroach on large areas of land.

Climate warmer and more moist.

Dinosaurs very common.
Other reptiles common in air and seas.
First birds.

CRETACEOUS — 70 million years

Much of southern Britain covered by sea.

Chalk deposits formed.

First flowering plants.

Many cephalopods in seas.

Horned and armoured dinosaurs abundant but becoming extinct together with many other types of reptiles at close of period.

CAENOZOIC ERA

TERTIARY — 63 million years

EPOCHS

PALAEOCENE 7 million years

EOCENE 22 million years

OLIGOCENE 11 million years

MIOCENE 12 million years

PLIOCENE 11 million years

Climate mild at first but becoming colder by end of period.

The Alps, Himalayas and other mountain ranges rising up.

Land areas at end of period about as present.

Mammals now the lords of the earth.

Modern types of invertebrates becoming numerous in seas.

Great migrations of mammals between North America and Asia, and between North and South America.

QUATERNARY — over 2 million years

PLEISTOCENE 2 million years

Pleistocene
Blue Area: Unglaciated

Glaciers so abundant that epoch called the Ice Age.
Four great advances of the ice separated by periods of warm weather.

Mammals and flowering plants the dominant living things.

First people.

Many animals pushed southward. Many plants killed by advancing ice.

HOLOCENE OR RECENT 20,000 years

Not yet time for great changes.

Man dominant.

MESOZOIC · · · · · · · · · · **CAENOZOIC** · · · ·

ᴱMIAN	TRIASSIC	JURASSIC	CRETACEOUS	TERTIARY	QUARTERNARY

AGE OF REPTILES — AGE OF MAMMALS — AGE OF MAN

HOW THIS
ANIMAL
IS
CLASSIFIED

CLASSIFICATION OF LIVING THINGS

In classifying plants and animals, scientists group the plants and animals that are very much alike into species. Species that are much alike are grouped into genera (the plural of genus). Genera are put together to form families, families make up orders, orders make up classes, and classes make up phyla. For an even more exact classification, classes may be grouped into subphyla and the subphyla into phyla. Subspecies are often called varieties.

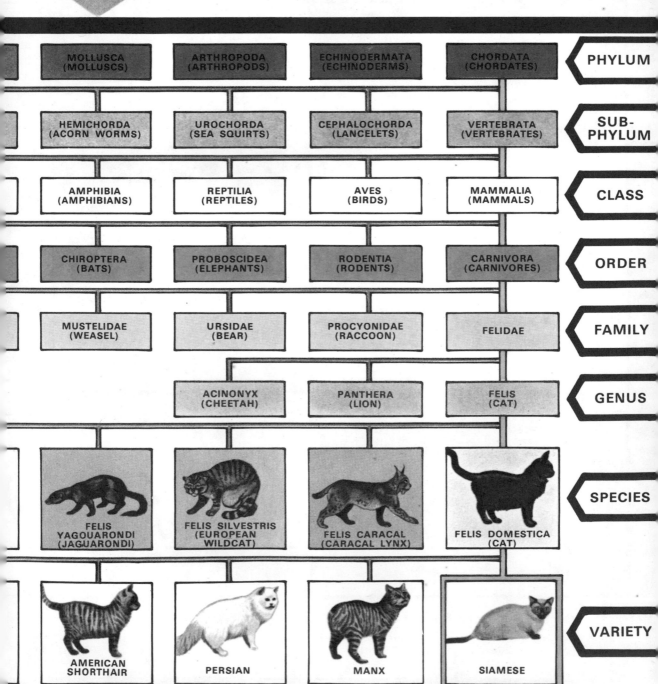

MOLLUSCA (MOLLUSCS)	ARTHROPODA (ARTHROPODS)	ECHINODERMATA (ECHINODERMS)	CHORDATA (CHORDATES)	**PHYLUM**
HEMICHORDA (ACORN WORMS)	UROCHORDA (SEA SQUIRTS)	CEPHALOCHORDA (LANCELETS)	VERTEBRATA (VERTEBRATES)	**SUB-PHYLUM**
AMPHIBIA (AMPHIBIANS)	REPTILIA (REPTILES)	AVES (BIRDS)	MAMMALIA (MAMMALS)	**CLASS**
CHIROPTERA (BATS)	PROBOSCIDEA (ELEPHANTS)	RODENTIA (RODENTS)	CARNIVORA (CARNIVORES)	**ORDER**
MUSTELIDAE (WEASEL)	URSIDAE (BEAR)	PROCYONIDAE (RACCOON)	FELIDAE	**FAMILY**
	ACINONYX (CHEETAH)	PANTHERA (LION)	FELIS (CAT)	**GENUS**
FELIS YAGOUARONDI (JAGUARONDI)	FELIS SILVESTRIS (EUROPEAN WILDCAT)	FELIS CARACAL (CARACAL LYNX)	FELIS DOMESTICA (CAT)	**SPECIES**
AMERICAN SHORTHAIR	PERSIAN	MANX	SIAMESE	**VARIETY**

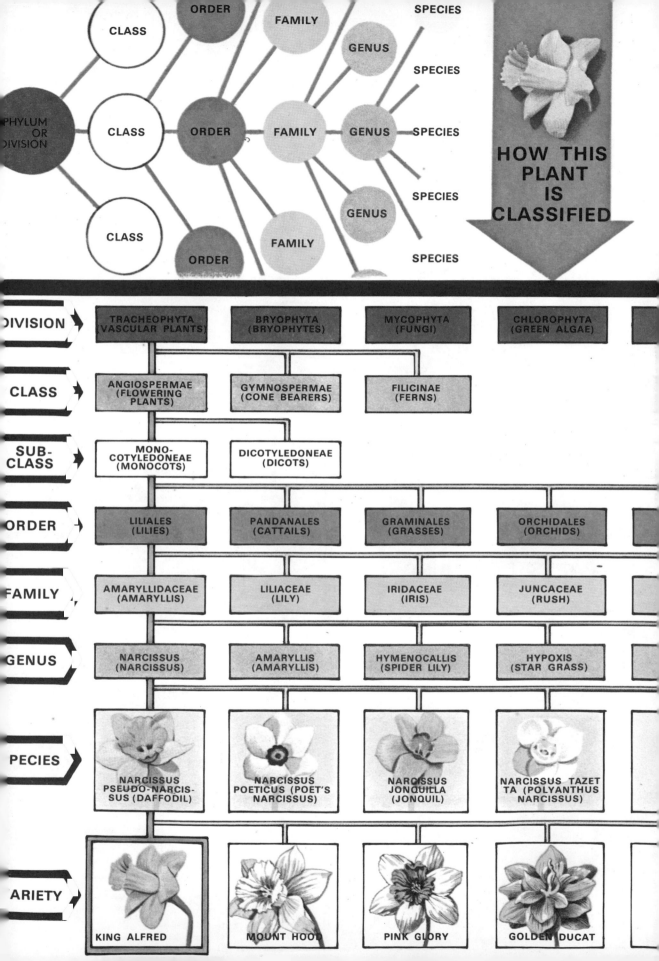

HOW THIS PLANT IS CLASSIFIED

DIVISION	TRACHEOPHYTA (VASCULAR PLANTS)	BRYOPHYTA (BRYOPHYTES)	MYCOPHYTA (FUNGI)	CHLOROPHYTA (GREEN ALGAE)
CLASS	ANGIOSPERMAE (FLOWERING PLANTS)	GYMNOSPERMAE (CONE BEARERS)	FILICINAE (FERNS)	
SUB-CLASS	MONO-COTYLEDONEAE (MONOCOTS)	DICOTYLEDONEAE (DICOTS)		
ORDER	LILIALES (LILIES)	PANDANALES (CATTAILS)	GRAMINALES (GRASSES)	ORCHIDALES (ORCHIDS)
FAMILY	AMARYLLIDACEAE (AMARYLLIS)	LILIACEAE (LILY)	IRIDACEAE (IRIS)	JUNCACEAE (RUSH)
GENUS	NARCISSUS (NARCISSUS)	AMARYLLIS (AMARYLLIS)	HYMENOCALLIS (SPIDER LILY)	HYPOXIS (STAR GRASS)
SPECIES	NARCISSUS PSEUDO-NARCIS-SUS (DAFFODIL)	NARCISSUS POETICUS (POET'S NARCISSUS)	NARCISSUS JONQUILLA (JONQUIL)	NARCISSUS TAZETTA (POLYANTHUS NARCISSUS)
VARIETY	KING ALFRED	MOUNT HOOD	PINK GLORY	GOLDEN DUCAT

BIRDS

FEATHERS

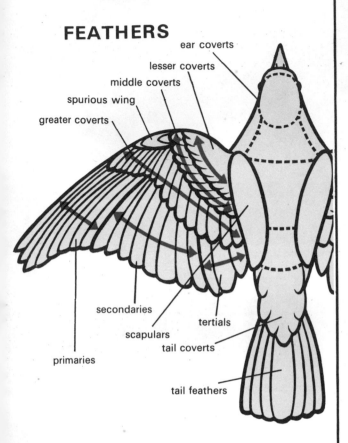

- ear coverts
- lesser coverts
- middle coverts
- spurious wing
- greater coverts
- secondaries
- scapulars
- tertials
- tail coverts
- primaries
- tail feathers

PARTS OF A BIRD

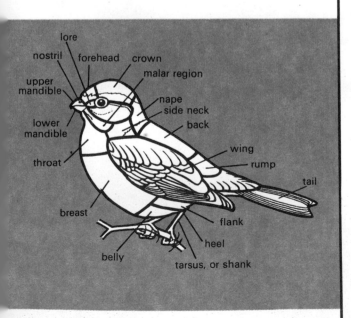

- lore
- nostril
- forehead
- crown
- malar region
- upper mandible
- nape
- side neck
- back
- lower mandible
- throat
- wing
- rump
- tail
- breast
- flank
- heel
- belly
- tarsus, or shank

BIRD ORDERS

RATITES (5 orders)
Cassowaries and Emus, Kiwis, Ostriches, Rheas, Tinamous

DIVERS

GREBES

TUBENOSES
Albatrosses, Petrels, Shearwaters

PENGUINS

PELICANS
Boobies, Cormorants, Gannets, Frigate Birds, Pelicans

STORKS
Bitterns, Flamingos, Herons, Ibises, Spoonbills, Storks

CRANES
Coots, Cranes, Gallinules, Rails

SHOREBIRDS
Auks, Gulls, Jacanas, Plovers, Sandpipers, Terns

WATERFOWL
Ducks, Geese, Swans

LAND FOWL
Chickens, Grouse, Partridges, Peafowl, Pheasants, Ptarmigans, Quail, Turkeys

FALCONS (Daytime Birds of Pre
Buzzards, Condor, Eagles, Falcons, Hawks, Kites, Ospreys, Vultures

OWLS (Nocturnal Birds of Prey)

DOVES AND PIGEONS

PARROTS
Cockatoos, Lories, Lovebirds, Macaws, Parakeets, Parrots,

CUCKOOS

GOATSUCKERS
Nighthawk, Whip-poor-will

SWIFTS AND HUMMINGBIRDS

TROGENS
Quetzal, Trogons

KINGFISHERS AND HORNBILLS

WOODPECKERS
Honey Guides, Toucans, Woodpeckers

PERCHING BIRDS Blackbirds, Flycatchers, Grosbeaks, Jays, Larks, Mockingbirds, Nuthatches, Shrikes, Sparrows, Starlings, Swallows, Tanagers, Thrushes, Warblers, Wrens

MAMMAL ORDERS

 MONOTREMES
Platypus, Spiny Anteater

 EDENTATES
Anteaters, Armadillos, Sloths

 AARDVARK

 MARSUPIALS
Bandicoots, Kangaroos, Koala, Opossums, Phalangers, Tasmanian Devil, Wombats

 PANGOLINS

 ELEPHANTS

 INSECTIVORES
Hedgehogs, Moles, Shrews, Tenrecs

 **RODENTS**
Beavers, Chinchillas, Dormice, Guinea Pigs, Hamsters, Mice, Muskrats, Porcupines, Prairie Dogs, Rats, Squirrels, Woodchucks

 HYRAXES

 FLYING LEMURS

 LAGOMORPHS
Hares, Pikas, Rabbits

 SEA COWS
Dugong, Manatees

 BATS

 CETACEANS
Dolphins, Porpoises, Whales

 ODD-TOED UNGULATES
Asses, Horses, Rhinoceroses, Tapirs, Zebras

 PRIMATES
Apes, Aye-aye, Lemurs, Lorises, Man, Marmosets, Monkeys, Tarsiers

 CARNIVORES
Bears, Cats, Civets, Dogs, Foxes, Hyaenas, Otters, Pandas, Raccoons, Sea Lions, Seals, Skunks, Walruses, Weasels, Wolves

 EVEN-TOED UNGULATES
Alpacas, Antelopes, Camels, Cattle, Deer, Giraffes, Goats, Hippopotamuses, Llamas, Pigs, Pronghorn, Sheep, Yak

INSECT ORDERS

 THYSANURA
Bristletails

 PLECOPTERA
Stoneflies

 NEUROPTERA
Ant Lions, Dobsonflies, Lacewings

 ORTHOPTERA
Crickets, Grasshoppers, Locusts, Mantids, Cockroaches, Stick insects

 ODONATA
Damselflies, Dragonflies

 TRICHOPTERA
Caddisflies

 DERMAPTERA
Earwigs

 ANOPLURA
Lice

 COLEOPTERA
Beetles

 ISOPTERA
Termites

 SIPHONAPTERA
Fleas

 LEPIDOPTERA
Butterflies, Moths

 THYSANOPTERA
Thrips

 HEMIPTERA
True Bugs

 DIPTERA
Flies, Gnats, Mosquitoes

EPHEMEROPTERA
Mayflies

 HOMOPTERA
Aphids, Cicadas, Treehoppers

 HYMENOPTERA
Ants, Bees, Wasps

MAMMAL FAMILIES

The several thousand species of mammals living today are grouped into 18 orders. These orders are divided into more than 100 families. This chart names 11 of the mammal families and shows animals that belong to each.

BEAR (Ursidae)

SUN BEAR   SPECTACLED BEAR   SLOTH BEAR   POLAR BEAR   GRIZZLY BEAR   BLACK BEAR (CINNAMON)

CAT (Felidae)

    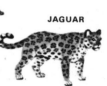

CAT
BOBCAT
OCELOT
LYNX
LEOPARD
CHEETAH
COUGAR, OR PUMA, OR MOUNTAIN LION
JAGUAR

DEER (Cervidae)

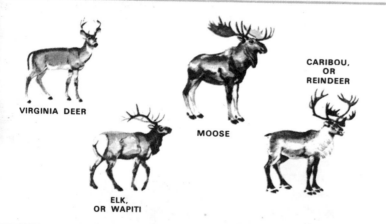

VIRGINIA DEER
MOOSE
CARIBOU, OR REINDEER
ELK, OR WAPITI

WEASEL (Mustelidae)

WEASEL
FISHER
MINK
FERRET
RIVER OTTER
MARTEN
SEA OTTER

CATTLE (Bovidae)

COW
WATER BUFFALO
ZEBU
MOUNTAIN SHEEP
BISON
CHAMOIS
MOUNTAIN GOAT
GOAT
GNU
MUSK OX
YAK
SHEEP

VOLE (Cricetidae)

DEER MOUSE   MEADOW MOUSE, OR VOLE   LEMMING   HAMSTER   MUSKRAT   PACK RAT

SQUIRREL (Sciuridae)

RED SQUIRREL   GREY SQUIRREL   FOX SQUIRREL   FLYING SQUIRREL   CHIPMUNK   PRAIRIE DOG   GOPHER   WOODCHUCK   MARMOT

DOG (Canidae)

TIGER

LION

DOMESTIC DOG

FOX

COYOTE

WOLF

CAMEL (Camelidae)

    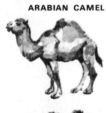 

SKUNK

BADGER

WOLVERINE

ARABIAN CAMEL

VICUÑA

ALPACA

BACTRIAN CAMEL

LLAMA

GUANACO

APE (Pongidae)

GIBBON

CHIMPANZEE

ORANG-UTAN

GORILLA

HORSE (Equidae)

ZEBRA

MULE

HORSE

DONKEY, OR ASS

PONY

SOME FAMILIES OF FLOWERING PLANTS

After flowering plants first appeared some 130 million years ago, they rapidly 'took over the earth'. Now there are more kinds of flowering plants than all other plants put together. There are perhaps as many as 250,000 species. They belong to several hundred plant families. In some families there are hundred of species; in others there are only a few.

Flowers are generally studied by scientists to find out how they are related to other similar plants. Without a study of their flowers it is hard to see why, for example, the wild rose and the apple belong to the same family or why the onion and the Easter lily are closely related. This chart names some of the many families of flowering plants and shows a few of the plants that belong to those families.

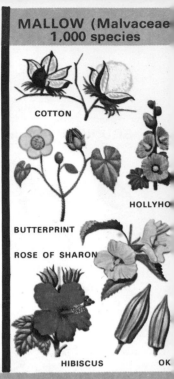

MALLOW (Malvaceae) 1,000 species

COTTON

HOLLYHO

BUTTERPRINT

ROSE OF SHARON

HIBISCUS

OK

PALM (Palmaceae) 1,200–1,500 species

PALMETTO

COCONUT PALM

ROYAL PALM

DATE PALM

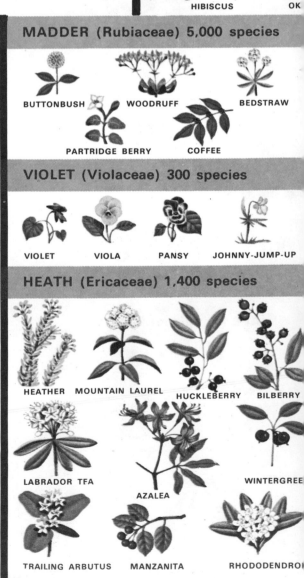

MADDER (Rubiaceae) 5,000 species

BUTTONBUSH   WOODRUFF   BEDSTRAW

PARTRIDGE BERRY   COFFEE

VIOLET (Violaceae) 300 species

VIOLET   VIOLA   PANSY   JOHNNY-JUMP-UP

HEATH (Ericaceae) 1,400 species

HEATHER   MOUNTAIN LAUREL   HUCKLEBERRY   BILBERRY

LABRADOR TFA   AZALEA   WINTERGREE

TRAILING ARBUTUS   MANZANITA   RHODODENDRO

ROSE (Rosaceae) 2,500 species

ROSE BLACKBERRY RASPBERRY CINQUEFOIL MOUNTAIN ASH

APPLE CHERRY PEAR PLUM PEACH APRICOT

AB APPLE ALMOND QUINCE HAWTHORN STRAWBERRY

BINDWEED (Convol-vulaceae) 1,000 species

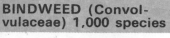

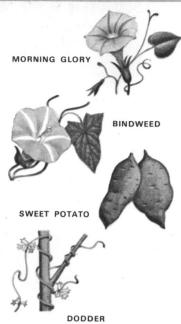

MORNING GLORY

BINDWEED

SWEET POTATO

DODDER

JE (Rutaceae) 900 species

EA (Theaceae) More than 200 species

RASS (Gramineae) 7,000 species

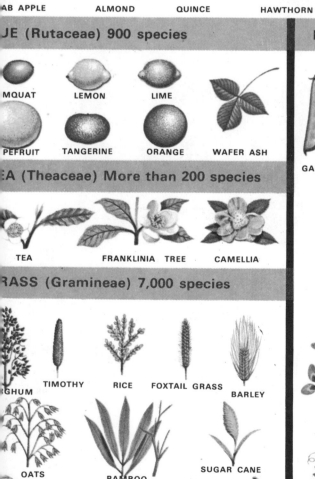

MQUAT LEMON LIME

PEFRUIT TANGERINE ORANGE WAFER ASH

TEA FRANKLINIA TREE CAMELLIA

GHUM TIMOTHY RICE FOXTAIL GRASS BARLEY

OATS BAMBOO SUGAR CANE

T CORN
MAIZE WHEAT BROOMCORN RYE MILLET

PEA (Leguminosae) 12,000 species

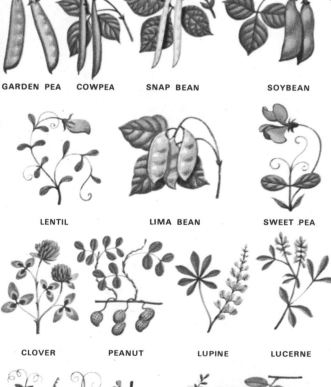

GARDEN PEA COWPEA SNAP BEAN SOYBEAN

LENTIL LIMA BEAN SWEET PEA

CLOVER PEANUT LUPINE LUCERNE

VETCH REDBUD BROOM CAROB TREE

POTATO (Solanaceae) 1,700 species

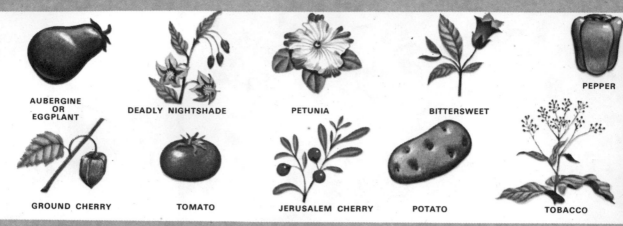

AUBERGINE OR EGGPLANT   DEADLY NIGHTSHADE   PETUNIA   BITTERSWEET   PEPPER

GROUND CHERRY   TOMATO   JERUSALEM CHERRY   POTATO   TOBACCO

MARROW (Cucurbitaceae) 700 species

CANTALOUPE   HONEYDEW MELON   SQUASH   WATERMELON   GOURD   CUCUMBER   PUMPKIN

OLIVE (Oleaceae) 500 species

FORSYTHIA

PRIVET   LILAC

ASH TREE

OLIVE

BUTTERCUP (Ranunculaceae) 1,200 species

PASQUE FLOWER   CLEMATIS   PAEONY   COLUMBINE   BUTTERCU

MONKSHOOD   LARKSPUR   BANEBERRY   HEPATICA   MEADOW R

ORCHID (Orchidaceae) 5,000–10,000 species

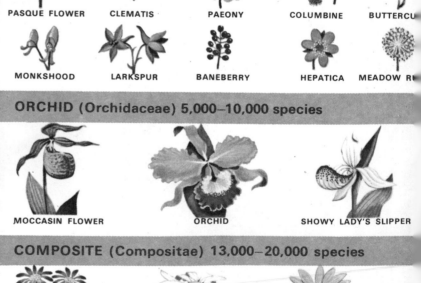

MOCCASIN FLOWER   ORCHID   SHOWY LADY'S SLIPPER

COMPOSITE (Compositae) 13,000–20,000 species

ASTER   DAISY   SUNFLOWER

THISTLE   LETTUCE   MARIGOLD

374

CABBAGE (Cruciferae) 2,000 species

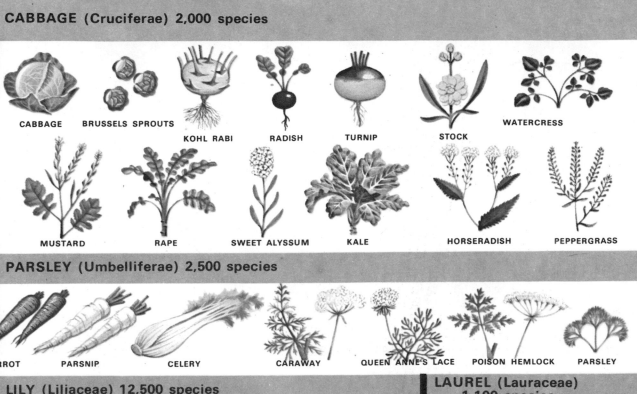

CABBAGE

BRUSSELS SPROUTS

KOHL RABI

RADISH

TURNIP

STOCK

WATERCRESS

MUSTARD

RAPE

SWEET ALYSSUM

KALE

HORSERADISH

PEPPERGRASS

PARSLEY (Umbelliferae) 2,500 species

RROT

PARSNIP

CELERY

CARAWAY

QUEEN ANNE'S LACE

POISON HEMLOCK

PARSLEY

LILY (Liliaceae) 12,500 species

LAUREL (Lauraceae) 1,100 species

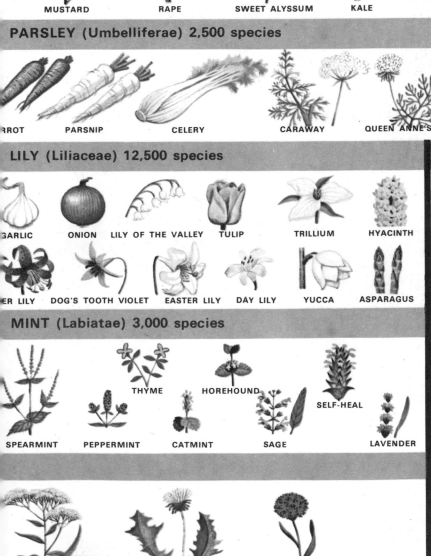

GARLIC

ONION

LILY OF THE VALLEY

TULIP

TRILLIUM

HYACINTH

ER LILY

DOG'S TOOTH VIOLET

EASTER LILY

DAY LILY

YUCCA

ASPARAGUS

MINT (Labiatae) 3,000 species

THYME

HOREHOUND

SELF-HEAL

SPEARMINT

PEPPERMINT

CATMINT

SAGE

LAVENDER

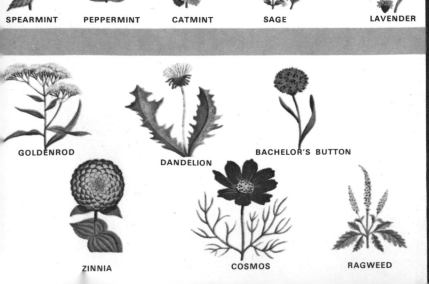

GOLDENROD

DANDELION

BACHELOR'S BUTTON

ZINNIA

COSMOS

RAGWEED

SASSAFRAS

SPICEBUSH

LAUREL

CINNAMON TREE

AVOCADO, OR ALLIGATOR PEAR

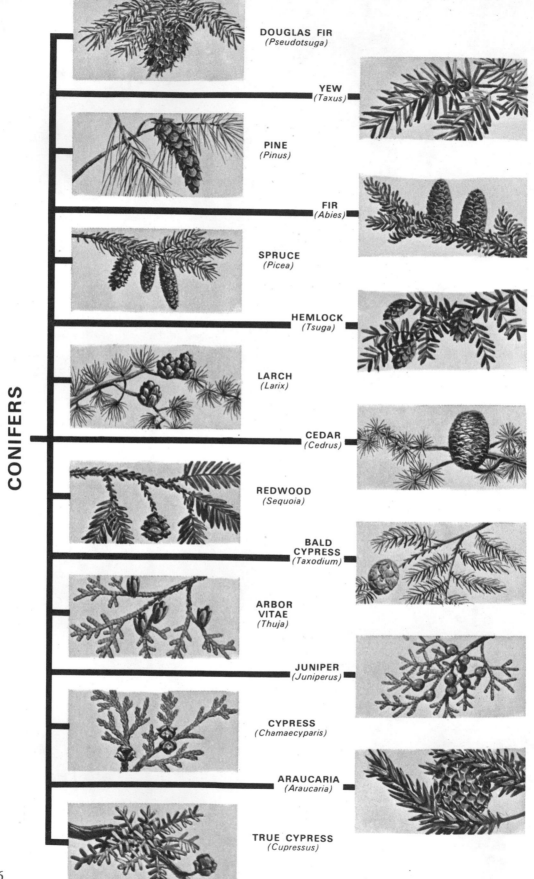

CONIFERS

DOUGLAS FIR
(Pseudotsuga)

YEW
(Taxus)

PINE
(Pinus)

FIR
(Abies)

SPRUCE
(Picea)

HEMLOCK
(Tsuga)

LARCH
(Larix)

CEDAR
(Cedrus)

REDWOOD
(Sequoia)

BALD
CYPRESS
(Taxodium)

ARBOR
VITAE
(Thuja)

JUNIPER
(Juniperus)

CYPRESS
(Chamaecyparis)

ARAUCARIA
(Araucaria)

TRUE CYPRESS
(Cupressus)

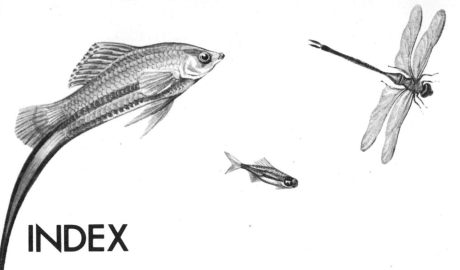

INDEX

Heavy type indicates those pages on which illustrations of the subjects appear.

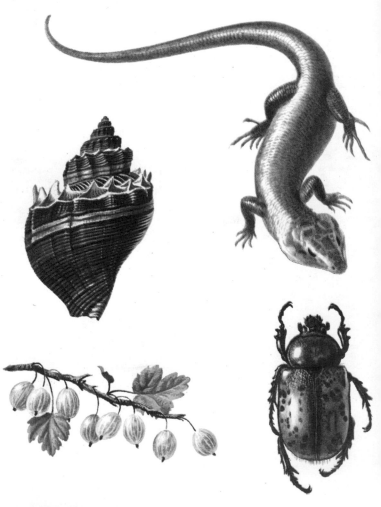